From Gags to Riches

JOEY ADAMS

From Gags to Riches

FREDERICK FELL. INC · 1946

PUBLISHED OCTOBER 1946.
SECOND PRINTING OCTOBER 1946.

The ham 'n' eggs cartoon on the title page represents, reading clockwise from the top, Joey Adams, Tony Canzoneri, and Mark Plant.

T O

MARIE *and* F. H. LA GUARDIA

who have been my inspiration ever since I was
strong enough to carry the Little Flower's hat

and to MARK *and* HELEN PLANT

and

RITA *and* TONY CANZONERI

without whom this book could never have
been written. They babied me and put up
with me as I wrote it on trains, in planes, in
restaurants between courses, and backstage at
clubs and theatres

TO THE ARTISTS WHO
ILLUSTRATED THIS BOOK

Through these pages pass the greatest cartoonists in the
world . . . only they stopped long enough
to make some wonderful illustrations.

This is to certify that they are on my Honor Roll forever.

DAVE BREGER	BILL HOLMAN
AL CAPP	KEN KLING
XAVIER CUGAT	JAY MCARDLE
PHIL DORMONT	STAN MACGOVERN
BOB DUNN	ZERO MOSTEL
GUS EDSON	RUSSELL PATTERSON
HAM FISHER	C. D. RUSSELL
RUBE GOLDBERG	OTTO SOGLOW
BOB GUSTAFSON	JACK SPARLING
LOU HANLON	HY VOGEL
FRED HARMON	DOW WALLING

FRANK WILLARD

Contents

From Gags to Riches

Foreword

BY F. H. LA GUARDIA

From Gags to Riches is the story of a New York City kid—written rather early, for Joey is still so young. I have not seen Joey's income tax return, so I do not know just what the significance is of that part of the title.

As a kid, Joey had what it takes to make a boy "rich" in health, happiness, and outlook. He had the good fortune of having intelligent parents. He was a healthy youngster, had a cheerful disposition, and always kept himself busy, getting a great deal of fun all through his

1

childhood. His good manners and politeness to older folks made him stand out and won him many friends in all groups of grownups. He was a leader among children —the kind of leader that is every teacher's joy and delight. It was always "Yes, Sir" or "No, Mam"—and no kid would ever call Joey a "sissy," for he knew how to take care of himself by persuasion or otherwise, and could get plenty tough in the manly art of self-defense.

I originally saw him around campaign headquarters when I first ran for Congress in an East Harlem district. My headquarters was always a favorite hangout for the small kids of the neighborhood. Joey stood out, though. His interest was in people. Even as a tot he would talk about tenements, poor kids who needed shoes. Later he got into the realm of real economics. He always wanted to do something, be useful—from holding my hat during speeches, when he was only a tot, to sticking stamps, running errands, writing jingles, policing kids at street meetings, and when he got into his teens he insisted on being a campaign orator.

From the very beginning, he was the "pet" at headquarters—always neat, hair carefully brushed, and clean hands. He would help the volunteers, mostly young ladies, who would shower him with candy, cake, and a great deal of kidding. "Do this, Joey, do that, and I'll give you a kiss." Little Joey would obediently respond and take prompt payment with a good deal of pride and satisfaction. It got to be a habit—one that seems to linger to this day.

Well, like all boys, Joey grew up. He wanted to go

into politics. I talked him out of that. He wanted to be a lawyer. He had the misconception so common that to be a "good talker," one "good on his feet," were the sole qualifications for a lawyer. It took considerable arguing. I finally resorted to presenting real, living examples. I pointed out the difference between the profound knowledge of law and the minimum requirements for admission to the bar. Well, that was over. Engineering? No, his dislike for mathematics and details ended that one. Medicine was out, and the pulpit had no appeal. Yes, he would be a businessman. So, we let it go at that.

The next time Joey reported, he had just completed a summer season in some inexpensive boarding house in the Catskills. A sort of combination all-around man, from dish-washer to bookkeeper—and, after a twelve-hour day, a bit of entertaining in the evening.

The next season he graduated from dishwashing and became a sort of assistant manager and official entertainer. This continued for several seasons, and finally I had to ask him if he intended to be a "mountain" ham actor all his life. This did not disturb him a bit. When I saw he was bent on being an actor, I tried to persuade him to go to dramatic school. He retorted that he acted the way I spoke: "Didn't you always say to be natural?" That was all the coaching I had ever given him for his public speaking. So he insisted that as long as he was natural and spontaneous, that was all he needed to be a good actor.

From then on, there was no holding Joey down. He

kept going up, up, and up. He loves his profession. He likes the people that are in it. He gets a kick out of his work and has much ahead of him.

His book is the story of a New York boy. Joey made it —others can. He may be a big shot, but to me he is only "little Joey," and if he ever gets a swelled head I shall take him across my knees and give him the walloping of his life—something I have been tempted to do on many occasions!

Another Foreword

BY TOOTS SHOR

JOEY ADAMS has asked me to sit down and write a foreword to this new book. The crum has a hell of a nerve asking me to do two things, so I decided not to comply. (That's a word I picked up from Tony Canzoneri.) I have, therefore, written this while standing at my

5

bar. No bum like Adams is going to tell me to sit down.

Most people who write forewords have read the book which follows. I am not at that disadvantage, so if I say anything about the stuff which Adams allegedly wrote, discount it. I not only have not read it yet, but the price is at least three to one that I will never read it.

However, I do not want you to think I am knocking the book. I am going to buy a copy to carry around with me, and I think everybody ought to.

The colors of the jacket go with any suit.

Let us take a look at the creep who wrote this book before we go any further. I first saw Joey Adams at a New York saloon called Leon and Eddie's. But I still like him. After all, that sort of thing is liable to happen to anybody. He was working with Tony Canzoneri at the time, which made him the first comedian I ever saw who was so bad he needed a bodyguard with him—on the stage.

I wouldn't have known that Adams was a comedian except that somebody who had been drinking asked him for an autograph. I saw him write:

"Joey Adams. Comedian. Now working at Leon and Eddie's. Three shows a night. 8:30, 12 and 2. Dinner very reasonable."

That Leon puts such strange clauses in his contracts!

I remember one night very well. I took a drink of brandy as Adams came on. He told a joke. I took another brandy. He told another joke. I took another brandy. After his fifth quick joke I thought he was great.

I went back to see him one night while I was sober,

though, and he proved to me that my favorite Adams was still the man who makes the chewing gum.

I think I ought to tell you how to read this book. While it is true that I haven't seen what follows this brilliant foreword, I have read books like this . . . if there ever was a book like it. I have found that the ideal way to read this kind of literature (okay, Joey?) is to take a large stack of Crosby and Sinatra records. Pile them near the phonograph. Open the book. Stop reading and play a record. Read another page. Play another record. Etc.

In that way at least you're going to hear a lot of records.

Maybe you think I am being cruel to Adams. I am, because I am a little mad at him. I told him he ought to let me read the book before I wrote the foreword. If nothing else, I figgured I could help him with the speling.

From here on, you're on your own, and remember that old French proverb, *Foreword is forearmed.*

P. S.: To step out of character for a minute and say something nice about somebody, I'd like to tell you that Joey Adams is one of the nicer guys of Our Town—and guys don't come nicer any place in the world.

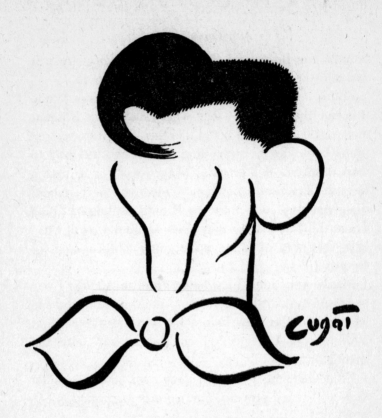

A Third Foreword

BY FRANK SINATRA

I CAN'T vouch much for Joey's gags, nor his riches. But I know the boy is loaded with luck. I know because a lot of us who grew up in my neighborhood were loaded with the same kind of luck. It's the kind that brought us into the world in Hoboken, New Jersey, instead of some place that's not in the United States.

When we think of this country as the land of freedom, we think of it as a place where we're free to express our opinions, free to vote, free to come and go as we please. But the freedom Joey and I understood best is the freedom we've both enjoyed most, the freedom to be anything you've got it in you to become. That's the most important freedom in the world. And unless you know what it's like to grow up in a neighborhood where on a clear day you get a nice view of the other side of the street, you'll never appreciate what it means when a guy discovers that his future is limited only by the horizon he sets for himself and his determination to travel as far as anyone has ever traveled in that direction.

Joey's come a long way in the direction he chose. It's one of the best directions I know. The competition's keen but there's always plenty of room at the top for a man who wants to pull himself up by his own resources instead of climbing on other people's. Joey's on his way. Unless they change the laws of the United States, it looks like a long happy road ahead. He's got his gags— I sincerely hope the latter half of his title comes as easy. If it *can* happen, it's got to happen here in the U.S.A. where a night-club emcee who grew up on the wrong side of the tracks can write a book and still maintain the best wishes of an ex-mayor of New York, an ex-ball-player who runs a restaurant, and an ex-Hoboken kid who gets a boot out of signing

Frank Sinatra

Foreword No. 4

BY GYPSY ROSE LEE

Dear Joey,

What's this I hear about you writing a book? A book
of memoirs, yet. What, may I ask, has a comic got to
remember? Unless it's another comic's jokes . . . As one
writer to another, I think you should put a switch on the

book right now before it's too late. Why don't you do like I did? I didn't have much to remember either—that is, not much they'd allow thru the mails—so I switched my memoirs to a murder mystery.

I had my character killed with a G-string. On you a G-string isn't so good, but you could kill off your character with a stale joke. You know how comics say, "This is a killer"? Well, you can use that premise. For a weapon you can use that gag from your act, "Cain and Abel were the first results of splitting the Adam."

Every successful mystery has to have more than one murder, so in Chapter Three you can kill off the likeliest suspect with "How do girls get minks? Like minks get minks." That one will kill them. I know because I'm using it in my own act.

And for another suggestion: Just because you've written a book, don't go literary and throw away the baggy pants. That's what I almost did. When my book hit the stands I was tempted to throw away the G-string. Then at the last minute I decided to keep it, just in case Princeton wanted to bury it along with the original manuscript in some damp archive. Bury it in an archive, huh? Two weeks later I took it out of moth balls and glued it on. I've worn it ever since. And not to keep me warm. Book royalties are very nice, but nothing takes the place of that salary check each week.

Good luck with the book, honey! Give my love to Mark and Tony and the bunch. Junie and I are so proud of your success . . . keep it up. I've been working saloons myself lately and it's fun. They've changed those

cards on the table from "No minimum at any time" to
"No cover at any time." Fine thing for a literary figure
like me!

                                        Love,
                                        Gyppo.

Pal Joey

BY EARL WILSON

MY PAL Joey Adams scribbled me a letter asking me to write a "forward" to his book. Joey is like Joe Laurie Jr. or Mark Twain or somebody who said he wouldn't give a damn for a man who could only spell a word one way. Anyway, I replied Joey should let Toots Shor write the forward, and I would write the precipice. I admit that's not very funny, but if you think that's not funny, wait till you really get into this book.

"This book is all about you, Earl!" Joey has been telling me for months. "ALL about you."

Being an author, he is entitled to tell a few lies, and evidently he did, for I next heard he told Toots Shor, "Toots, this book is all about you. ALL about YOU!"

I have a sneaking suspicion it is about Joey Adams.

However, Joey is an interesting subject for a book, because some people contend that he is the funniest man working in a night club today. Why worry about what the other ninety-nine percent say? I met Joey very early in my Saloon Editor career. I believe Joey says I met him the very first night of my Saloon Editor career. Now I ask you, if you had just started covering the night clubs five minutes ago, and had all the night-club entertainers in New York City to choose from for your first night, would you go to see Joey Adams? The answer, of course, is you would in the pig's posterior! I went to see June Havoc, I think it was, that night, and there was Joey Adams calling on her (no, no, not *falling* on her) and we became close friends and have continued close friends right up till tomorrow when Joey reads this.

Despite his false stories which you are going to read in the ensuing pages, Joey Adams got his start in life at the age of nine when he sold shin guards to lower East Side school teachers around 1902. He was then idle from 1902 until 1942. (This was the only time in his career he wasn't working.) In 1942 he saw a great future and began peddling ear stops to voice coaches around Steinway Hall. This was during the Frank Sinatra or "God damn that noise" period. He quickly cleaned up a small fortune, not to be confused with the large Fortune that sells for a buck a copy, and has since been clipping coupons or, at times, paper dolls.

Joey is a great Don Juan and many girls have gone crazy over him, some of whom were not crazy already. He is handsome, electrifying, brilliant, gay, sweet, strong, clever, smart, at least five feet four inches tall, weighing a good 135 pounds with his joke books under his arm and his Adler heels on, witty, pungent, well-dressed, and you can be sure whenever you meet him he will have a wisecrack on his lips—and don't go spoiling it by asking whose wisecrack it is! What do we care whose it is? Joey is my pal and I have of course been kidding in the above essay because I happen to like him and think he will go far. He is a mighty funny comedian and if you haven't seen him, go right over and get your ticket to the Flea Circus now!

I intended to write something personal about Joey Adams here but I gave it up. What is the use of both of us talking about how much we like him?

INTRODUCTION

Signs of Success

SUCCESS on Broadway is recognized in the oddest ways. You have "arrived" on the Main Stem when Winchell gives you an orchid and Earl Wilson talks about your *derrière*, when Toots Shor calls you a crum-bum, Nick Kenny rhymes your birthday and your anniversary, Swifty Morgan picks you out to sell you fifty-cent ties

16

for five dollars, and Lindy's and Reuben's name sandwiches after you . . .

You're a "hit" on Whoopee Boulevard when Leon
& Eddie's, La Martinique, and the Havana-Madrid
run celebrity parties for you; when Adam Hats puts
your picture on their ads and Broadway Rose embraces
you . . .

You know you're in the "big time" when Lee Mortimer
calls you the Woo-Woo of the Week and a man twice
your age greets you with "When I was a kid I used to see
you from the balcony of the Bedford Theatre in Brooklyn". . .

You're a "headliner" on Mazda Lane when headwaiters recognize you and give you a ringside table and
you talk about "my friend, President Truman." When
you table-hop at the Stork and you have at least one feud
and ten enemies that you hate . . .

You're the "white-haired boy" of the big town when
press agents whisper in your ear while you're sitting in a
night club with a gal, asking, "What's the girl's name?"
so they can give it to some columnist. When photographers take your picture at openings and Leonard Lyons
relates an anecdote about you . . .

You're a success on the Great Watt Way when you are
pointed out as the anonymous phony in Dorothy Kilgallen's column, *You Can't Print That* . . . And when
Ed Sullivan is reminded, right in the middle of his
column, to call you. And when Louis Sobol reminisces
with you and Danton Walker puts you on his preferred
list—*and you write a book* . . .

Well, Winchell has or-kidded me and Earl Wilson has said I made an ass of myself. Toots Shor has called me a crum-bum and many other names that I can't mention, even in a book about Broadway. Nick Kenny has mentioned my birthday, anniversary, and divorce in rhyme, and Swifty Morgan has stuck me with ties that I wouldn't wear to see Milton Berle in a Billy Rose show.

Leon & Eddie's has given me a nonentity party and Havana-Madrid has run a smellebrity night for me. Lindy's and Reuben's have named sandwiches after me —ham—and I've hired a press agent to keep my name *out* of the Adam Hats ads.

Broadway Rose has embraced me so hard, I couldn't get rid of the odor for weeks. Lee Mortimer has called me the Wow, the Woo-Woo, and the *So What* of the Week; and headwaiters recognize me immediately when I hand them a ten-dollar bill.

I am the only Broadway character that doesn't know President Truman, and I'm not angry at any of my enemies—after all, I made them. In the columns "on the way to the altar," "license shopping," "looking for a preacher," etc., press agents have tied my name up with those of June Havoc, Judy Garland, Gypsy Rose Lee, Shirley Stevenson, Betty Jane Smith, and Jane Kean, all in one week! And photographers have taken my picture at hundreds of openings, but one has yet to appear in a paper.

Leonard Lyons has used many anecdotes about me, which, in the vernacular of baseball's famous Tinkers-to-Evers-to-Chance, have gone from Adams-to-Lyons-

C. D. RUSSELL

*Headwaiters recognize me immediately—when
I hand them a ten-dollar bill*

to-Cerf. Louis Sobol says I have nostalgia—"I can listen
to those old gags over and over again"—and *Variety* and
Billboard agree with night-club critics Virginia Forbes,
Gene Knight, and Robert Dana that I have something no
great comedian has—bad jokes.

And here is my book . . .

Well, they laughed at Edison, they laughed at Bell,
and they laughed at Fulton. I wonder who wrote *their*
material?

I have often reprimanded hecklers in night clubs and
theatres with "I don't butt into your business, stay out
of mine," and very often quote a story to punctuate that
statement:

"In Brooklyn there is a famous bank that transacts
millions of dollars' worth of business a day. In front of
that bank is a little frankfurter stand, operated by an old
Italian peddler who sells his franks for five cents apiece,

C. D. RUSSELL

including mustard in the middle and a pickle on top. One day a man approached the old peddler and asked to borrow ten dollars. The peddler's answer should make you think: 'I nonja can do. I make-a up wid-da bank—dey sell no hot dogs, I no lend-a money'."

Well, here I am, not heeding my own advice, in the big business of writing a book when I should be selling frankfurters . . . or ham . . .

Do you want to know *my* biggest success? No, it wasn't at Loew's State or the Coronet in Philly or the Capitol Theatre in New York. It was in a little hospital in Miami Beach. We were entertaining a soldier in a private room. He was a lieutenant in the Air Corps, and they told us he hadn't talked or smiled for months. He just looked into open space and stared. Even his loved ones, who had come from California to be with him, couldn't get him out of his stupor. They were beside themselves with grief.

Nick Kenny, whose heart is as big as the battleships he writes about, had heard about it and made up a show to see what he could do to make the war hero normal again. We brought a piano into the room and put on a show that lasted for hours. Nick recited his poems and Harry Link played his song hits. Leo Durocher, the famous manager of "dem bums," told his best baseball anecdotes, and Mark Plant, the handsome giant baritone, sang a dozen popular songs, but the boy just stared. Then I introduced Danny Kaye and he put on a show that would have ripped apart any Madison Square Garden audience. He danced, gagged, and sang, but the boy still showed no signs of life, just kept staring straight ahead.

I told every joke I knew, old and recent, clean and dirty, but the hero of a hundred missions over Axis territory only looked through me. Next I introduced Tony Canzoneri, the ex-champ turned actor, and we went through our routine. I slapped and cuffed Tony all around the room. We tried every trick we knew to make some impression on our little "audience of one." I was beginning to lose hope, when Tony, as he usually does near the end of our act, slapped me gently across the face. The boy smiled. At last, a spark of hope. I whispered to Tony to do it again. This time the boy showed a wide grin. Every eye in the room was focused on the lieutenant. "Hit me harder," I told the little champ. With each wallop the lad laughed more loudly and with each laugh Canzoneri hit me harder. "Boy oh boy!" the kid finally blurted out, "it's about time that ham got it."

To the young officer's glee, Tony gave me the beating of my life, and the six-times world champion certainly knows how to administer a licking. The kid left the hospital soon after that, and I stayed there . . . to take care of my contusions and lacerations. Every bone in my body ached—I was in the punk of condition—but my heart felt good.

We saw the soldier boy many times after that and still keep in touch with him. He is quite normal in every way, which is more than I can say for myself . . .

That's why we like to appear at every veterans' hospital, in every town we play, to try to bring the boys laughs. Even if it means working it in between the five and six shows a day we must do in vaudeville theatres around the country. It's the least we can do for those swell kids who won the peace for us and saved our four freedoms.

That's why I take my hat off and bow from my heart to the people of show business, the "soldiers in grease-paint" who gave and are giving their time, their talents, their efforts, and yes, their very lives that "our boys" might laugh.

That's why this book, too. If we bring one good laugh, then our efforts will not be in vain. But as Jimmy Durante would say, "I got a million of 'em". . .

I'd like to tell you about Broadway after dark and the fun and heartache that go with each step forward and each step backward. Don't misunderstand, this is not an autobiography. If anything, it's an alibiography. It is merely a picture of the Great White Way (with all its

*One comic's impression of another: the author
as he looks to Zero Mostel*

side streets) as it looks to me—its habits and its characters, its chorus girls and its stars, its wits and above all
its *laughs*.

Dean Inge said, "There are two kinds of fools. One
says, 'This is old, therefore it is good,' and the other
says, 'This is new, therefore it is better'."

As far as this book is concerned, I feel more like a
bride as I write it. "Something old, something new,
something borrowed, something blue." Something old?

I have some old jokes to refresh your memory—some of them so old they don't remember Henny Youngman. Something new? Some new jokes for some real laughs. Something borrowed? After all, an original wit on Broadway is the guy who sees it in the Broadway columns before you do. Perhaps I can beat Bennett Cerf to some of these. Something blue? Well, we've got to keep the women amused, too . . .

Anyway, this story about show business will come to you as I see it, straight from the shoulder. Yeah, I know —you'll say it should come from a little higher up . . .

CHAPTER ONE

On My Way to the Waldorf

EVER since I was knee-high to a grasshopper, I've had an ambition to live at the Waldorf-Astoria. Somehow, that was the way I would really feel success. As a kid, living at the Waldorf meant "a house full of toys" or "all the candy I could eat." As I grew older in show business, it had an even stronger meaning for me. The famous

Park Avenue hotel meant "top billing" and "my name in lights." It was equivalent to ★ ★ ★ ★ in the *News* and a rave notice by George Jean Nathan.

After all, you can't wear two pairs of pants at a time, even if they come with the suit. You only wear one pair of shoes at a time, no matter how high Adler elevates you, and you can eat only three times a day. In fact, as you grow older, your diet gets stricter, particularly in show business. To keep looking well you must take care of your figure. Actors who have a lot to eat, wind up with the biggest seat.

At any rate, the way I could feel success was to live at the place I always connected with the "big time."

And then, after all these years on Broadway, looking for work—I signed a contract to appear at the Capitol Theatre in New York. I was going to appear at the "Palace" of present-day vaudeville. Until then the only Broadway run I'd had was chasing street cars. Appearing at the Capitol meant two thousand a week and my name up in lights next to Guy Lombardo's.

There was another dream come true. When I was a kid I had two idols, Guy Lombardo and Fiorello LaGuardia. (Now that I'm grown up, I make speeches like Lombardo and I lead a band like LaGuardia.)

My first thought on receiving the Capitol contract, was to wire the good news to my Mom and Dad and my brother Sol.

Then I sent a wire to the Waldorf for reservations. I think when I got the okay from George Lindholm, its managing director, it was one of the biggest moments in my life. That sounds silly, doesn't it? But it did mean a great deal to me.

And I was coming to my own New York. Brother, after traveling all over the country, working in almost every vaudeville theatre, big and small, playing all those bars and alleged night clubs in every one-horse town— and some of those burgs looked as though the horse really gets around—it was a thrill coming back to Broadway. Believe me, there's no place like home (if you find one), and my home was going to be the Waldorf . . .

We had just finished at the Oriental Theatre in Chicago and were flying into New York, brag and baggage. It was the eve of my appearance at the Capitol.

I couldn't help thinking of the broken-down flat where I was born, in the Brownsville section of Brooklyn. (Of course, a lot of funny things happen in Boston, too.) I was a fifteen-pound boy, a healthy pink and a loud yeller. I joined a family of three brothers, a sister, an uncle and aunt, and a mother and father so wonderful, they couldn't be any better if I had chosen them myself. Eight of us in three rooms! I guess no matter how crowded they were, there was always room for one bore. And anyhow, I was there and there was nothing they could do about it.

It wasn't easy, crowding all those hungry people into three cold rooms and feeding them. But we got along somehow. At times it didn't look as if we would. We had more troubles than a radio serial.

Our apartment was four flights up at the rear, and steam heat was "only for the rich." My mother and dad slept in a room by themselves and my three brothers slept in another bedroom with my uncle. My sister and aunt slept on cots in the kitchen. No wonder my uncle and aunt never had any children . . .

I joined my folks in their bedroom. After all, I was the *moozinick*,[1] as my father called me.

And now I was going to live at the Waldorf in a suite for myself.

The plane was passing over the Bronx and I could just see the little Chinese restaurant at 170th Street and Jerome Avenue—Munn's—where I used to entertain on Saturday night for free chow mein. What shows we used to put on for nothing! Jackie Miles, Lenny Kent and Betty, his dancing partner in those days, Leon Fields, Phil Rapp, who is very successful today as a writer, Bill Castle, who has become a famous director, Jackie Phillips, Robert Alda, the Warner Brothers picture star, and so many others. If we had pork with the chow mein, we had to do an extra number. Remember, fellas?

I thought about all those years of going to agents' offices and hearing "Nothing today" or "Sorry, they want names" or "That job I promised you at the Baumgarten Beer Garden is out; the waiter is doing master of ceremonies."

Sometimes the agent didn't want to spend a nickel to call you, if you had a phone, and would make you come back fifteen or twenty times—"in case" a client needed

[1] *Moozinick.* The youngest member of the family and the one that gets all the attention; the favorite.

an act. After fifty or sixty hopeful trips, he would tell
you, "Sorry, they wanted a colored act, instead" or "They
can't use your type." How did he know what "type" I
was? He never bothered to see me work. I was beginning to forget what type I was, myself! In those days I
was George Jessel one day, Al Jolson the next, and Eddie
Cantor the following day. Whoever I happened to see
work that day, that's who I tried to be that night. Even
if it was only in front of the mirror at home or for my
faithful "fans," my family.

"Fasten your belts and no smoking, we're landing at
La Guardia field in five minutes." Those were the sweetest words I had heard in years. Now my only interest
was in the future; after all, I was going to spend the
rest of my life there.

My buddies, Tony Canzoneri and Mark Plant, un-
fastened my safety belt and shoved me into a taxi. Before going to the hotel I wanted to drive past the Capitol
Theatre to see my name up in lights. What a thrill, after
twenty-three years of M.C.'ing [1] at weddings and *bar-
mitzvahs* [2] and *brisses*, [3] after all those years of "social
directoring" on the borsht circuit [4] for room and board

---

[1] *M.C.'ing.* Acting as Master of Ceremonies.
[2] *Bar-mitzvah.* Confirmation ceremony. In Jewish families, when a
boy reaches the age of 13 it's usually the occasion to give him a big
blowout—dinner, show, and all.
[3] *Briss.* Cutup party for boy infants.
[4] *Borsht circuit* or *borsht belt.* Borsht is a Russian beet soup that is
served almost daily in Jewish summer resorts. For years it has been
the cause of gagging among actors, who call it "consommé with high
blood pressure." After a summer of borsht in the mountains, they never
want to see another plate of beet soup again.

and a few a week, enough to pay for your tips and laundry! Sometimes the hotel owner would let you run an "affair" to make a few extra for yourself to get you out of hock.

I remember all those "Circus Screeno," "Bingo," and "Amateur Nights" on the Loew Circuit in the Bronx, Brooklyn, and Long Island—my first big theatre, Loew's Pitkin, a beautiful house seating 3800 people (although I never did prove it).

I could see again all those years of night clubs in Scranton, Hazelton, Trenton, etc., working for weeks and not getting paid off, and—if I asked for money—being threatened by the gangsters who ran the "joints." Stranded in Albany, no room rent in Hartford, hitchhiking from Utica . . .

Working in "flash acts" [1] for half-salary. Always half-salary "until you play the de luxe houses." Even the full salaries, which we never got, weren't enough to pay for traveling, decent food, and room rent.

The night clubs were the places that really brought you grief. Some of the joints were unbearable. The salary was just enough to keep you eating. "If you do good in my club, I'll double your salary after the first week," was the usual cry of the club owner. But they were always "too weak" to pick up my option.

But it was all worth it. I wouldn't trade one day of it for all the "silver spoons" in the world.

---

[1] *Flash act.* The big opening or closing act on a vaudeville bill, built up to make the show look big. The lowest-price act, in general, it usually comprised a group of dancing girls plus a singer or a comedian.

Anyway, at long last, I was going to open at the Capitol Theatre in New York.

"Hey, am I supposed to guess where yer goin'?" The cab driver took me out of my trance. "Dis cab ain't for sleepin'." Of all the cab drivers in New York, I had to choose one who was impersonating a human being. What a sweet disposition! Like the guy who pours cement into life preservers. His face looked as if it belonged on an iodine bottle.

"Don't be angry, everybody can't be normal," I sent back in my best M.C. style. I forgot for a moment that Canzoneri and Plant weren't with me.

"I'm only kidding," I said, when I took a quick glance around and saw the empty seats next to me. "Take me to the Capitol Theatre, Fifty-first Street and Broadway."

"Okay, Schmo,[1]" said the driver, and we were off.

When we got to Broadway and Fifty-first Street, I said, "Drive slowly, will you, pal?" As we approached the theatre, I looked out to see my name up in lights but I couldn't find it.

"Hey, driver, why isn't the marquee lit up?"

"Watcha tryin' t' do, brush up on yer ignorance, jerk? Don'tcha know dere's a war on, ya moron? All da teayter lights is blacked out."

Bad enough I have to take the blow of the lights, I have to be stuck with a cabbie who has charm like the inside of a fountain pen.

"Take me to Fiftieth Street and Broadway for a moment, will you, angel face?" He looked as though his

[1] *Schmo.* A jerk; term of derision.

face had stopped a kick and he had a haircut that looked
as if he'd caught it in a pencil sharpener.

"Okay, but don't be long. I ain't got all night, ya
know."

Joe Vogel, Marvin Schenck, and Jessie Kaye had told
me my pictures would be on the billboard in the subway, advertising the theatres. I took three steps at a
time as I leaped down the stairs of the subway station.
This might still save the night for me.

I looked around for three or four minutes without success when I got a bang on my shoulder and turned
around to see "my pal" the cab driver, red in the face
and yelling at the top of his lungs:

"Watcha tryin' to do, beat de cab bill? I got a good
mind ta hit yer so hard, ya'll wind up wit' a payfect set
o' gums."

I was as embarrassed as the guy who looks through a
keyhole and finds another eye. All I could blurt out was,

"Do you realize who you're talking to, young man?"

"Don't tell me, I wanna hate ya incocknito," said the driver.

Oh well, I realized I was talking to a victim of jerkumstances, so I said, "I'm trying to find my picture on the billboards. Furthermore, you have all my luggage up there in my cab."

"Not t'ree dollars' wort', bud." All of a sudden he'd become my buddy!

"Just one moment till I find my picture, will you, pal?" I returned the affection. And there it was right behind me all the time. My face had a moustache painted on it and the word "Stinks" written across the poster, with an arrow pointing to my face.

This put the hack driver in convulsions. He banged me on the back and laughed till I thought he'd choke.

How can a fellow with such a low mentality have such a high voice?

"You belong in a home for idiots," I yelled.

"Do ya have any room at *your* house?" he snapped back.

C. D. RUSSELL

That was the cruelest blow of all. Him "topping" me! The evening was a complete bust . . . "Okay, let's go to the Waldorf, and make it snappy," I said nonchalantly, trying to impress him with *that*.

"Yer going to the Waldorf, buddy? Ho, ho, that's rich! Ya want the servants' entrance?" That made him howl even more.

"No, the Park Avenue entrance, and I happen to live there, wise guy." I tried to console myself, "So I didn't have my name in lights and one guy wrote 'Stinks' across my picture—it was probably some ignorant kid, anyway. So what if the cab driver thinks I'm a dope and an idiot?" I kept mumbling to myself. "I'm going to open at the Capitol tomorrow and I'm moving into the Waldorf tonight. The Waldorf, do you understand?"

"What are ya sayin', Schmoey?" asked my pal.

"Nothing, I was talking to myself. Just drop me off at the Park Avenue entrance."

As he started to drive east from Fiftieth and Sixth Avenue to Fiftieth and Park, my whole life came before me. It was like a man going down for the third time, who remembers everything in that split second . . .

CHAPTER TWO

Adams Meets the Hat

WHEN I was six years old, I lived in Harlem at 104th Street and Madison Avenue. I was making a speech on a soap box, one night, to a group of youngsters ranging from five to ten years of age.

It was election time, and I was talking about "The Workingman" and "The Proletariat" and "Relative Proportion," using the expressions I had heard my father use many times at home. I was waving my hands frantically and screaming at the top of my voice as I had seen the campaigners do on street corners in our neighborhood.

A little dark man with a big black hat joined "my audience" and stood there listening to me. When I was through, he walked over to me.

"I like your sentiments, son. Where do you get them?"

"My father feels the same way. Are you for the proletariat, too?" I asked the chubby little stranger.

"Yes."

"Do you believe in fighting for the workingman?" I pressed him further.

"Yes, Sonny, I do."

"Do you believe in helping the underdog?"

"That's my life's work."

"Okay, you're on my side," I said. "Shake, pal, what's your name?"

He straightened up to his full five feet and said, "Fiorello H. La Guardia."

That's how I met "The Hat" or, as he is called by millions who know him and love him, "The Heart." I introduced him to my audience. He loves children. He

made a speech to us kids that night that will stay with me always. He became the inspiration for everything I ever did . . .

I became a "pet" around campaign headquarters for the "Major," as we affectionately called him. He was a Major in the first World War and very proud of the title.

Any night at "headquarters" you might see school-teachers, bricklayers, doctors, fighters, newspapermen, artists, and actors, all working for the election of the Little Flower.

Attillio Piccirilli, the world-renowned sculptor; Lowell Limpus, the newspaperman; August Bellanca, and a great many others were constantly there.

Some would address envelopes, some sorted the "dollars" that came in from the poor people of the district for the "Major's" election. Others ran errands or folded literature. Some would sweep the office while others served coffee.It wasn't odd to see a famous musician or a champion fighter serving food or sorting mail. Only party politicians were conspicuous by their absence.

I saw F. H. elected as congressman, president of the Board of Aldermen, and finally as Mayor of New York City on the Republican, Progressive, Socialist, and finally the Fusion party ticket. He changed parties, he always said, "because I don't want to be a rubber stamp for any party boss; and as soon as those clubhouse politicians start giving me orders, I drop them like a hot potato."

I watched him in Congress as he fought for each bill for the underdog. I listened to him fight the landlords when they tried to raise the rent of the tenants in his district. I saw him picket, shoulder to shoulder with the needle workers in the garment center.

He fought for the farmer and the factory worker, for the Post Office employee and the Soldiers' Bonus, the coal miners and the cotton pickers.

He was the first to fight prohibition and even made 3.2 beer to prove his point. He fought the power trusts and the monopolies and was the first to fight Hitler in the open.

He fought for the four freedoms with his heart and soul.

He fought for all the things he promised us kids on the corner that night . . .

He gave New York City the most honest and most efficient administration in its history. He made it the show place of the world by beautifying its highways, and gave it La Guardia Field, one of the greatest airports in the world.

He gave the city wonderful playgrounds and ran the "tinhorns" and "grafters" out of the town so that "his kids" would not grow up in the wrong environment.

All the world knows this and respects him for it, but I love him for many other reasons . . .

I love his sense of humor. Like the time he tied the knot for Mary and me at City Hall. After the ceremony he cautioned my wife, "If he gives you any trouble, let me know and I'll give him a good spanking on his *tuches*.[1] He may be bigger than me now, but I did it before and I can do it again."

His love for children is unequaled. When the newspapers in New York went on strike, his only concern was the kiddies' missing the "funnies," so he read the comics to them on the air and later on in the newsreels. Everybody, everywhere, laughed with him as he delighted children all over the country . . .

He can cook, and speak seven languages. He loves music and can direct any orchestra and do a good job,

[1] *Tuches.* The part of the chicken that goes over the fence last; or, as Earl Wilson would say, the *derrière*. It's a Jewish word.

too. He used to sit in the audience of a Gilbert and Sullivan operetta and direct the entire score from his seat, much to the annoyance of the people sitting around him. He keeps score at ball games and loves all sports.

I love the way he is always looking for his glasses—and they are invariably on his forehead. I loved him even when he yelled and screamed at us and sometimes threw inkwells when he couldn't find something in the files. Nobody ever felt bad because we knew that his heart is as big as his hat. When he finally found the mislaid papers (they had probably been in his pocket all along) he would send out for corned beef or pastrami sandwiches and everybody was happy again . . .

I love him because when he was at City Hall, anybody without a connection could see him. An old lady with a problem, or a young fellow with some troubles, or a poor old man with an idea, always found the Little Flower's ear or there would be hell to pay.

However, if you came with a connection, that was a different story. "I'm a friend of so-and-so and I gotta see the Mayor" was always the easiest way to miss him or, more aptly, for the attendant to get instructions to "throw the bum out."

The only way one of those political-connection guys could get a chance to meet the Mayor was to set fire to his house. "Patience and fortitude" was his credo. Patience for the poor and their troubles, fortitude to fight the enemies of decency.

I love him because he's got "guts" or, as he calls it, "intestinal fortitude." I saw him stick his forefinger in the chest of a racket guy twice his size in Harlem—with only an eleven-year-old boy to "protect" him—and say, "You tell your crooked bosses that if they send you around here again, you'll go back in a box!"

As a congressman he made $200 a week and was given $90 a week for a secretary and clerk. He kept $50 a week for himself and added $150 to the $90 for clerks and for the office to help the poor of his district.

Even as Mayor, at $25,000 a year, part of it went as "salary" to many admirers in Harlem who had believed in him but who he felt would not make capable city employees and would be a burden to the taxpayers.

I love him because he admits his mistakes. As he puts it, "When I make one, it's a pip!"

Even when "the passing of the Hat" became a fact at City Hall, Butch still took his fight to the people. "I am leaving politics for good, but if the tinhorns and grafters come back and the poor people don't get a square deal, I'll be back and there will be hell to pay." Again, patience and fortitude . . .

Even in his first broadcast after leaving the office of Mayor of New York City, his eyes sparkling, ready for a fight when he heard that his sponsors might try to weaken his stuff by disclaiming any responsibility, he said:

"If they announce that the sponsor is not responsible for their commentator's sentiments, I'll announce that the sponsor's product is not necessarily endorsed by the commentator."

And so the Little Flower turned up his hat and be-

came an actor—possibly the one guy in show business
who knows enough about horses not to bet on them.

In fact, it was the "Major" who made me become an
actor. The incidents are as vivid to me as when they
happened twenty-three years ago . . .

"I want to be in politics like you," I often said to the
"Major" when I was a kid, but he even discouraged me
from studying law. I worked hard at school and graduated as the valedictorian of my class at P. S. 171. That
still didn't impress him. "Why don't you become an
engineer?" he suggested. That needed an expert at
math, and all the figures I admired were in dresses. I
couldn't convince him that politics was what I really
wanted.

I introduced him at all the open-air meetings in Harlem. There it was the custom for one speaker to start,
introduce the next speaker, and go on to the next gathering. In that way, we could have six or seven meetings
going on at one time.

Vito Marcantonio usually spoke before me. He would
then introduce me and go on to the next meeting, leaving me to introduce "our congressman."

I had a four-minute speech that Marc had written for
me. I knew it backwards and forwards. I would always
end by saying, "And now I would like to present the
past, the present, and the next congressman of the 20th
Congressional District—Fiorello H. La Guardia."

One night, when all the speakers had left and I was
alone and had finished my speech, I started to introduce
the major as I had done a thousand times, "And now the

past, the present, and the next congressman of the 20th Congressional District, Fiorello H.—," but the words got stuck in my throat. The Little Flower wasn't there and all the speakers had gone.

I was only eleven years old and all I knew was the speech that I was taught—I couldn't ad-lib a belch after a Hungarian dinner. Waiting for the major, I tried to think of something to talk about, but all I could think of were the things he used to say. So I made his speech, word for word and intonation for intonation. He was my idol and I had watched him so many times I could repeat every word, every gesture. "My speech to you tonight is not through any mechanical device but comes to you from the heart," I shouted and put the microphone on the side, as I had seen the major do a thousand times.

"And the trust companies . . ." I yelled. "If you don't like the sodas on the corner, you go to the other corner and pay less, but if you don't like the gas, you've got to buy it anyway."

That kept on for forty minutes. I did all his pet stories and used all his expressions, even to the high voice and the hands in the air . . .

Finally I saw a big black hat coming around the corner. I was saved at last. I introduced him as I usually did and stepped off the platform, exhausted.

The first words out of his mouth were, "My speech to you is not through any mechanical device but comes to you from the heart." The audience began to titter. "And the trust companies . . ." he began to shout. "If you don't like the sodas———." By this time the audience was

screaming with laughter and I was scurrying home to
a safe hiding place. I knew the Little Flower's temper.
I didn't show up at campaign headquarters for days until the major finally came and got me and made me
apologize. I didn't know until years later that little Butch
laughed and laughed that night when he found out the
whole story. That was my first experience as a gag
stealer and, eventually, a comedian . . .

A few weeks later, after this had died down, I went to
Marie Fisher, the Little Flower's secretary and one of
the most wonderful people in the world (she later became his wife), and told her that I would like to sing our
campaign song on the lucky corner at 116th Street and
Lexington Avenue on the night before election. Ed
Koehler and I had written a song to the tune of *Avalon;*
it went something like this:

> Fi-*or*-el-*lo* La *Guar*-di-a
> Harlem needs a man like you in Congress,
> You voted for . . . the soldiers' bonus,
> Helped the immigrants,
> And fought in Congress *for* us.
> Fiorello La Guardia,
> With a record like yours,
> Harlem needs you.

Marie heard me sing it and then made me repeat it in
front of the major. In a small room, without music, I
didn't sound too bad and they decided to let me do the
song.

They hired a band for the occasion—one of those

typical street bands with red coats and caps and walrus moustaches to match. Nobody thought about having a rehearsal or finding the right key for me.

I knew nothing about an eight-bar introduction or a pickup or a keynote, and when the leader asked me what I wanted, about ten minutes before I went on, I said, "Just play the La Guardia song for me."

My big moment arrived. The Little Flower himself introduced me. Ten thousand people crowded the streets and I was the center of all eyes. I started full of confidence. After all, the major and Marie thought I was great.

For ten minutes I tried to get into the song. The band started and I followed, my voice changed and I tried to get into tempo, they started again and again I came in too soon or too late. We stopped and started all over, and again I loused it up. By this time everybody was on the verge of collapse and laughter. I was never so embarrassed in all my life. Only Marie and the major tried to keep from laughing so as not to hurt my feelings.

Later, when I went to the restaurant where we usually gathered for a snack before going home, I noticed that "the gang" was particularly quiet. I found out later that they didn't want to embarrass me. They couldn't compliment me and they didn't want to bring up my "flop" performance. The major had warned them about that.

I sat there for about three minutes and finally blurted out, not knowing how to cover my embarrassment, "Major, didn't I put that over? You know I purposely did that to make them laugh."

The major leaned over and gave me a kick in my *derrière* that I think I still feel to this day. "You dirty little Eddie Cantor," he said. (That was the only theatrical name he could think of.) "You little phony—from now on you're a ham actor."

CHAPTER THREE

The Borsht Belt

A ND so I became an actor. Maybe it's because I wanted to sleep late.

At the beginning I was nervous when I went on stage; now the audience gets nervous.

When the critics blasted me for this or that and I went to La Guardia to complain or cry, he would say, "Don't worry, son. Critics are like parrots, they only repeat what everybody is saying."

I went through some very lean years in show business. I wanted to get along on my own.

There were times when my blue serge suit was so shiny that if I fell down, it would be seven years' hard luck.

I lived in rooms so small that if I dreamed, I had to dream about midgets. One night Lew Parker came to visit me in a little hotel cubbyhole that I called home. "Hey, this is some room," he barked. "This room is so small, when a girl comes to visit you, she's *got* to lie down."

For a time I lived by my wits, and you have to be clever to live on such small capital.

I took part in the shows at P. S. 171, Patrick Henry

Junior High School, De Witt Clinton High School, and
City College.

La Guardia introduced me to Major Benjamin Namm,
who gave me a job in his famous department store in
Brooklyn. I worked in Namm's hat department for about
a year, and spent most of my time at the store putting on
shows for the employees. I concentrated all my efforts
on entertainment and little if any on the hat department.
One day I received a letter from Major Namm offering
me a share in the store, so I quit. His letter said in part,
"If you don't take an interest in our business . . ."

I'll always be proud that I am a member of the Namm
family. They were the first to "listen" to my jokes. I used
to put the shows on during the lunch hour—they couldn't
walk out unless they wanted to starve. Whatever they
ate, they were always treated to a goodly portion of
ham à la Adams . . .

For me, and for a lot of other actors, the borsht belt, in
the Catskill Mountains, was a lifesaver during the summer months. The salary wasn't big, but you got free
room and board and a chance to get at an audience.
Many of our great comedians were "born" at some of
those resorts. Danny Kaye and Henny Youngman
worked in them for years and are still doing some of the
material they developed there. Milton Berle, Jackie
Miles, and Lenny Kent are products of the Catskill
Mountains. Robert Merrill of the Metropolitan, Robert
Alda, and Phil Silvers are other alumni. Jan Murray, a
very clever comedian, still reminisces about his days at
the Hotel Nevele, where he used to take shower baths

in sour cream. Moss Hart, Luther Adler, and John Garfield are also sons of the Great Borsht Way.

Charles Previn started in a small band at the Morningside Hotel in the Catskills and became one of the outstanding men in music. He is now the musical director of Radio City Music Hall. Garson Kanin and Beatrice Kaye are others who are proud of their up-state Alma Mater.

Jan Peerce, the Metropolitan star, used to play the violin and sing in a band at the President Hotel and in smaller hotels in Kiamesha. Sammy Levine was an athletic director up the Catskill way.

Jan Murray was working at a place called "Paul's" in Swan Lake and was very unhappy because he didn't have a straight man. He complained loud and long to the producer and the owner of the hotel. Finally, one of the hoofers in the show offered his services. "I never did this before, but I'll be glad to try," said the good-looking blonde lad. "The only trouble is, I'm a Swede and I don't know those Jewish words for the blackouts." "I'll teach you," said Jan. "Don't worry about a thing. I'll make a star out of you. Just do what I tell you."

The blonde Swede did become a star—his name is Van Johnson.

At these hotels we had to keep the guests happy, day and night. We gave calisthenics in the morning and then got into funny outfits to "entertain" at the pool or the baseball field. Then on the porch, before and after each meal, we would tell stories and "make fun" as the guests often suggested.

I "kibitzed" the card games and danced with the old women and the ugly daughters. I took them on hikes and played games with the children. I arranged camp fires and hayrides. I was a human vitamin pill.

All this, in addition to doing a show every night of the week. I had to use guests and chambermaids and other employees to fill out my cast for the shows. Some of the shows were "not so hot" and the customers walked out, particularly the "lovers" who wanted a reserved seat in the bushes. The only act they worried about was the Mann Act. It never bothered me when they walked *out* on me; it was when they walked *towards* me that I started to worry. I didn't want applause after one of these bad shows; all I wanted was a ten-yard head start.

Of course, there were those who loved every show because they would recognize "Sarah" or "my roommate, Irving" in the cast. Seeing their own bus boy or waiter in the show was enough to insure a big laugh and a cheer from the customers at his table.

After the shows, I would go out to "mingle with the guests." That was very important. If you were a good "mingler," the success of your show was assured.

One thing always drove me crazy, and it would invariably happen right after a show. A big "cloak and suiter" would call me over and pat me on the back. "Say, dot was very good." For him, that was a big compliment. "You weren't bad. So tell me, what do you do in the wintertime?"

Julie Oshins, a wonderful comedian and another borsht-circuit graduate, who since became the star of

This Is the Army and one of the favorite comics of G.I.'s all over the world, suggested a reply that made me happy. After that, when a guest asked me what I did in the wintertime, I answered, "I wear an overcoat."

Today the borsht circuit has become "big time," and the "casinos" up there have become the summertime Loew's State, Roxy, Capitol, and Paramount.

Part of my job was to mingle with the guests

Al Beckman and Johnny Pransky were the pioneers who started to bring Broadway to the Catskill resorts. They had a lot of trouble convincing some of these farmers that Harry Richman and Sophie Tucker were important for their business.

"I never heard of Harry Richman," was the answer one owner gave. "Is he a good mixer?"[1] When the name of Paul Draper came up, one owner asked, "What does he do?" Al and Johnny had a lot of patience, "He's a dancer," they explained. This didn't stop the proprietor.

[1] Meaning, does he mingle with the guests and kid with them all day?

"Well"—and this was the killer—"has he a good partner?"

Little by little the hotel owners became educated to "names," and today in any of the borsht resorts up there a week-end vaudeville show has some of the biggest stars in show business. Any night at Grossinger's you are apt to find Belle Baker, Eddie Cantor, or Milton Berle doing their stuff on the stage and Leonard Lyons, Louis Sobol, and Earl Wilson watching out front.

A regular Concord show might have Willie Howard, Sophie Tucker, and Bill Robinson, all in one week end. The Nevele, Evans, and Nemerson are others that have big stars regularly. The Grand Hotel in Highmount has had the stars coming up there for years; the Wesson brothers, Henny Youngman, Benny Fields, Jack Durant, and George Jessel are only some of their Broadway regulars.

A summer on the borsht belt was a great lesson in romance, too. More *schidachs* [1] were made there than in all the matrimonial bureaus in the country. The Catskills provided an ideal place for a girl to find a husband and for a boy to find a girl with a large *nadan*. [2]

After all, where else can you pick an apple off the trees and a tomato off the grass? The Catskills, where the birds are flyin', the girls are sighin', and the boys are tryin'.

Most of the girls wanted to go with every Tom, Dick, and Marry, and brought their baiting suits along. They changed their clothes more times a day than my nephew

[1] *Schidach.* A match between a boy and girl.
[2] *Nadan.* Dowry.

who is three months old, and used enough perfume to hold you smellbound. They were dresstitute. Anything to attract a man.

The boys had different ideas, however. They wanted results, but no consequences. They sat around dame-dreaming about their wolfing at night. A Catskill wolf is sylph-conscious, and marriage is only talk to gain a point.

Of course, if the girl had money—well, that was different. Those guys were interested in money up to a certain point. The decimal point. When they found out a girl had plenty of loot, they would immediately go on the make. Very often they would ask you to be the *schadchen*.[1] "Tell her I'm a big executive in the dress business," one of them would say. You could probably find him any day pushing a truck in the garment center.

The girls did the same thing. "Tell him I'm a dietician or an executive at Macy's." That meant a waitress or a behind-the-counter girl. Talk is cheap—that's why there's more supply than demand—so I lied to each about the other.

In the Catskills, when a girl goes out with a fellow, she doesn't spend an evening, she invests it. She wears lovely bathing suits but never goes in the water with them; her tennis rackets and golf clubs are all unused. Anything to make an impression and find a husband.

"What kind of husband do you want?" I once asked a girl who was looking to get married. "First, he must be a man," she answered; "after that I don't care."

[1] *Schadchen.* Matchmaker.

The food is part of the deal in the borsht belt. Three meals a day and all you can eat and, brother, some of those guys eat anything that doesn't bite them first. One guest sitting at a table with me ate so much for dinner I didn't know where he put it. "Are you still eating?" I asked, after he had been served five portions of chicken. "I can still chew, but I can't swallow," he replied.

A lot of married men go up there as "single" boys just to have a holiday. They figure, "Every dog has his day, and the Catskills' nights were made for wolves."

Some of them send their wives to the country so they can do their wolfing at home, and as one wag put it, "I regret that I have but one wife to send to the country."

Don't get me wrong. Many beautiful romances have started on the borsht belt; and some of the most wonderful friendships that I have to this day, I first made in the Catskill Mountains.

One incident stands out in my mind from my fifteen years in the Catskills. Johnny Pransky and Al Beckman booked me to be the "Social Director" at the Plaza Hotel at Fallsburgh for the summer of 1934. Besides room and board, my salary was to be $1500 for the summer, a twelve-week period. Out of that money I was to pay Dudley Gilbert, a great comedian, who has remained my pal all these years; Bob Alda, now making $3000 a week at Warner Brothers; Bill Castle, the Columbia director; Elizabeth Royce, now with M.G.M.; and three other entertainers.

I was nervous about working at "such a big hotel" and complained to my friends, Beckman and Pransky,

"After all, I have to follow Lou Saxon, the king of the mountain entertainers, who was such a big hit there last summer."

"It's like any other hotel, you dope," Johnny lectured me; "only it's easier because there are more people to laugh." He showed me how to comb my hair to make me look taller, gave me a good pep talk, a bus ticket, and sent me on my way.

It was at the Plaza that all the "racket" guys spent the summer with their wives and children, and I was to entertain them. Lepke Buchalter and Gurrah Shapiro were there with their families. Harry Strauss and Abe Reles and all the rest of Murder, Inc. were guests. (Most of them have since died in the electric chair.) I danced with their wives and mothers and they all treated me nicely.

Mrs. Shapiro, who was the mother of Gurrah Shapiro, one of the heads of Murder, Inc., was the "Queen Bee"

Among the clientele were the Murder Inc. gang

at the Hotel. Everybody catered to her. Her son, in jail at the time, lined her path with gold. She was a lovely woman but only aware that her son must be a big man because everybody was so nice to her and she got everything she wanted.

My Mom was with me, too, and Leonard Lyons, the famous columnist of the *N. Y. Evening Post,* sent his mother up there. Our Moms became great pals; they were constant companions. They rushed into the casino every night, right after dinner, to make sure they had front seats, and very often waited two hours before the show went on. Leonard's mother, one of the sweetest women I ever met, went to night school so she could learn enough English to read her son's column in *The Post.* She was very proud of him.

Every night, the conversation before the show was the same. Mrs. Lyons would talk about "my Lennie," and my Mom about "my Joey."

Mrs. Shapiro, who invariably sat behind them, was getting "fed up" with listening to "my Lennie" and "my Joey." One day when Lennie came up to visit us, Mrs. Lyons said to my mother, "At last you'll get a chance to meet my Lennie."

Mrs. Shapiro couldn't stand it any longer. She yelled to her friends, so everybody in the casino could hear, "That's all I hear, Leonard Lyons, Leonard Lyons. He's only got his name in small letters in one paper. My son got his name in big letters and his picture on the front page of all the papers almost every day, but do I say anything?"

CHAPTER FOUR

"So, What's New?"

IN BROOKLYN, they always answer all questions with a question. If you ask a Brooklynite how he feels, he invariably will answer, "How should I feel?" If the question is, "What's new?" your answer will usually be, "So what could be new?" "How's the family?" will always get, "How could they be?"

That's why, when Marvin Schenck and Jessie Kaye asked me if I'd like to run the amateur shows at Loew's Pitkin and Loew's Premier in the Brownsville section of Brooklyn where I was born, I answered, "Why not?"

What's so wonderful about Brooklyn? All a night-club comedian has to do is crack the name of that borough, and the drunks forget about trying to make the cigarette girl and laugh themselves sober.

The home of "Dem Bums" has a personality all its own. The people there are real, honest, and friendly. They stick together and fight for their borough, their city, or their country at the drop of a bagel. They love their borough even more than the bobby soxers love Sinatra.

When Noel Coward, who has a one-crack mind, insulted the borough of my birth by insinuating that

Brooklyn boys aren't brave, the people from "over the river" rose up as one to fight the Coward and show the world the deeds of the Meyer Levins and the other heroes of their proud community.

No matter how much Brooklynites are ribbed and kidded, they always come up laughing. Their sense of humor is out of this world.

They laughed with delight when Eddie Foy remarked, in discussing the engineering feat of the Brooklyn Bridge: "All that trouble, just to get to Brooklyn?" When a doctor was examining a soldier in a recent picture and asked him, "Where were you born?" and the kid answered "Brooklyn," they screamed as the doctor asked, "Any other defects?"

They loved the story of Peter Minuit, who bought Manhattan from the Indians for $24. As Earl Wilson tells it, Minuit had closed the deal and was standing on the banks of the East River, staring across. "Say, wait a minute," he said, "isn't that Brooklyn over there?" "For $24," said the Indian chief, a lower East Side boy, "are you expecting the place to be perfect?"

Brooklynites kid about their own community, too. One soldier from the Flatbush section of Brooklyn was in London seeing the sights after a heavy battle, when an Englishman, who was making the rounds with him, asked, "How do you find our English women?" His answer was straight to the point: "The same as in Flatbush, by whistling."

Dr. Louis Satter, Brooklyn College professor, noted on the campus for his sense of humor, told a class after an unsatisfactory showing, "If this class were to stand up and form a circle, I'd be liable to arrest under the Federal statutes."

"Why?" they all asked.

"Because I'd be harboring a dope ring."

DAVE BREGER

The following story is supposed to have originated in the borough of Brooklyn. I have it from the reliable Al Buck, the famous sports writer of the *N. Y. Post:*

Leo Durocher, the temperamental leader of "Dem Bums," took Peter Gray, the one-armed outfielder of the St. Louis Browns, to get a shave. The barber knicked him five times. After it was over, the barber looked at Gray and said his face sure looked familiar. "Haven't I shaved you before?" he asked. "No," said Pete, "I lost this arm in an auto accident."

The people from "over the river" have a language all their own. When the great pitcher, Waite Hoyt, now a

Cincinnati radio announcer, got hurt in Brooklyn, papers headlined the story, "Hoyt hurt." Brooklynites reading the headlines excitedly pronounced it in their native tongue just the reverse, "Hurt Hoyt."

Sure they laugh with you when you poke fun at their borough, but don't challenge their courage or their civic pride or their great patriotism.

All over the world, any real Brooklynite signs the register, "Brooklyn, U.S.A."

I know you've read about Brooklyn as the home of Murder, Inc., but did you know that Brooklyn sold more war bonds than almost any city in the world? Have you heard about Dave Soden, who has dedicated his life to the poor and the unfortunate of every race, creed, and color? Did you know that men like Abe Stark and other merchants spend all their spare time helping the unfortunates of their borough, that Samuel Leibowitz and Mayor Bill O'Dwyer won't live any place else? Did you know that Brooklyn's casualty list in World War II was one of the biggest? That Brooklyn is the city of churches?

I've already mentioned one community in Brooklyn, called Brownsville, that is a city in a borough of a city. Brownsvillites have their own character and manner. They have their own way of speaking. A Bostonian is an American broadly speaking, but a Brownsvillite is an American badly speaking.

That's the neighborhood in which the Loew office decided I should start my career as a Master of Ceremonies for their amateur shows. I took the job for a good cause —'cause I needed the money. The Pitkin Theatre was only a stone's throw from the place where I was born.

At one time, to work in a theatre in Brownsville you had to be pretty tough. Anybody with ears and teeth was a sissy. You had to be a bass in order to live, and I was born a soprano.

But they told me all that had changed now. So I took the subway to Utica Avenue, and, brother, that is something! The motto of the I. R. T. is "The public be jammed." It was so crowded it was beginning to be fun.

The Pitkin audiences treated me very warmly right from the start. They went for me right away . . . but I managed to keep a safe distance away. I put them in the aisles that very first night: they were shooting craps.

One little gray-haired lady saved the night for me. As the band played the introduction to my music and the spotlight hit me as I walked on stage, she hollered, "Wonderful! Oy, goot!" When I went on with my specialty, near the end of the show, she was more excited than ever. She kept yelling, "Oh boy, is that goot! Wonderful, wonderful!" After the show I made it my business to wait for my little old fan and talk to her.

"How did you like the show?" I asked.

"Hmm, not bad," she answered nonchalantly.

"How did you like me?" I asked excitedly.

"Well, Eddie Cantor didn't die," she cautioned, "Al Jolson is still alive, George Jessel still makes a living, you're fair."

"Yes, but lady, all through the show you kept hollering, 'Wonderful, marvelous, sensational!', especially when I was on the stage."

"Why not?" she answered. "I have rheumatism. I was sitting in the front row and the spotlight was baking my back—wonderful, marvelous, sensational!"

It was at Loew's Pitkin, too, that I received my first fan letter, but that didn't discourage me. Little by little, the Brownsville gang began to like me and took me to their hearts. After that, I could do no wrong. They sent me presents and cheered for me even when the material was not so good. They laughed at the same jokes and waited to see me when I came out of the stage door.

Many of them brought me home-made candy or halvah or Indian nuts. My friend Jack Fischer of the Little Oriental sent me home-made *kishke*. It's a sort of breaded lead pipe. If you can't sleep and you toss in bed all night, go to the Little Oriental and eat some of the *kishke*. No more tossing in bed. No more jumping around. You'll just lie there, dead to the world.

Leaving the theatre, I would often be greeted with, "That was a swell show, Joey boy. Well, good luck! See you next week. If I live I'll see you Wednesday, if not, Thursday."

I'll never forget the faces of the two local partners who came to present me with a gift in token of their esteem. They got so mixed up in making the speech that they started fighting. "Who needs you as a partner?" shouted the smaller of the two. "Who needs *me*?" yelled the other. "Yeah, who needs you?" "I wish you the hardest luck in the world, you shouldn't have bread to eat and you should come to me and I shouldn't have it to give to you." The little man countered with, "You should lose every tooth in your mouth except one, and that should be left for a toothache!"

Many women even came to me with their problems. "I found my son in bed with the maid last night," said one woman, quite disturbed about it. "You're an actor, you know about such things, what do you think I should do?"

"Nothing," I advised her. "After all, it's a human thing."

"Yeah," she said, "before you know it, he'll be smoking cigarettes."

How could I get laughs? These people were funnier than anything I could ever say, so I decided to try some of their dialect and mannerisms on stage. Again Brooklyn's sense of humor came forward in a big way. They laughed and screamed at anything that poked fun at them in a good-natured way.

Myron Cohen, one of the greatest Jewish and Brooklyn dialecticians I ever heard, has made a study of the people of Brownsville. Some of his stories are the funniest I ever heard because they are so true to life.

Myron tells the story about the "candy-store cowboy" who walked into a soda fountain at Pitkin and Saratoga Avenues in Brownsville and told the clerk, "I want a chocolate banana-split sundae with whipped cream and melba, Indian nuts and halvah mixed."

The clerk said, "Vot da hell is dat?"

"Well," said the unabashed youth, "on the bottom you'll put three slices bananas, on top three scoops ice cream, then melba, Indian nuts, whipped cream, halvah, chocolate covered, more whipped cream, and a cherry on top."

"Please," said the clerk, "maybe you'll got time to come back Friday for a fitting?"

Myron swears this happened in front of Abe Stark's in Brownsville: Two friends were conversing. "You're so crooked," said one, "that the wool you're pulling over my eyes is fifty percent cotton."

His story about the three naughty girls who were brought before a Brooklyn judge for soliciting is a classic. A little peddler from Brownsville was in the same court that day for peddling without a license.

"What do you do for a living?" asked the judge of the first lady of the evening.

"I'm a hairdresser," lied the tart.

"Thirty days," said the judge.

"What do you do for a living?" he asked the second girl.

"I'm a dressmaker, your honor."

"Thirty days!" said the judge, angered.

"What do you do?" he asked the third one.

"I'm a prostitute," admitted the last of the three.

"For telling the truth, sentence suspended," said the old judge.

Then the little peddler was brought before the bar of justice. "What do you do for a living?" the judge asked.

"To tell you the truth," answered the street merchant, "I'm a prostitute."

Earl Wilson tells about the delicatessen store owner in Brownsville who was asked for some *lox* (smoked

DAVE BREGER

salmon). "Vot kind of lox," he inquired, "for itting or vashing?"

Walter Winchell relates an argument by two women in a tenement in that same neighborhood. "Who do you think you are?" yelled one. "Drop dead, that's who I am," answered the other.

Lou Holtz swears this happened: Sam Lapidus was talking to some friends in his store. "You know, I was just thinking that if I had Rockefeller's money, I'd be richer than Rockefeller."

"How do you figure that out?" asked Holtz.

"Because," explained Sam, "I'd also have my store."

Harry Hirshfield tells me the following happened to him at the St. George Hotel in Brooklyn, and he's been telling it ever since. He was in the elevator, going to do a benefit on the roof, when a woman approached him. "I'm glad you're doing such a good job for all the people and making them laugh. All people are good, no matter what the nationality. Look at me, I'm not anti-Semitic to the colored people!"

Peter Donald relates the story about the clothing manufacturer who was married thirty-five years and came home one day to find his wife in bed with his best friend. He looked at his pal sympathetically. "Jake," he said, "*I must* . . . but *you?*"

One incident that stands out in my mind is a story I've been telling for a long time. It actually happened while I was riding in the subway to Brooklyn, on my weekly trek to the Pitkin. It was Lincoln's birthday and I was looking at Honest Abe's picture on the front page of my evening newspaper while hanging on to a strap. For about five minutes I stood there admiring our sixteenth president; beard and all, he was a wonderful figure. From the corner of my eye I noticed an elderly lady, about seventy, standing next to me, leaning over my shoulder. She looked at the picture of Lincoln, then she looked at me, then back to Lincoln and back to me. Finally she got up enough nerve to tap me on the shoulder, and pointing to Honest Abe she said, "He looks like a familiar man from Brownsville—who did he kill?"

Henny Youngman tells of the woman who stayed through four shows when he was playing at the Pitkin. "Did you really like me so much?" he asked when he met her later. "No," she replied bluntly, "I just couldn't find my shoes."

Louis Sobol describes the two chaps who went to a funeral parlor to see an old friend who was laid out.

DAVE BREGER

"Hm," hmmed one of them, "he looks good."

"Why not?" answered the other. "He spent the whole winter in Florida!"

I must go back to my favorite dialectician, Myron Cohen. His stories about the two partners are classics.

Two partners were sitting in a restaurant having dinner, when one of them suddenly sat up startled. "My God!" he screamed, "I left the safe open." The other yawned, "So what, we're both here, ain't we?"

He also tells about the two Brownsvillites who met in the street. "Lend me ten dollars till I come back from Chicago, will you?" one of them pleaded.

"When are you coming back?" asked his friend.

"Who's going?"

The Little Oriental was crowded with customers one night. "What kind of lobster is dis to bring me?" hollered one of the customers, "it's only got one claw."

"I'm sorry," apologized Jack Fischer, the proprietor, "he was in a fight."

"So, you dope," screamed the diner, "bring me de winner."

Two women met on the street and one noticed that the other was wearing a V-neck sweater. "That V, that's for Victory?" asked the inquisitive one.

"No, for virgin," answered her friend.

DAVE BREGER

"You're a virgin?"

"It's an old sweater."

Brooklynites, and particularly Brownsvillites, laughed with the wits at all these quips. No matter how troubled they were, their sense of humor always came out ahead. Of course, most people in Brooklyn don't talk that way. The wits naturally look for the one they can "make fun" with.

Brooklynites are warm, sincere, and faithful people, and sentimental to the last.

The party they gave for me when I left the Pitkin

Theatre after two years as master of ceremonies will always be remembered by me as one of the sweetest things of my entire career. Ten thousand people showed up in a theatre that seats 3800. Thousands more were turned away and thousands heard the show and the ceremonies from the street where Al Weiss, the manager, had placed microphones. Almost every merchant in town presented me with gifts. Jewelry, suits, haberdashery, flowers, shoes, radios, luggage were only some of the gifts I received. They made a *tsimmes* [1] over me that brought tears to my eyes. Everybody from Borough President Cashmore to the manager of the theatre made a speech.

Dozens of stars came to the "farewell" party. Bill O'Dwyer, Abe Stark, and the Non-Pareil Club made me presentations. Judges, senators, congressmen, and all my friends from Brownsville showed up.

You can imagine how terrible I felt later on when circumstances made it necessary for me to hock some of those wonderful presents to pay a lot of debts. The darkest hour is just before the pawn.

[1] *Tsimmes.* Stew, fuss, to-do.

CHAPTER FIVE

Indoor Tan

"W<small>HY</small> don't you change your name from Abrams to Adams?" suggested my friend Bill Pludo, who was then vice-president of Adam Hats. "It might bring you luck."

"W-e-ll," I stammered, "I—."

"Well, nothing," Bill interrupted. "If it was good enough for two presidents of the United States, it's certainly good enough for you. And look at Adam, he started out naked, now he's got hat stores everywhere."

I decided to try the new name. If I flopped, I could always go back to my original name and they would never know me from Adams . . .

"You need more than a change of name," Harry Hershfield decided. "You need a change of gags." The dean of story tellers gave me new gags and timely stories. In a few weeks I went from Joe Miller to Harry Hershfield.

I took advice from everybody and tried everything. Colonel Jay C. Flippen cautioned me about working hard. "You've got to put your whole heart into what you're doing," said Jay, "and you can't miss. All work and no play makes Jack. You've got plenty of time to play when you're on the stage."

*"You've got to put your whole
heart into what you're doing"*

I did what the Colonel suggested. I was to my gags
what Betty Grable was to her sweater—we both put
everything we had into it.

I had very little time for fresh air or exercise. When I
felt like exercising I lay down till the feeling went away.
I was beginning to get an "indoor tan." I developed a
traffic-light complexion—red eyes and green face.

"Each new show under your belt is another step up
the ladder," was Bert Lahr's advice. "Play any place and
anything that has an audience."

I worked every little vaudeville theatre in almost
every little town in the country. I ate in so many one-
armed joints, I was beginning to get purple-heartburn.
The rooming situation was terrible, too. Some broken-
down hotels and rooming houses charged seven and
eight dollars a day, if you slept sideways. They could fit
more people that way.

I found myself in places like Lynn, Mass., on New
Year's Eve. Let's face it. Lynn is a helluva place for a

New Yorker to be on New Year's Eve or New Year's
Day or, for that matter, any day.

With me, acting is a gift, but even as a gift, the Lynn
audiences didn't want it.

But all the time I was learning new gags, trying out

*Jimmy Walker taught me the importance of
dressing well*

new stories, and getting experience, "more shows under
my belt."

Jimmy Walker taught me the importance of dressing
well at all times. I went to Kolmer-Marcus, where my
good friends Willie Kolmer and Jack Marcus spent
weeks trying to find the right type of clothes for me,
to make me look good, or as good as I could look.

I bought Beau Brummell ties, Adler Elevator Shoes,

Beau Brummell toilet water—everything to give me a "front." Clothes certainly "fake" the man.

It was my father who warned me about drinking to excess. "Stay away from booze," my dad drilled into me, and he certainly knew how to drill. He believed in the axiom, "A pat on the back develops character if administered often enough, hard enough, and low enough."

Even as a kid, I found out that drinking doesn't drown your troubles, it just irrigates them. It's all right to drink like a fish if you drink what a fish drinks.

Chuck Hamilton, the fabulous Broadway character and pal of Damon Runyon, was also generous with his counsel. "Wilson Mizner gave me this advice many years ago and I'm passing it on to you. Hear me good, so I won't have to show you slides," he continued in his own vernacular. "Always make 'em think you have money. If they think you're broke, they'll cross streets to avoid seeing you. If they think you're loaded with dough, they'll smile and say 'How are you?' and shake your hand even when they hear you have leprosy."

"Have confidence in what you're doing," my pal

Horace MacMahon, the movie villain, stressed to me, "but don't get big-headed. Conceit is a form of I-strain that doctors can't cure."

Horace gave me the confidence and the affection I needed. The man who had killed Humphrey Bogart thirty-two times on the screen worked with me and cautioned me about Broadway in general. "Remember what Winchell said," he reminded me: " 'Look out for the guy that pats you on the back, he's looking for a place to put the knife.' And don't worry about being the greatest comedian—just make 'em laugh."

Sammy Walsh, one of the better comedians, bills himself as "America's No. 2 Comedian." When anybody asks him who is No. 1, he says, "I dunno, they're all fighting about it."

Horace, too, impressed me with the importance of humility. "Don't let applause, good notices, and laughs go to your head. Compliments are like perfume, to be inhaled but not swallowed."

Jessie Kaye, the Loew booker, and one of the nicest fellows in all show business, cautioned me about my rapid-fire delivery. "You talk so fast, I can't even tell who you stole the jokes from."

I tried to remember all these chunks of advice. I tried to make my memory a storehouse instead of a lumber room. Things started to get better. Perhaps the change of name was lucky. Even the wolf at my door was beginning to gain weight.

That's when I met my first romance. Her name was Sara Taitz, an elocution teacher, pretty as a picture.

Her father was the Reverend Taitz, a wonderful little man who was very fond of me because I used to sing him his favorite folk songs.

He cautioned me about my future. "My wife will never let Sara marry an actor," he told me in confidence.

I really knocked myself out

I guess she didn't know I was an actor when she permitted me to visit their home so often. She probably thought I smuggled dope.

"Please come and see me at the Mt. Morris Theatre tonight. It's only a couple of blocks from your house," I pleaded with the little preacher. "Maybe after you see me work, you can make Mrs. Taitz change her mind."

When I saw him in the audience that night, I really knocked myself out. I did my entire show for him, with a lot added. After the show, I ran straight to the Taitz home. "How did you like the show, Reverend?" I asked with great pride.

. "That's all right, you can marry my daughter," he said. "You're not an actor."

I didn't receive the Reverend's praise or his daughter's hand, but that didn't discourage me.

I was booked to play my first good night club in Utica, New York. Would I lie to you? I was a big hit. They held me over for six cancelled checks. One of the owners ran away with the money and I was stuck with my first "good notices," a lot of compliments, and six hunks of rubber. But I was happy. The audience laughed.

Wolfe Kaufman, who was with *Variety* at the time, gave me my first good notice in that famed theatrical weekly. I was working in a flash act with sixteen girls, at the Grand Opera House at Twenty-third Street and Eighth Avenue, in New York City. He'll never know the encouragement and happiness he gave "the unbilled youth who looks like a comer."

Jackie Osterman, one of the great wits of all time, saw the same show and remarked in his column in *Variety*, "Joey Adams at the Grand Opera House does an imitation of Milton Berle, that's certainly covering a lot of territory."

Leon Fields, an old friend, suggested we do a double act in vaudeville. We convinced the manager of the Bronx Opera House that we were local boys and if we got "top billing" we could pack his theatre every day.

He took a chance with us and put our name up in

lights, "Fields and Adams and Co." The "company" was Mary Rose, an adorable and talented dancer, who later became my wife and my ex-wife. Our act laid the biggest egg in the history of the theatre, but Mary stopped the show cold with her great dancing. After the first show, the manager changed the billing on the marquee to read, "Mary Rose and Co."

I went back to doing a "single," and from then on things really started to come my way. I finally played Loew's State and worked with some great stars. Lucille Ball, Desi Arnaz, Harrison and Fisher, Sheila Barrett, Smith and Dale, and Jean Parker rounded out the bill,

From then on, things really started to come my way

with me as Master of Ceremonies. They gave me this wonderful show to introduce, just in case. . . .

Every time I think of that incident with Jean Parker, I blow my top. It was one of the funniest things that ever happened in a theatre. At the end of her act, at every show, she did a cancan number. On the last day, just as she was about to pick her skirts up to do her high kicks, she accidentally slipped and fell. She walked off stage, embarrassed, without doing the number.

After the show I went to her dressing room to console her. She was doubled up with laughter. "What luck!" she screamed. "When I got back to my room I was in tears until I discovered how lucky I was not to do the cancan number. For the first time in my life I had dressed in a hurry, and I'd forgotten to put my panties on!"

It was at the world-famous Leon and Eddie's that I started my climb into the big money. I entertained at one of their famous Sunday night celebrity parties, and Leon and Eddie took me into their private room and offered me the job as M.C. to replace Eddie Davis who was going on vacation.

"I'm scared to follow you, Eddie. And furthermore, when I did a benefit with Tony Canzoneri, the champ, the other day, I promised him he'd work with me from now on."

"Okay," said Eddie, "I like a guy who admits he's afraid; sign him up, Leon, and Canzoneri, too, before he wants me to hire the whole Brooklyn Dodgers team."

And so began one of the pleasantest relationships and

the most important step in the theatrical careers of Canzoneri and Adams, and Mark Plant, who was to join us later on.

It was at Leon and Eddie's that I started to crash the Broadway columns. Until then I couldn't even crash the telephone directories. The day I started there, a little guy from Ohio started as the Saloon Editor of the *N. Y. Evening Post*. My show was the first one he covered, and he was one of the first men to sing my praises. We became great friends. I'll always be grateful to Earl Wilson for being in my corner right from the beginning.

Lee Mortimer, the famous night-club and motion-picture editor of the *Mirror*, was another member of the fourth estate who encouraged me and stayed on my side. Virginia Forbes of the *Sun*, Bob Dana of the *World-Telegram*, Frank Coniff of the *Journal-American*, Bill Smith of *Billboard*, Joe Cohen of *Variety*, Abel Green himself, all cheered me on. I'll never stop being grateful to them.

It was at Leon and Eddie's that I met George Raft and Bob Hope. All the stars were regular visitors: Cesar Romero, Billy DeWolfe, Bing Crosby, Joe E. Lewis, Frank Fay, Bert Wheeler, Belle Baker, Sophie Tucker, Ella Logan, Phil Baker, Bert Lahr, Frank Sinatra, Monty Woolley, Art Waner, the talented pianist-composer, and many others. All of them helped me with advice and words of encouragement.

Lois Andrews, the former Mrs. George Jessel, was a regular visitor for the late show every night. I tried to impress her with a dance one night as she was sitting

ringside. "Can Jessel do this?" I threw at her, as I did
an intricate step. "Are you kidding?" she kidded. "He
can't even walk."

Joe Pasternak, Dorothy Kilgallen, Danton Walker,
and Ed Sullivan were others who were nice to me with
precious compliments. One night Mark Sandrich, the
Paramount producer-director, came in, and after the
show signed me to do the comedy lead in a picture
with Bing Crosby called "Blue Skies." I was all packed
to leave for the Coast when I heard on the air that Mr.
Sandrich had died that very day.

I met a lot of characters at the famous Fifty-second
Street bistro, too.

The guy that annoyed me the most was the out-of-
towner who waved a $20 bill in my face. "Get me a
dame and it's yours." He would usually find himself on
his *derrière* on the sidewalk. Leon and Eddie's never
allowed "mixing" at the Club between patrons and
chorus girls.

Of course, other little clubs on the East Side flourished
because of mixing. One of them even fired a talking dog
because he couldn't mix.

Some characters brought their girls into the club, not
to watch the show but to get them drunk fast at the bar
so they could take them home. They told me, "Candy is
dandy, but liquor is quicker."

It was at Leon and Eddie's that I encountered one of
the most spine-chilling incidents of my entire life. It was
in 1943 and the audience consisted of many men in uniform. Eddie Davis was entertaining, and the audience

was screaming with laughter. That is, everybody but one table next to me. Three people were sitting there— a marine colonel, a corporal, and a private. They were watching Eddie with somber faces, not a smile on their lips. The "boss" was in great form that night. The packed crowd was hysterical at his gags and songs, all but the solemn three at the table to my right. I couldn't take my eyes off them. I noticed that Eddie looked in their direction, too.

After the show I went over to compliment the Fifty-second Street minstrel on his great performance, when I saw the colonel approach us. "I want you to know I enjoyed your show very much, Mr. Davis," said the leatherneck officer.

"Well, you certainly didn't show it, sir," said Eddie.

"I feel you deserve an explanation," said the elderly officer. "There were two thousand of us on Guadalcanal. We had been on the island for months. Our ammunition and food were getting very low, with no help in sight. The Jap snipers were picking us off daily. The only amusement we had was a copy of *Esquire* with pictures of Leon and Eddie's and all its gaiety. Every man on the island read that magazine at least fifty times. It was our only contact with home and fun. And we all made a vow, from the smallest private to the commanding officer, that if any of us ever came out of this alive, we would all meet at Leon and Eddie's on our first day on American soil. So you see, Mr. Davis, there are only three of us left, and we were watching and enjoying the show for two thousand dead marines."

We played many hospitals in the afternoons to try to bring a little fun to some of those kids who had done so much for us. At Halloran Hospital I met a little Brooklyn boy who was completely out of hand. "Why don't you talk to him, Joey?" one of the nurses asked me. "He's from your home town and maybe he'll listen to you. He gambles, drinks, talks dirty, grabs all the girls that pass, and is an all-around character."

"Why don't you behave yourself, son?" I cautioned the youngster. "You've got plenty of time to knock yourself out."

"Aren't you Joey Adams from Loew's Pitkin?" asked the kid.

I was thrilled that he recognized me, and figured that now maybe my errand would be easier. "Yes," I answered.

"Didn't you give blood to the blood bank about six months ago?" he inquired further.

"Yes, I did."

"Well, meet the guy that got it."

We entertained at all the Army camps we could reach in the afternoon. At Camp Dix we played to thousands of servicemen: fifty thousand G.I.'s and fifty nurses in one camp. In the vernacular of Winston Churchill, never have so many chased so few, for so long, for so little.

One day a comparatively unknown and unimportant actor received an invitation to meet the President of the United States, Franklin Delano Roosevelt. It was the most important thing that has ever happened to the little vaudevillian. The appointment was for 3:05 p.m. and for five minutes.

He idolized the great president. Roosevelt was the one man, in all the world, that he would get on his knees to. He arrived at the White House at 1:05, two hours before the appointment. He made up his mind to remember every word the sponsor of the four freedoms would say. Each word would always live in his mind.

The actor's blue serge suit had a crease in it like a knife, and his white collar was starched for the first time. He didn't sit down in the two hours that he waited; he wanted to look just so.

When the President's secretary called him to enter, the actor's heart was in his mouth. What could he say?

Tell me some of your Roosevelt stories.

He forgot all that he had planned. As he entered, the greatest American stood up and said, "Come in, son, welcome! How's the family? I hear you're good at dialect stories. Tell me, do you know any good Roosevelt stories?"

The President stood up for the little actor! The little vaudevillian told him stories for thirty-five minutes. Roosevelt laughed and laughed. "Come to see me again, will you?" he said as the boy was leaving.

"This is a great country," replied the actor, "when a little nobody like me can come and talk things over with the No. 1 man."

"That's why this is a democracy worth fighting for," said our commander-in-chief.

After that, how could anybody ever think himself important? Who could ever get "big-headed?"

Several months later, when the actor was playing at a theatre in Washington, he received a note from Marguerite LeHand, the President's secretary. "The President wants to know if you can spare a few moments to tell him your latest Roosevelt and dialect stories."

Could *the actor* spare a few moments?!

Our country was in the middle of the worst war of all mankind and the President found time to send a note to a little comedian who had amused him!

There was a grand lesson in humility for all of us to heed. The greatest man of our times was the most humble, most human person of all.

CHAPTER SIX

At Last, the Waldorf

"OKAY, Schmo," shouted the cab driver. "Here's da Waldorf. Geez, are yiz dreamin' again?"

For the second time that night my pal took me out of a trance. "Thanks, Buddy," I sarcasmed, "just put my bags on the curb."

At long last, the Waldorf. This was the tomorrow I had looked forward to, yesterday . . .

As I started to enter the Waldorf lobby, a phony streak hit me from nowhere. I put my hat at a Jimmy Walkerish angle, fixed my muffler in the form of an ascot, and strolled into the famous Park Avenue hotel.

This was the moment I had waited for. All the ham in me came out as I entered with the assurance and tread of a Barrymore. As I got to the middle of the lobby, I got a bang on my back and a voice yelled, "Well, I'll be a son-of-a-b——!! Joey Abrams, what the hell are you doing here?" I turned around to see a bellboy grinning from ear to ear, his dirty hand outstretched.

"How do you do?" I nodded, still trying to keep up my front.

"What are you, a big shot?" said the bellhop. "I re-

member you from Loew's Pitkin when we used to throw
spitballs at you."

"Okay, okay," I squirmed, "see you later."

I continued to walk proudly over to the desk to register. "Look who's here!" said the girl behind the desk.
"Remember me from the Plaza Hotel in the Catskills?"

"Oh yes," I said very quietly. "Where do I register? I
have a suite reserved for Joey Adams."

"I remember you when you were Abrams," said my
new friend. "Tell us that joke you used to tell about
the—"

"I'm sorry, I've been traveling all night and—."

"Oh, come on," she pleaded, "just one joke." And she
called over all the charwomen, bellboys, and clerks to
listen to me. I had no choice. There I was at 4:30 in the

morning, telling jokes to all the night staff at the Waldorf-Astoria. And I wanted to be a big shot. I had to tell them about twenty jokes before they'd let me register and go to my room.

I made one last effort at being a big shot. When the bellboys took my bags to my room, I nonchalantly whipped out two five-dollar bills and offered it to them.

"Are you kiddin'?" said one of them. "You're one of us; we can't take money from you."

Success has made failures of many men. Thank goodness, I was taught my lesson in time.

The next morning when I entered the elevator, everybody around me was wearing jewels and sables. The elevator operator spied me and shouted, "Hey, Joey, there ain't no benefit shows in the building today. What the hell are you doing here?"

That's all, brother . . .

CHAPTER SEVEN

The House That Crum-Bums Built

As I turned the corner, on my way over to Toots Shor's, I was thinking of Joe E. Lewis' classic warning, "Don't let failure go to your head."

"Oh, well," I kept mumbling to myself, "I'm going where I'm wanted. I'm a celebrity at Toots Shor's. All the stars are pals of mine and Toots is my buddy."

I was anxious to see the famous oversized proprietor of the world-renowned Fifty-first Street restaurant. He's a character in his own right and has a profile like a set of keys. All the polish he has, he can wear on his fingernails. But he has more class than all of society put together.

He's very easy with a buck—he'll pay anything but a compliment. He loves to tease and rib his friends, and his friends include the biggest in politics, business, and the show world.

Frank Sinatra gave Toots a beautiful watch inscribed, "Any pal of Sinatra's is a pal of mine." Yet when they met in front of a theatre in Philadelphia, Toots ribbed the bobby-sox favorite with "Here, boy, get me a paper," and handed Frankie a dollar bill. And a little bobby-soxer who overheard him, said to Shor, "You fat thing!"

Bob Hannegan gave Toots a "medal" on the day he took office as Postmaster General. "Now maybe you'll respect me as a member of the Cabinet." "You're still a crum-bum," answered the fat man.

When Truman was vice-president, he loved to eat at 51 West 51st, just to listen to Toots' lingo and insults. The big boy has no respect for titles or names. All his customers are alike.

Charlie Chaplin was waiting in line one day and insisted on a table. "You'll have to wait, Charlie," said Toots. "In the meantime, make funny for the customers."

He admits he was a bum in Philly and that he has chronic palpitation of the tongue, but his gruff sense of humor has really paid off.

I have it from reliable authority, his adorable wife, that it's not fat he has around his waist, it's a money belt. He will insult anybody but his wife, "Baby," who is as lovely today as when she worked in the front line of the Ziegfeld Follies. Toots admits he married her when she wasn't looking. She is the only person he takes orders from. He led her to the altar, but from then on, his leadership stopped.

His "crum-bum" expression, used on all customers, is finding its way into dictionaries. Tootsie once used the term to apply to a great political figure, then an opponent of Franklin D. Roosevelt. F. D. R. heard about it and roared with laughter, asking for the spelling of the word, and said, "Spell it out again."

His insults are quoted in columns every day. "He's become such a celebrity," said Earl Wilson, "he'll soon be too big a man to hang around Toots Shor's."

He slaps Ann Sheridan and Carole Landis on the back and follows up with, "Hiya, Babe." To Lana Turner he said, "Put yer skirts down, kid, my waiters can't concentrate on their work." When Milton Berle comes in and walks from table to table, he screams, "Sit down, hammy, we saw yer suit."

"My waiters can't concentrate on their work"

Any noise irritates him, yet he is as soft-spoken as a train announcer, and as quiet as a traffic cop when you pass a red light.

No matter how many comedians are in the room, it's Toots who is always "on." I've seen him at a table with Jack Benny, Bob Hope, Bert Lahr, Eddie Cantor, and Danny Kaye, and Toots was getting the laughs.

He loved Roosevelt and was one of his biggest boosters, contributing to his election and soliciting votes even from the renowned Republicans that frequent his place. Toots never asks personal favors of any of his political pals, but never refuses anything that is asked of him.

Every member of his capable staff loves him. He's a two-fisted fighter and a four-fisted drinker, a man's man. When all the night-club owners were complaining about the curfew and hollering "Twelve o'clock and all is hell," Toots screamed, "Anybody who can't get drunk by twelve o'clock ain't tryin'."

His friend, Col. Nicky Blair, who operated the Carnival, escorted his precocious eleven-year-old son, Eddie, over to Toots Shor's restaurant one night. Eddie sought out the quiet, retiring political adviser. "Uncle Toots," he piped up, "why do folks up my way make such a fuss about Roddie Rockfeller? He goes to my school in Riverdale and plays on my football team. He plays okay, but shucks! he's no All-American candidate in *my* book."

His father murmured, "Well, his pop is kinda important, son."

"Important!" bellowed Toots, making certain that Gen. Hap Arnold and Brig. Gen. "Rosie" O'Donnell, who were at the adjoining table, could hear every word. "Important! Listen, Eddie, I own a saloon, right? Well, this Rockfeller kid's pop used to own a saloon right across the street—the Rainbow Room—and you wanna know sumpin', the joint is closed. That kid's pop couldn't make the grade as a saloon keeper!"

Toots Shor wears plain, well-tailored clothes but never evening wear. "I like to wear my own clothes," he says.

When a movie writer asked him, "Who writes your insults?" He sarcasmed, "Are you making a personal appearance to apologize for these last pictures you wrote?"

He is a great lover of sports and knows the record of every baseball player, particularly the Giants, his idols. Mel Ott, the famous manager of the team, is his pal. Leo Durocher is always around to rib Toots when the Dodgers beat the Giants. That doesn't stop the fat man. "I saw your team play tonight," he ribs Lippy. "Why, ya creep, ya was just lucky. Those crum-bums of yours couldn't whip potatoes in my kitchen."

Irving Hoffman, eating some pot cheese in the restaurant, complained about it to his pal, Bob Goldstein. "He says it doesn't taste right," Bob said to Toots; "come on—taste it." "Why should *I* taste it?" hollered Toots. "Let *him* get sick!"

If he's sitting with celebrities of the theatre and someone asks for his autograph and ignores the stars, that's Toots' cue to tell them, "Why ya crum-bums, ya think yer important—why don'tcha open a candy store?"

C. D. RUSSELL

"Let's go to the round table at Shor's—he lets all the other crum-bums in"

When La Guardia accompanied Gen. Ike Eisenhower
to the Polo Grounds for the Giants' baseball tribute to the
great general, Toots Shor sat in the same box with them.
"Your little pal, Joey Adams, is opening at the Capitol
Theatre," Toots whispered, "and he's getting $2000 a
week."

"That's wonderful!" the mayor commented. "But on
second thought, he's making four times as much as I am."

"Why not?" retorted the brusque Toots, who's no re-
specter of titles. "*He's* got *talent!*"

When Toots appeared on Jack Eigen's program on
WMCA, he admitted, "Last week the radio was on the
bum; this week the bum is on the radio."

He attends all the fights at the Garden and is always
on hand when any of his crum-bum pals opens in a night
club. He goes to all the Mike Todd openings, but last
year when Todd presented Maurice Evans in *Hamlet* he
didn't want to go. "I hate that high-brow stuff, and this
guy Shakespeare never eats in my joint, anyway." When
Todd pleaded with him to attend because "You're lucky
for me," Toots finally accepted.

At the first act intermission, or as Toots calls it, "between halves," he expressed his admiration for the play:
"It's cops-and-robbers stuff." And when he returned to
his seat, he looked around the theatre and said, "I'm the
only guy in da joint who don't know what's goin' to happen from now on."

He doesn't like to see his famous crum-bums annoyed
by autograph seekers. He chased a would-be autograph-
seeker away from Jerry Lester when Jerry was having

dinner. "Thanks, Toots," said the fiery little guy. "Don't thank me, ya bum," yelled Toots. "I just didn't want my customers ta carry worthless things away with 'em."

Only once have I seen Toots lost for words. The Giants had won six straight games in a row and he was in wonderful spirits. He was giving all the guests drinks on the house and slapping everybody on the back. All the celebs were target for his insults that night. One woman, who couldn't understand his ribbing of her favorite celebrities, finally approached the roaring host and said angrily, "You're the kind of bum you try to keep out of your place!" And Toots didn't utter a word.

No person who ever met the big fellow has failed to fall for his gruff but lovable charm. I was no exception. The night I went over I hadn't been there for months. I was anxious to see him again, and I knew that he would be glad to see me.

"Hiya, Tootsie old boy," I greeted as I entered the door.

"Why, ya bum, where ya been? La Guardia is out of office, screw, we don't want ya here. What are ya, a big man 'cause you're opening at the Capitol?"

Well, I said to myself with an easy breath, here we go again. It's good to be home.

I'm anxious to see all my old pals. I hate to table-hop, but I've been away a long time. I must go over and say hello to Earl Wilson. "Earl, it's good to see you," I greet. "I got a great story for you."

"Yes?" says Earl. "What is it?"

"It's about the woman who was driving along hitting

everything and everybody in sight, passing red lights, and finally winding up around a pole. 'Let's see yer license,' said the cop when he finally got to her. 'You mean,' said the lady, 'with that kind of driving, they'll give me a license?'"

"O.O. McIntyre used it in 1908," Earl squelched. "But keep tryin', kid. See you later."

I must go over and see Jimmy Walker. "Jimmy, I'm writing a book. Do you—."

"Why not buy one, it's cheaper," the former mayor interrupts.

My pals are certainly glad to see me. "When did you get back?" says Leonard Lyons.

"Just today, Lennie. Say, I got a good story for you. A man and woman were brought before the bar of justice, looking for a divorce. The judge asked how many children they had. 'Three' was the answer. 'Why don't you wait another year?' suggested the judge. 'Then you'll have four children. You'll take two, you'll take two, and everybody will be happy.' 'Supposing we have twins, your Honor,' said the husband. 'Look at him, twins!' shouted the wife. 'If I depended on him, I wouldn't have these three either!'"

"I can't use it," says Lennie.

"Why not?" I shout. "It's a good story."

"Yeah, but I don't think Bennett Cerf can print it."

Bert Lahr is at his regular table doing his usual moanalogue. "I bought a car from the Smiling Irishman," he complains, "and now it's all falling apart."

"Why don't you put an ad in the paper?" suggests

Nicky Blair: "Just bought car from Smiling Irishman; who would like to buy it from a sad Jew?"

"Hiya, fellers," I greet. "I just got into town. Did you know I was writing a book?"

"I didn't know you could read," heckles Bert Wheeler. They've all caught it from Toots.

Oscar Levant is having his eighteenth cup of coffee. "Hey, Joey, tell the waiter to bring me another cup of coffee. Explain to him that I'm not normal, will ya?"

"Did you hear about my book, Oscar?" I return the greeting with pride.

"That's like Broadway Rose writing the society column for the *Herald Tribune*."

I must say hello to my old friend Monte Proser of the Copacabana, who ran a fortune into a shoestring. "Howya, Monte, you look like ya had a big night."

"It was awful drunk out last night," the little producer answers. "What are you doing in town?—as if I cared."

"I'm opening at the Capitol and—."

"Geez," he sneers, "that place is certainly going down."

Toots is telling Frank Sinatra about his visit with General Eisenhower. "That guy is in a different spear," shouts the reticent Shor. "Meet a real entertainer, ya bum," he yells at me as I approach the table. "Ya think yer makin' a lot of loot when ya open at the Capitol? He makes more with one song than you do in a year."

"That's not true," says the boy with the swoon in his mouth, remembering the taxes. "All that I am or ever hope to be, I owe."

"Didja know," shouts Toots, "that inmates in loonatic asylums don't think they're Napoleon any more? They all think they're Sinatra!"

Jimmy Cagney, the Irishman, is there, telling Maxie Rosenbloom the correct way to pronounce some Yiddish words.

Levant is still looking for his nineteenth cup of coffee when the Goldstein twins, Bob and Leonard, join him at the table. "I wish you wouldn't go around together," he tells them. "I can't tell which one of you doesn't like me. Not that I have any enemies—I haven't—but all my friends hate me."

Ex-Sgt. Broderick Crawford, the film actor, was in New York for months, even after he received his army discharge. His mother, Helen Broderick, who knows just where Crawford can be found any time of day, sent him a message. He was reading it as I approached his table: "Son," it read, "haven't you got enough points to get out of Toots Shor's?"

"Hell-o, kid," says Milton Berle, holding my arm and looking all around the room for recognition. "I hear you're writing a book. Well, don't steal any of the gags from *Out of My Trunk*." That's the title of Milt's joke book.

"I won't, I don't go in for petty larceny." I'm beginning to get the Toots Shor "feel." "By the way, I hear your book is selling like hot cakes."

"Yeah," Berle admits; "I wish they would sell like books."

"Truthfully," I inquired, "is your book any good, Milton?"

"Any good!" he spouted. "Last year I had a million copies printed."

"Can you spare one?" I asked.

"One? I got a million of 'em."

Bing Crosby joins Frank Sinatra and Toots Shor at the corner table. "Is it true, Bing," roars Toots, "that you bought your horses a mirror so they could see what a horse's head looks like?"

"I don't have to do that," flings Bing. "I can bring them in here to look at you."

"You're just sore," hollers Toots, "because Frankie is my favorite singer, ya crum-bum."

"Joey, darling," greets Gypsy Rose Lee when she spies me wandering around the room.

"Hiya, Gyp," I reply to the girl who ekes out a bare existence. "How's June? I hear your sister's in a dither over her opening at the Capitol with me. This is her first appearance in vaudeville in years. Is she sick or nervous?"

"You know Havoc," said Gypsy, "—one part sickness, one part nervousness, and two parts ham."

Before I sit down to eat, I must say hello to one of my

all-time favorites, Fred Allen. "I thought you were going to Hollywood to make a picture, Fred."

"Hollywood is no place for a professional comedian, kid," said Fred. "There's too much amateur competition. California is a fine place to live if you happen to be an orange."

As I pass by Barbara Stanwyck's table, Earl Wilson is saying, "Are you going to see Frank Fay in *Harvey*?"

"No," says the former Mrs. Fay, "I've seen all the rabbits he has to offer."

"It's about time ya stopped takin' bows around the joint," shouts Toots. "Sit down and pay a tab for a change, ya bum. Join those other crum-bum comics at the round table."

The "other crum-bum comics" are Jerry Lester, Jay C. Flippen, Joe E. Lewis, Bert Lahr, and Bert Wheeler, a handful of the most famous clowns in the country.

"Which of my gags are ya going to do at the Capitol?" heckles Lester, when I sit down.

"So you're writing a book," annoys Lahr. "Who is translating it into English?"

"I'm the only comedian not writing a book," says Joe E. "That makes me a celebrity."

"That Adams has a lot of talent," ribs Flippen, "but it's in Bob Hope's name."

"Leave the kid alone," singes Bert Wheeler. "He's as happy as if he were in his right mind."

Gee, it's good to be back with your friends . . .

CHAPTER EIGHT

"Everybody Wantsa Get in duh Act"

A REGULAR session of the "round table" at Toots Shor's always has a handful of comedians, Earl Wilson, Jack O'Brian, the young and talented drama critic of the Associated Press; Jack Eigen, Broadway and Hollywood reporter of WMCA; a couple of press agents, a few show girls, Chuck Hamilton, the fabulous Broadway character who never was on a stage in his life but knows everything about everything and is always the last word, Orson Welles, and Toots himself.

Frank Young, the writer; Paul Douglas, Nicky Blair, Harry Bloomfield, the producer; Paul Denis, and Jimmy Walker are others who join the "heckle sessions" from time to time. They discuss everything and everybody. Nobody in show business ever escapes their scalpels.

"I just pulled the greatest heckle line on the stage of the Capitol," I said to the gang at the round table one night. "Some character in the audience annoyed me and I told him if he disappeared suddenly, it couldn't happen to a nicer guy."

"The greatest!" shouted Chuck Hamilton. "He's around Broadway a hot second and right away he pulls 'the greatest heckle line.' Did you ever hear of Frank Fay? I

100

go away back with hecklers, you know. A couple of guys sitting around this table aren't spit either."

"The best ad lib. I ever pulled on a heckler," interrupted Joe E. Lewis, "happened at the Copacabasement where I work. Some alleged friend of mine was annoying me all through my act. I finally squelched him with, 'I don't know what I'd do without you, pal, but I'd rather.'"

Bert Lahr uttered his pet sizzler to a punk who passed Bert's table one night at Howie's and cut him dead. Some of the others at the table teased him about it. "Makes no difference," squelched Bert. "If that punk had said what was on his mind, he'd still be speechless."

"I was working at the Roxy," added Jerry Lester, "and wearing my best Beau Brummell tie, when a wise guy hollered, 'Where did you get that tie?' I stopped him dead with 'I can change my tie, but how about your face?'"

"We were at Leon and Eddie's one night," chimed in Jay C. Flippen, "and they asked me to M.C. the celebrity night. Eric Blore came on stage and he was a little high. I couldn't get him back to his table. Finally I suggested, 'Will somebody at Blore's table please open the bottle so he can find his way back?'"

"I think Jack Waldron's answer to a drunk," suggested Earl Wilson, "is my prize for the best topper of the year: 'Let's play horsie; I'll play the front part and you stay as sweet as you are.'"

"Are ya through, fellers?" interrupted Chuck Hamilton. "The kid here," he said pointing to himself, "will now

tell you a little about the art of heckling, if I can get 'on'
for a minute. A guy called Jack White, who used to work
at the Club 18—do you hear me good?—was annoyed by
a woman heckler. His back talk fractured the woman and
the audience: 'You wouldn't like it if I came where you
worked and turned out the red light.' That'll do, won't
it, fellas?" said Chuck. "Now you can close the book."

Down through the years, the heckler has been a can-
cer in the life of showpeople. Some of their answers are
classics in the art of ad lib. You might be able to use some
of their retorts on your nagging wife or your stay-out-
late husband.

Remember 'way back in 1945 when the war was on
and cabdrivers and waiters were nasty? When the guy
behind the nylon and kleenex counters gave you dirty
looks and your butcher closed the door in your face?
Remember the abuse you took from the cigar-store salesman and the conductor in the bus who let you off four
blocks too late? Here is your chance to get even. Mem-
orize some of these squelches and use them on your
former hecklers. Does your hotel clerk act sarcastic, does
your maid still give you trouble? Are you annoyed by
drug-store cowboys who whistle at you? Here are my
favorite ad libs. hurled by my favorite wits:

Fred Allen described a man as "so small he's a waste
of skin."

Walter Winchell sent a wire to Senator Bilbo on his
birthday: "I would have sent you a present but there is
no way of wrapping up a Bronx cheer."

Dwight Fiske at the Versailles was telling about the

parents' meeting at a village school, at which a proud and patriotic parent got up and announced, "I am the father of fifteen children and I never left the United States." "It seems to me," commented Winchell, "that Mr. Laubermacher never left home."

Jan Murray's ad lib. is a pip. When a bald-headed heckler wouldn't stop annoying him, he cried, "That guy blew his top."

In Ciro's one New Year's Eve, Bill Stern, the famous sports announcer, made a threat that was resented by a drunk. "You'll do it over my dead body!" challenged the latter. "That," cooed Bill, "could become my favorite route."

Milton Berle complained to "Kup," the famous columnist, "Chicago is so crowded this week that every place is jammed." Kup answered, "Every place but the theatre you are working in."

Lenny Kent's retort to a customer was really poisonous: "Happy heart attack!"

Jimmy Durante bangs his hands on his sides and yells, "Everybody wantsa get in duh act."

Vince Curran of Club 66 is famous for his cutting sarcasm. Meeting an actor who usually annoyed him with self-praise, Curran gushed, before the actor could open his mouth, "I think you're great." "Really!" said the ham. "You're great," Vince went on, "with cold cuts."

One night Vince was bothered by an intoxicated female from Hollywood. "Don't mind her," was Curran's demolisher; "she's here incognito without her leash." He once called a dame visitor at his club "Dame May Half-Witty."

Frank Hyers and Pat Harrington are experts in the art of slapping people down. Frankie said to an annoying female, "Why don't you take the 1:30 broom out of town?" To an inebriated heckler, Pat sarcasmed, "You've got more nerve than an abscessed tooth."

Corporal Harvey Stone, whom Ed Sullivan called "the No. 1 G. I. comedian of the war," had to stop in the middle of his act at Madison Square Garden to answer a pest, "If you want the floor so much, why don't you crawl back under it?"

Beatrice Lillie is known for her vitriolic tongue. She remarked about a famous floozy, "She's a lady in her own wrong." When the woman got too bothersome, Auntie Bea added, "Can I drop you off somewhere—off the George Washington Bridge, for instance?"

At the 400 Club a song plugger had too much to drink and was starting to be a bore. "Oh," oh'd Lenore Lemmon, the Broadway madcap, "climb back into your flask."

A well-known drunk was reported suffering from a brain concussion. "Wonder how that happened?" someone asked. "I think," said Fred Allen, "he was hit on the head by a falling napkin."

Walter Winchell, who hates street-corner hate spreaders, as most of us do, tells about the corner prejudist who was screaming, "There ain't enough room in this country for furriners and us Americans." And a lumbering giant among the listeners retorted, "Yessiree, especially pale-face foreigners!" The squelcher was Jim Thorpe, American Indian Olympics star.

Several years ago Monty Woolley played Kris Kringle on a department-store platform during a bond rally. Suddenly he burped. One woman in the crowd was shocked. Woolley leaned forward and oiled, "And what did you expect, madame—chimes?"

Jack Durant, another of my favorite friends and entertainers, has been up against many situations in clubs and theatres. His best comment, I think, was on an ugly pest who insisted on following him home: "She's got the kind of face you don't want to remember, but can't forget."

Jack Waldron had a good silencer for a heckler who was razzing his act. "Look," said Jack, "why don't you be quiet and see how bad I *really* can be?"

Harry Lewis was being heckled by his wife and philosophized, "Some men don't realize what happiness is until they get married, and then it's too late."

Mickey Alpert, one of the best-loved guys in show business, is also prey for the table comedians. One of them he stifled with, "You'd make a good actor playing human beings, but you'd need plenty of rehearsing."

A past master in the art of ad lib. is Joe E. Lewis, whose

poisonous darts at would-be an-
noyers could alone fill a volume.
Here are a few of them:

To a girl pest, known for her loose
living: "Look, girlie, let me make a
buck, too."

To a gambler: "You look like a deck
of cards that's been shuffled all night."

To a sailor: "Why don't you go
heckle Admiral Nimitz?"

To a blabbermouth: "The last time
I saw a mouth like yours, there was a
fish hook in it."

To a wise guy who tripped a chorus
girl: "That's the first time I ever saw a
pair of shoes with three heels!"

To a fat annoyer: "Oh, bore a
hole in your belly and let the sap
run out."

To a drunk: "He'll sober up
when he gets the check."

To a bald-headed ribber:
"Didn't I shoot you into the side-
pocket some place?"

Bob Burns, the Arkansas trav-
eler, used to paralyze an audience
with laughter when he was bothered with a continuous heckler.
He would tell a long story to do it,
but it was worth it. "When I was a

kid," he would start from nowhere, "I used to live on a farm with my Aunt Minnie. One day I accidentally killed our only donkey with an ax . . . You know," Bob would finish, looking straight at his heckler, "my Uncle Jed told me that some day that jackass would come back and haunt me."

One night, Hi Sands found a tough audience; he couldn't get a laugh or a hand for any of the acts. Finally he nastied, "I know there's an audience out there; I can hear you breathing."

The younger comedians, who came up the hard way, working the borsht circuit, club dates, and local night clubs, have had to face table comedians all their life. It sharpened their wit and their poison became stronger.

Jackie Miles "killed" a candy store cowboy with, "He came up from the gutter, and is he homesick!" Another time, the Sinatra of the comedians was annoyed by a loud guy with a foghorn voice. "If I need a stooge," said Jackie, "I'll get one with a college education."

Morey Amsterdam, the author of *Rum and Coca Cola* and a famous radio wit, often gets hecklers even on his radio show. He devastated one of them with, "As I leave the studio I'll pass you, and there'll be a piece of mistletoe hanging at the end of my coat."

Morey once had to stop in the middle of a show at his night club when a nuisance went too far. "You now have thirty-two teeth," barked the comic. "Would you like to try for none?"

Jackie Winston flattened a noise-maker at Maxine's in the Bronx with, "There's a guy with a brain marked *tilt*."

Larry Best inquired of a pest, "When do you let the air out of your head?"

Annoyed with a would-be comic who never works, Jackie Phillips asked, "Why don't you learn a trade so you'll know what kind of work you're out of?"

Benny Baker, the Shakespearean comic, was once hissed while appearing at a celebrity night. He was prepared. "There are only three things that hiss," he insinuated: "a goose, a snake, and a fool—come forth and be identified."

As Romo Vincent stepped on the stage of the Coronet in Philadelphia, a drunk shouted, "Le's see shome women! Get off, fatty, le's see shome women!" Romo looked at him and said quietly: "May I say I enjoyed you in *The Lost Weekend*?"

Allan Drake: "Go stick your head out of the window, feet first."

Red Buttons: "Why don't you take a long walk on a short pier?"

Joe Frisco was having dinner at the Havana-Madrid one night while Jack Eigen's celebrity party was in session and Milton Berle was on stage, throwing jibes at Frisco. "Don't eat so much, Joe," he kidded, "just because you're getting it for nothing." "I couldn't take you on an empty stomach," Joe replied.

Julie Oshins is mellowing lately, but the star of *This Is the Army* used to pray for hecklers so he could use his poisonous answers. "Are you a victim of sex experiments?" he asked one crackpot. Of another character, he said, "There is the main reason for twin beds!" "Only God can

make a tree, but it took your parents to make **the sap**,"
he whipped at another.

Lew Parker, the radio and stage comedian, has been
in vaudeville ever since he was a baby. His trip around

A comic faces his audience

the world sharpened his wit. Entertaining all those G.I.'s,
you had to be on the beam or they really let you have it.
One soldier was very annoying and Lew didn't want to
rib him, but he finally had to say, "I would make a mon-
key out of you, but why should *I* take all the credit?"

Tony Canzoneri has standard answers to all would-be pests: "I had 250 fights; what's your excuse?"

Mark Plant answered a wack with, "When your face comes to a head, have it lanced."

Frances Faye, our favorite piano pounder, whose jive and swing is sharp as a tack, was approached by the friend of a Broadway wise guy. Trying to convince Frances that his pal was a fine feller, he said, "His word is his bond." "Zatso?" countered Faye. "Who put it up for him?"

Billy Vine, an old pal of ours from the lean days, was working at Lou Walter's Latin Quarter when a "hep-cat" decided to challenge him. "Let's have a battle of wits," yelled the sucker. "Okay," squelched Billy, "I'll check mine and we'll start even."

Joe E. Ross to a bad audience: "Is this an audience or a jury?"

Archie Robbins answers taunts in a quiet, dignified manner. "You're suffering from an interferiority complex. Why don't you go home and write yourself some threatening letters?"

When Frank Fay is attacked he stops cold and stares at his antagonizer. "Sir," he says, "you are annoying the man I love."

Milton Berle, the poor man's Bob Hope, was bothered by a chap sitting at a table alone. "I see you're here with all your friends," Berle said brightly.

Henny Nadel heckles himself in his act: "I will now do an imitation of a Broadway phony, which is very easv for me to do—I don't need any practice."

Alan Gale lets them have it with, "I never forget a face, but in your case I'll make an exception."

Peter Donald, the renowned radio comedian who is loved by everybody, is very seldom annoyed by audience pests. But even Peter was irked by a jerk one night while on the floor at La Martinique. "The next beer you have," Peter countered, "have the bartender put the head on you."

Even little "Mousey" Bert Wheeler, who wouldn't harm a soul, was forced to tell a character who annoyed him when he was doing his warm-up for his "7-Up" broadcast, "If you have your life to live over again, don't do it."

The famous dialectician and pal of the bigs in show business, Patsy Flick, was doing a benefit at the Astor Hotel one night when some ass kept interrupting him. "Don't look now," remarked Patsy, "but there's a dope standing in your shoes."

Eddie Schaefer answers audience moans with, "Don't mind him, he got drunk on Scotch tape."

So you see, it doesn't pay to heckle a comedian. It's his business to be on the ball. Unless you want Jackie Gleason to tell you to "walk east till your hat floats," or Lou Saxon to make a dope out of you with, "If Moses had seen you there would have been another commandment," or Doc Marcus, "You don't have to worry about getting ahead, you're doing very well without one."

Gene Baylos loves to heckle comedians with, "I saw your act, save your money," while Zero Mostel is a little more subtle: "Some people get up bright and early; he only gets up early." Leo Fuld always apologizes that he is a foreigner from Holland and doesn't understand the language, but then he lets you have it right between the eyes with, "Too bad birth control isn't retroactive."

All the big comics have favorite answers ready when they are annoyed. George Jessel might tell a pest, "In biblical days it was considered a miracle for an ass to speak; now it's a miracle if one keeps quiet."

Phil Baker likes to cut hecklers with, "Why don't you go out and buy a car and have an accident?"

Bob Hope told an audience who laughed at him, "If you think I'm funny, you should come up here."

Buddy Lester, one of the funnier clowns, was annoyed at an audience that wouldn't laugh. He finally let out with, "Who does the embalming here?"

Eddie Cantor has been answering hecklers ever since he worked as a singing waiter, too many years ago. When one bothered him the other night he let go with, "You came in here with an empty stomach and it went to your head."

Henny Youngman is my choice as one of the funniest natural comedians. His sense of humor is super. He is always on the rib, even likes to heckle himself. "When I was born, people came for miles around to look at me; they didn't know what the hell I was," or, "My mother sent my picture to Ripley and it came back marked, 'I don't believe it.'" He answered a would-be wise guy with, "He has a B.A. degree; he mastered the first two letters of the alphabet." Another time in Philadelphia when he couldn't get a laugh: "I wasn't born here but I'm sure dying here."

These are swell gags to use on your enemies or on your better half, perhaps the store clerk or the cab driver that you've been "gunning" for, but make sure you got a couple of guys like Tony Canzoneri and Mark Plant to protect you. The other fellow might not see the humor of it, and you're liable to wind up in the hospital, reading the rest of this book from a horizontal position.

CHAPTER NINE

From Punches to Punch Lines

THE boys at the round table were discussing fighters who had turned actor, when I entered Toots Shor's one night. "Pull up a fighter and sit down," yelled Henny Youngman.

"Who's the subject of destruction tonight?" I asked.

"We're talking about the guys that are now flooring people with jokes instead of their fists," Jay C. Flippen explained. "You should know a little about that. In your act you've got the greatest little champion of all time, Tony Canzoneri."

"Tony has gone from punches to punch lines very successfully," I said. "Ed Sullivan calls him the greatest straight man since James J. Corbett."

"I heard that you were a fighter, too. Is that right, Joey?" asked Earl Wilson.

"Yes, for a while," I answered. "I was the roughest, toughest fighter that ever hit the canvas. Fighting is all right providing you do it intelligently, but you can't always find a smaller man."

"I'd rather go a few rounds of drinks at the bar, than a few rounds of hits in the ring," Earl laughed.

"It's easier to tell jokes," I suggested. "All you have to

do is keep moving, and you're not a target. A ring is too confining."

"What made you quit the ring?" asked Earl.

"When I was at City College," I answered, "I fought a guy forty pounds heavier than me. His name was One-Round Murphy. He knocked everybody out in the first round. But not me—he knocked me out in the dressing room. I'm the first guy they ever carried *into* the ring.

After that, I decided to take singing lessons instead of boxing lessons. I'd rather get belly laughs than belly punches."

"What makes most fighters take to the stage?" asked Bert Wheeler.

"Some of those guys," answered Jimmy Cannon, the renowned sports writer of the *N. Y. Evening Post,* "put on funnier shows in the ring than any comedian in the business. Max Baer, Maxie Rosenbloom, and Tony Galento, for instance, were more comical in the squared circle than they ever were on the stage. Other fighters, when they took dives, put on a dramatic performance that out-Barrymored Barrymore. All they had to do when they went behind the footlights was to put on a little greasepaint."

"If they made so much money in the ring, as you news-paper guys claim," interrupted Bert Lahr, "why do they have to open restaurants and bars and go into show business? With all the dough those mugs made you'd think they would retire."

"Most of them leave the ring broke," answered Jimmy. "While they're on top, they get more phony propositions than a chorine. Everybody wants a piece of them, and gets it, too. A ring champ is a body of steel, completely surrounded by relatives and hangers-on. The horses take a few, the girls on the hip parade take some, a few bad investments in the stock market, and they're through! When the champ's brain becomes pregnant and he real-izes what's happened, it's too late. His ring career is finished and so is his money.

"A man is never a hero to his wallet," Jimmy concluded. "As the gang leave his bandwagon he must look for a place to earn a living, and the usual thing is to go on the stage or open a restaurant or night club to cash in on his popularity in the ring."

Some of the boys have been quite successful as pub owners and actors. Back in the days when they fought with bare knuckles, the stage and the restaurant busi-ness was the next step.

John L. Sullivan owned a saloon on Sixth Avenue, Jim Corbett had one where Saks now stands, Tom Sharkey was on Fourteenth Street near Third Avenue, and Kid McCoy held forth in the basement of the Continental Hotel.

The great John L. was a pretty good actor too. If he didn't go over too big he would tell his audience, "I may not be too good on the stage, but I can lick anybody in the house." John L. liked his liquor straight and his women curved. His bar was one of the most successful in town. But the liquor finally got him and he went broke. Later on he took the oath, and toured the country lecturing on the evils of liquor.

James J. Corbett was the best of the fighters-turned-actor. He worked in vaudeville and dramatic shows all around the country.

Practically all the boxers of this generation tried their hands at running bistros after hanging up their gloves. They figured if they could make money hand over fist in the ring, they could do the same over a bar. Some of them fared very well, others went broke.

Fight fans like to see their heroes at close range. They like to come into a saloon and throw punches at their idols, just to tell the folks back home that their favorite champ knocked them out. Jack Dempsey has had to flatten dozens of pests.

Any night, in any number of bars and restaurants around the country, the boys are gathered around talking about their past ring battles. The champs have gone over each round of their career a million times.

Abe Attell is telling a group at the bar in his little restaurant on Fifty-third and Broadway, about his twelve

years as champion in the featherweight division. Tony
Galento is bragging in his bar in Orange, New Jersey,
"I'll kill that bum Joe Louis the next time we meet. I'll
fight him winner-take-all. That bum hit me when I
wasn't lookin'." Frankie Bradley is reminiscing in his
Steak House in Philly about the time he almost won the
bantamweight title.

Jack Sharkey owned a bar in Boston. Lew Tendler,
Benny Leonard's perennial opponent, runs two success-
ful restaurants in Atlantic City and Philadelphia. Jimmy
Goodrich, the former lightweight champ, runs a pub in
Buffalo. Barney Ross has a bar in Chicago, and Mickey
Walker is the boss of a restaurant and bar in Elizabeth,
N. J. Kid Kaplan is happy with his place in Hartford,
Connecticut; and Pete Herman, the former little bantam
champ who went blind, is the boss of a very prosperous
night club in New Orleans, named after him. Joe Mad-
den's restaurant on the East Side of New York has been
a profitable enterprise for many years. Maxie Rosenbloom's night club in California, Slapsie Maxie's, is one
of the most famous spots in the country. Former light-
heavyweight champion, Bob Olin, followed the pugi-
listic tradition by opening a steak house on Fifty-eighth
Street. Al Singer and Tom Heeney both opened bars
in Miami Beach.

Some boxers have found it's easier to make money by
working in night clubs than trying to run them. Former
champions have tried every phase of the entertainment
field, and from the looks of things, being an actor or
night-club performer is the most lucrative.

The old-timers tried the vaudeville circuit with more or less success. Like John L., when their acts failed to go over, they usually offered to fight anyone in the house. Knute Rockne once went on a barnstorming tour of this type, and had the daylights knocked out of him by a frail

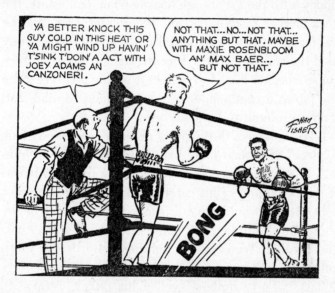

little youngster. After the show, Rockne tried to convince the boy to turn professional, but the lad elected to continue his schooling and go to West Point. The "skinny kid" was Dwight Eisenhower.

In addition to running his tavern in Orange, N. J., Tony Galento also tried Tin Pan Alley for a while and wrote a few songs. His efforts got a lot more circulation in the papers than in copies sold. When two-ton Tony appeared at Loew's State with his manager, "Yussel" Jacobs, they hit the all-time low in that theatre. It took them two years to get rid of the egg they laid.

Benny Leonard, considered the greatest champion in the history of the lightweight division, tried his hand at almost everything when he left the ring. He lost so much money with the Pittsburgh hockey team, real estate, the stock market, restaurants, and other enterprises, that he was forced to make a comeback at the age of forty. Benny tried the stage with little success. He is a brilliant after-dinner speaker but always does it on the cuff. He did a fine job as a commander in the Merchant Marine, and is now a referee and a great one.

Like so many of the greats of pugilism, everybody took a "piece" of Leonard. He likes to tell this story on himself: His father objected to his going in the ring. It was at the beginning of his career, and on the evening of a fight, Benny would have to sneak his tights out of the house. One night he came home with a black eye. "Aha!" said his dad. "You've been fighting again. I told you a million ti—" "But pop," Benny interrupted, "I made forty dollars." "Forty dollars!" yelled his father. "When do you fight again?"

Georges Carpentier now owns one of the most famous night clubs in Paris, the Lido on the Champs Elysées. He played host there to thousands of Americans during and after the war.

Jack Dempsey has his finger in many pies and puddings. He owns a hotel, a restaurant, and a night club. He has real estate, and a brand of rye is named after him. He was in pictures and vaudeville, and in his late forties is still one of the best-liked champions of all time. He would give it all up just to give a pal a "hotfoot."

George Raft tried boxing first, and then went in for dancing in night clubs before he finally became a movie star. Carl Brisson had seventy-two ring battles and was light-heavyweight champion of Europe before becoming the singing idol of two continents. Victor McLaglen

was a great heavyweight fighter, and so was Victor Jory. Mark Plant had twenty professional fights before he realized singing was much easier, and Fritzi Zivic is starting to "steal" jokes from comedians to brush up on routines for his night-club jobs.

A great many champs of the ring have made good in pictures. The former middleweight champ Freddie Steele is doing great in Hollywood. So are Jackie Fields, who was welterweight champ, and Johnny Andrisano, a great fighter from Boston. The diminutive Fidel La

Barba, former king of the flyweight division, is now a writer in Hollywood at a very fancy figure.

Canada Lee is doing very well as an actor, and even the Shakespearean Gene Tunney appeared in several pictures. The distinguished Sam Harris once managed Terry McGovern. Jack Renault did a lot of work on the screen.

Max Baer is one of the greatest personalities in or out of the ring. He has the physique and brawn of the greatest champion of them all, but he has the heart of an actor. He would rather get one good laugh from an audience than win twenty titles in the ring. The lovable Maxie made a picture with Myrna Loy, called *The Prize-Fighter and the Lady*, that was one of the greatest pictures to come out of Hollywood.

Now Baer is working with Slapsie Maxie and together they make a sensational laugh team. They don't have a rehearsed act, and maybe it's better that way. Whenever one of them gets a big laugh in the show with a gag, the other is bound to steal it and do it himself the next show. To hear them argue off-stage is a show in itself. Each thinks the other is "nuts." Maybe both Maxies are right, but at five thousand a week it's very becoming . . .

Sid Silvers, veteran vaudevillian, screen writer, and comedian, worked with Baer in the ill-fated musical, *Hya, Gentlemen*. When Baer read his lines for the first time, Silvers complimented him and said, "I'm going to teach you everything I know about show business, Max. I'm going to make you the biggest star on Broadway." "Yeah," Baer grunted as he patted the tiny comic, "and

I'm going to make you the world's heavyweight champ."

Once in a while a fighter turns out to be a "bad" actor. Max Schmeling made a fortune fighting in this country. He was treated royally by all of America. When he went back to Germany he joined the Nazi party. Irving Mandell, the sports editor of the Miami Beach *Sun Tropics* has proof that Schmeling was a member of the Gestapo. Even the rats in his own outfit hated him and gave the "superman" a super-licking on more than one occasion. He lost more than the heavyweight title, he lost the respect of sportsmen all over the world.

Poor Primo Carnera, the gargantuan heavyweight, did most of his acting in the ring. Hangers-on took most of the fortune he made in this country, leaving him practically penniless. When he went back to Italy, he did a little acting to try to recoup some of his wealth, but his stage performance could never compare with the act he used to put on in the ring.

Jack Johnson, the retired Negro heavyweight champ of yesteryear, made a lot of money doing fifteen and twenty shows a night in a flea circus on Forty-second Street. Right up to his recent death in an auto accident at the age of sixty-eight, he was still a big favorite and a tremendous draw wherever he appeared.

Some ring immortals have gone in for physical culture, and with great success. Philadelphia Jack O'Brien, Charlie White, and Packy McFarland were three of the most famous in that line.

One of the greatest fighters of all, Mickey Walker, didn't fare so well as a master of ceremonies. He threw punches faster than he threw jokes. He opened a bar and grill opposite Madison Square Garden, but the fans who used to love to see him dish out lickings to his opponent didn't come in to see him dish out drinks over the bar. He finally opened a bar in Elizabeth that clicked in a big way. The "toy bulldog" is now using his championship "mitts" to paint. He **is a** very fine artist; his exhibit

last year drew the acclaim of art experts all over the country, and on *Information Please* he told how he taught himself to paint.

Joe Louis was always as mum as the proverbial oyster, though lately he has doctored his personality with doses of showmanship. Joe's many years as champion of the world, meeting so many people, forty-five months in the Army, and a bit of tutoring by his friends Rochester, Bill Robinson, Duke Ellington, Canada Lee, and Count Basie, have taught him the tricks of a showman. The result is a Joe Louis you'd hardly know.

While he retains the unaffected simplicity that has

always been his trade-mark, the Brown Bomber now writes love lyrics, does a few dance steps, indulges in practical jokes, and even heckles his friends in show business. During the war, Joe toured the United States and the rest of the world giving exhibitions and lecturing to the boys in uniform. To amuse battle-weary veterans he started to inject some lightness into his routine, and little by little began telling more and more jokes. "I get a kick out of making a crowd laugh," says the modern Louis.

Before the second Billy Conn match the sports writers asked Louis what he would do if Billy ran all through the fight. "He can run," said Joe, "but he can't hide."

That kind of conduct was foreign to the Joe Louis of former years, who rose from the cotton fields of Alabama to one of the most outstanding members of his race. A veteran boxing writer who interviewed the World's Champ when he first won the title, reports, "I talked to him for a full half hour and all I got out of him was three yesses and two noes." Today the Brown Bomber might hit him with his latest stories or perhaps a hotfoot. The accolades thrown at him all over the world have given him the confidence to use his sense of humor. Now he slays 'em—with wisecracks.

It was a fighter who helped me on my way in show business. He taught me the meaning of humility and courage. His brand of decency, honor, and gentlemanliness was an inspiration to me . . .

Tony Canzoneri and I became great pals from the very first day we met. I always wanted to be a boxer, and he wanted to be an actor. When I was boxing at City College, Tony was my idol. He was not only a great champion but a great showman. I taught him the little I knew about the stage, and he showed me as much as I could learn about the ring.

Like so many great fighters before him, after his fighting days were over, the little champ tried dozens of enterprises with no success. He went through a million dollars in the fur business, a dress factory, haberdashery and clothing stores, several restaurants, a liquor store, and his farm in Marlboro, N. Y. He was very good to his family and loved to live well. The horses took a few, and when he hung up his gloves, after sixteen years and 370 ring battles, he was completely broke.

So when Tony received an offer to open in a show called, *They Shoulda Stood in Bed*, he jumped at the idea. I went to see my boxing idol on the opening night. Furious at the way they handled my little champ, I rushed backstage after the show to meet Tony for the first time and tell him so. That's how I met my partner and pal.

We appeared at a lot of benefits together after that, and finally decided to do an act together. We toured the country playing night clubs and theatres. Everywhere we played, his faithful fans turned out in droves. The mayor, the leading businessmen, and the "mob" were his stage-door Johnnies, besides the hundreds of young hopefuls of the ring who came to seek his advice. The newspapermen all gathered around him. I never saw such adoration for one benign, taciturn gentleman who had only gone to the seventh grade in school. The racketeer and the merchant, the fighter and the politician all loved the little champ.

Ed Van Every called him "The Little Babe Ruth," Dan Parker tagged him "The Walloping Wop" and "The Little Pizon." Ed Sullivan nicknamed him "The Boy Dempsey."

Tony's confidence in me and his complete trust in my judgment spurred me on to do bigger and better things for both of us.

We roomed together when we were on the road and would often stay up all night talking about the days when he was the great featherweight, junior lightweight, lightweight, and junior welterweight champion of the world. His sense of humor always sent me to bed laughing. Then his snoring would wake me up again.

He seldom talked about his great victories, but always kidded about his few losses. He fought Harry Blittman in Philadelphia and took the one real beating of his long career. It was the first time he had fought a southpaw. Even then his sense of humor came to the fore. When he came back to his corner after the eighth round he said to his manager, Sammy Goldman, between bruised lips, "As things stand now I gotta knock this guy out to get a draw."

"I was too selfish in that fight," gagged Tony in the dressing room after it was over; "I took everything. Maybe I should join the Brooklyn Dodgers as a catcher."

Tony couldn't do much with Jimmy McLarnin in the first round of their first fight. The microphone hit him as he went to his corner before the round, and he walked out to a barrage of fists before he could compose himself. He kept getting hit with everything that McLarnin could throw. All his own punches missed their mark. But when he finally got into a clinch he whispered to Jimmy, "Wait till I get you outside!"

When he got back to his corner after taking a terrific licking for three minutes, his manager yelled at him: "What's the matter, Tony, you looked bad!" That was all he needed. He couldn't "look bad" for his fans. He rushed out in the second round and nailed McLarnin with a right in his own corner and sent him to the canvas. After that he gave McLarnin a beating for the rest of the fight.

In his battle with Kid Chocolate he was showing off for a beautiful dark-haired actress, Rita Angel. His eyes kept searching for her in the fourth row ringside. For four rounds Chocolate kept punching "The Boy Dempsey" unmercifully. "I'm not worried," Tony kidded between rounds. "I'm winning on the radio—Sam Taub, the announcer, is a friend of mine."

In the fifth round Tony was hit with a jolting left that sent him up against the ropes. He forgot about the doll in the fourth row, went to work on the Chocolate for fair, and won the rest of the fight with the greatest of ease.

That same beautiful doll now watches him almost every night from a "ringside" table as he entertains in night clubs. He still likes to show off for her in spite of the fact that she has been his wife now for almost ten years.

Is Tony proud of her! Whenever anybody compliments him about his performance on the stage, his eyes light up as he says, "The real star in my family is my wife, Rita Angel. She's a great actress, and some day she'll be bigger than any of 'em."

She soon was, and when a little actress was born to "The Walloping Wop" and the little dark-haired Jewish doll, Tony was jubilant. He became very attached to his little "Litwop," and even now he calls her twice a day from whatever part of the U. S. A. he happens to be in.

Denise Canzoneri never saw her daddy fight. Since both Rita and Tony are now on the stage, the talk around their home is constantly of show business. Denise herself is being tested for movie and stage roles.

On her eighth birthday I took my adopted niece to Toots Shor's for dinner. "So you're da daughter o' Tony Canzoneri, da great fighter, huh?" Toots remarked as he stroked her head.

"Oh, no sir," she replied, "I'm the daughter of Tony Canzoneri the great actor!"

In his sixteen years in the ring the "Little Babe Ruth" never saved one clipping or write-up, and he had millions of notices on the front pages and sports sections of newspapers all over the world. Now that he's in show business, he saves every scrap written about his acting talent.

He was always a great showman. When he fought Johnny Dundee at Madison Square Garden his manager told Tony to try to knock Dundee down and then go over and pick the aging champion up off the floor. It would be great showmanship. Dundee was an old man at the end of his career, and Tony was just starting. Canzoneri did his best to knock the great Dundee down, but the old champ had too much "heart." The next day the papers said, "Canzoneri held up Dundee." Tony denied it vehemently to anybody that would listen. "I did my best to knock him down," he asserted, "but he's a great champion. I take my hat off to one of the greatest of all time—Johnny Dundee."

After he lost his title to Barney Ross in Chicago, Tony and Barney became great friends. Barney went on to win the lightweight and welterweight titles. Soon after that, at Guadalcanal, he annexed another title—champion of human rights.

We were working at Leon and Eddie's when two navy lieutenants asked Tony and me to join their table. "We have been following you around the country trying to catch up with you and give you some regards," said the younger-looking of the two.

"About eight months ago," continued his friend, "we were in Guadalcanal and became fast friends with a marine sergeant. It was Christmas Eve and he was the only person on the island who knew how to use the organ. He's a little Jewish lad and he sat in the church all night, with bombs falling all around, and played the only tune he knew, *My Yiddishe Mamma.* Most of the church was ripped away but he continued to play as the rest of us prayed. We will never forget him."

"He often spoke about you boys," said the other lieutenant. "He never saw your new act and made us promise that if we ever got to the U. S. A. before him, we would look you up and send his love and best wishes. His name is Barney Ross."

Sitting just three tables away was the former champ and war hero. He had just returned to the States and finally caught up with us, arriving ten minutes before the lieutenants entered the club. The reunion was the most touching scene I ever hope to witness. There were war hero Barney Ross, two rugged lieutenants, Tony Canzoneri, and myself, all singing *My Yiddishe Mamma,* with tears running down our faces.

Barney has given up the fight arena and entered the

business arena as publisher, columnist, radio commentator, fight promoter, referee, actor, and manufacturer. Now when he goes into action he carries a leather briefcase instead of leather mitts.

The biggest flop of our career was when Tony and I played Chicago, Barney's home town. It all came about because the Windy City fans loved Canzoneri too much. Sounds funny, doesn't it? We opened at the Latin Quarter, and all the mob bought out the club for the first night. The champ received an ovation that lasted five minutes or more. Everything went great until I slapped their idol, as I usually do in the act. A hush came over the entire audience. After that we couldn't get a snicker out of them.

After the show, Tony had to stay by my side for fear the gang would kill me. He tried to explain to "the boys" that it was "in the act," but it didn't do any good. From that night I could never get started in the Latin Quarter again. Even now, every once in a while, I wake up in the middle of the night and see those faces glaring at me.

Tony's father was his most rabid rooter. If Tony was given a bad decision—which happened quite often, because the little champ never let them buy off a referee or judge—it would need twenty cops to hold his father down. Once when Canzoneri was floored, his pop swallowed a cigar, band and all. When Tony came up, so did the cigar.

In 1940 the hands of fate reached out and struck a sad blow to the Canzoneri household. Tony needed

money badly and, against the wishes of all his friends
and admirers, decided to make a comeback. He was
matched to fight "Bummy" Davis at Madison Square
Garden. All the Canzoneri fans stayed away in droves—
they didn't want to see their champ beaten. Tony was
K.O.'d for the first time in his career, and on that same
night, a few blocks away at the St. James Theatre, his

wife opened in a show called *Summer Nights*. It was her
first starring role and it was K.O.'d by the critics. And
that very day up in Marlboro, N. Y., they had foreclosed
his farm.

But true champion that he is, Tony came through
with flying colors. They could never floor his spirit or
his courage. His Marlboro Hotel and farm is now a thriv-
ing business, his wife has played fine roles on the stage

—and very successfully, too—and the champ is still in the entertainment world.

It was Canzoneri who taught me never to be nervous or afraid. It happened on our first professional job together, at the Steinway Theatre in Astoria, L. I. It was a very small theatre, seating about six hundred people. We received fifty dollars for four days to break in our act. We rehearsed for two weeks and finally were ready to open. The first show was scheduled for 11 a.m. I asked Tony to meet me at nine o'clock that morning so that we could rehearse our act backstage before going "on."

Canzoneri got there at 10:55, only five minutes before the show started. I never was so nervous in my life, and when I saw him I really blew my top. "Are you kidding?" I yelled. "Don't you realize this is our big chance? What the hell is the matter with you? Aren't you nervous?"

"Don't get excited," said the champ in his usual reticent manner. "Why should I be nervous? Once I fought a guy called Barney Ross at the Polo Grounds for the lightweight championship of the world. I was getting $45,000 for the fight, 50,000 people packed the arena to see the scrap, friends of mine bet millions on me to win, my family all came to see me take back the title. Ross could knock your head off with a right or a left, and I slept for four hours before the fight. Here I'm getting $1.25 a show, there are eleven people in the audience, and nobody can hurt us—so what the hell do you want me to be nervous about?"

CHAPTER TEN

I Gaze into My Hate Ball

THE boys at the round table were stirring up "the belting pot" one early morning.

You can't sit down at a table near Two-Time Square without noticing that somebody has his back turned to somebody else. There are worse feuds on the double-crossroads of the world than there ever were with the Hatfields and the McCoys.

Almost every Broadwayite has some destructive suggestion to offer about someone. Comedians who are usually loud and glib, become as silent as a Harvard man in the Yale cheering section, when another comedian shows up on the scene.

Most of their arguments are sound—merely sound. The average person around the Main Stem is a magician—he can turn anything into an argument.

"I'm so glad that our gang never give each other the 'louse-up,'" I was telling the boys at the table. Jackie Miles, Joe E. Lewis, Jerry Lester, Jay C. Flippen, Bert Lahr, Bert Wheeler, and Peter Donald all nodded approval.

"Then how come," bellowed Toots Shor, "you creepy comedians are afraid to leave da table?"

135

"All actors are alike," cut in Chuck Hamilton. "Yer always shootin' yer mouth off and jealous of somebody. Look at me, I've been around here a long time and I never fight with nobody. Everybody loves me."

"So how come, ya crum-bum, ya don't talk ta yer best pal Frank Fay?" chided Toots. "I'm the only guy around here that has no dislikes. I love everybody."

"So how come," Chuck retorted, "you and Sherman Billingsley of the Stork Club don't talk?"

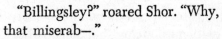

"Billingsley?" roared Shor. "Why, that miserab—."

"So ya love everybody, eh?" Chuck heckled.

"I've been on Broadway for forty years," interjected Bert Lahr, "and I have no enemies. Oh, maybe one or two, but I don't have a bad word to say about them or anybody else."

"By the way," slimed Flippen, "have you seen Billy Rose lately?"

"That little punk," Lahr sneered, "he's one guy—."

"Oh, yes," interrupted Bert Wheeler, "I bumped into Brian Donlevy and Kate Smith today and—."

"Why," Lahr choked, "don't mention their names to me. Those ph—."

"Take it easy," ejaculated Joe E. Lewis. "Jack Benny told me—."

"There's one guy that I can't stand," belted Lahr. "He and I were pals until—."

"What do you think of Mike Todd?" asked Jackie

Miles. "I hear he's doing a show for you."

"Now there's a great man," Bert purred. "He's a guy I love."

"Will ya love him in December as ya do in May?" laughed Toots.

"Look at me," suggested Jerry Lester. "I don't have an enemy in the world."

"Then how come," zinged back Toots, "ya don't talk ta yer own brother?"

On the Hardened Artery it must be fashionable to have a feud. Some of them are real and bitter. Others are fancied, just good publicity, dreamed up by a press agent.

The Buddy and Jerry Lester feud is no press agent's fancy. The brothers really hate each other. The funny thing is, they always work in the same cities at the same time. Recently in Philadelphia, Jerry was at the Walton Roof and Buddy at the Coronet. They glared when they passed each other on the street. They turned their backs in restaurants. *And in the City of Brotherly Love!*

Jerry ribs Buddy in his routine: "This act has built me a home. It built my brother a home, too. Oh, well, Buddy is doing my act, but it's better than sending him money."

Each hates to be mistakenly introduced as the other, but the error will happen. Buddy appeared at a benefit and for the first time made mention of his older brother's name. It was a very tough audience and Buddy didn't do so well. And so he signed off, "This is Jerry Lester saying good-night."

"I'm so tired doing two jobs," sullied Jerry one night.

"My brother is at the Paramount and I'm at the Roxy."

Dick Haymes and his brother, Bob Stanton, have the Hollywood rights on the Lester family feud.

Allan Cross and Henry Dunn have been working together as a team for sixteen years. They share the same dressing room when they have to, but never say an unnecessary word to each other. The cause of their dispute is lost but the feud lingers on.

A couple of years ago the team thought they had enough and decided to split. Dunn continued in show business, while Cross opened a delicatessen in Providence, R. I. After several months, Cross decided he'd had enough pastrami. Back they went into partnership. After all, as a team they made a minimum of a thousand dollars a week, which they shared equally. It takes a lot of salami to bring in that kind of money! As I'm writing this, Cross and Dunn are a big hit in Chicago, but they might be split up before you turn the page.

The most celebrated show-business feud was that of Gilbert and Sullivan. The famous collaborators rarely saw each other, but turned out some of the sprightliest comic operas extant.

One of the most successful teams of all time, Weber and Fields, feuded through years of big-time show-stopping.

Abbott and Costello went from burlesque at almost nothing a week to an income of a million dollars a year. Fame and fortune brought them a lot of personal unhappiness. Everybody in America tried to patch up their feud. Every columnist claimed his advice brought them together again, only to find the next morning that they were fighting once more. They don't talk to each other, only *about* each other.

When Walter Winchell is feuding with somebody—and that is all the time—he likes to embarrass his opponent by poking fun at him. Lately he has confined his fights to national figures away from Broadway. "If I can cause some of those un-American rats enough aggravation so they can't eat their dinner, then I have a good night's rest," fumes Walter.

His feuds with Hamilton Fish and Senator Bilbo, Rankin, Hoffman, Nye, and Wheeler are public knowledge. "Anybody that fights against my country," rages Walter, "fights against me." He likes to change his antagonists' names to make them look silly. He calls them Westbrook PIGler, H. V. KaltenBORE, JERK McWilliams, Congressman RANKin, GER K. Smith, and Argenti-NAZIS.

His first international feud was with Adolph Hitler. Winchell was proud that he was No. 1 on the Fuehrer's hate parade. Walter tried to laugh him off the map by referring to him as a "whoopsy" character. Hitler was finally wiped off the map but it took more than laughs.

Winchell likes a good fight, and he has feuded with everybody from the Shuberts to Martin Dies, from his own publishers and censors to Danton Walker, Ed Sullivan, and Westbrook Pegler.

The "orchid man" has his comedy feuds, too. Years ago, he started a make-believe feud with Ben Bernie that brought the beloved maestro world-wide recognition. When the late Bernie appeared in Chicago, Walter belted him on the air: "No wonder they call Chicago the Windy City; Bernie is always working there." Ben cuffed back, "There are three things to keep away from your door—the wolf, the river, and Winchell."

The most famous "friendly enemies" are Fred Allen and Jack Benny. Jack looks like an insurance salesman and Fred looks like the guy he sold it to. Their feud has helped make both of them millionaires. And like Winchell and Bernie, they have always been pals.

Allen's famous line, "Benny is tighter than the top olive in a bottle," has been repeated all over the world. He said, "Jack has been known to pump up quarters and try to pass them off as half-dollars."

"I used to regard Benny as the greatest single menace in radio," Fred monotones, "but now new evidence has come along to convince me that Benny is just a minor irritation." Fred says they put pickets in front of Warner Brothers Studios in Hollywood, because "they're afraid Jack will get in there again and make another picture."

Benny counters with: "Fred Allen looks good in front of everything but a mirror." Jack praised Fred at a benefit: "He's the star of stage, screen, and radio, so whether you go out or not, he's got you trapped."

Bob Hope and Bing Crosby are another Damon and Pythias team that put on the rib for publicity. "You're solid, Bob," slaps Bing, "solid, but all in one place." Hope loves "Der Bingle" but he once introduced "the groaner" on his radio program with: "Bing is a hale fellow, all wet."

Morey Amsterdam, the comedian's comedian, is always ready to "make with the louse-up." He loves to have fun feuds. He says about his fellow worker on the Gloom Dodgers program over WHN: "When Ward Wilson gets in a taxi, they leave the vacant sign up." Ward banged back with: "The doctor took Morey's brains out because of a headache, but he doesn't need them—he's running the Gloom Dodgers program."

Morey started a feud with the King Features columnist. "I got a smart dog," mired Morey, "he reads the papers. The other day I found him poring over Westbrook Pegler."

The girls at La Martinique were angry at Lee Mortimer because the *Mirror* columnist said they all had double and triple chins. Lee fought with Jay C. Flippen because Flip had no "midnight manners" and wore white shoes, after dark, in a night club. Lee and "The Voice" are on the outs. Lee gets a kick out of picking on "Frankie Boy." He says Frank ought to have a microphone with arms, to hold *him* up.

The friendly-enemy feuds have been famous down through the years. Rudy Vallee and Will Osborne, Bing Crosby and Russ Columbo, Crosby and Sinatra, Eddie Cantor and George Jessel, Sophie Tucker and Belle Baker—all were good friends but gagged up a fight for the public.

A lot of feuds have reached the "knife-throwing" stage. Dean Martin and Sonny King were pals for years. They were managed by the same agent, Lou Perry. As soon as success started to reach them, they tried to outshine each other. Martin had his nose fixed and Sonny, a former fighter turned singer, copied some of Dean's mannerisms in singing a song.

"He's a nice guy," smeared Dean, "but all those fights he had gave him a cauliflower throat." Sonny heeled back, "Don't think I don't know you just because you're singing under an assumed nose."

The Lenny Kent-Jackie Miles fracas has got completely out of hand. Jackie ignores the thing completely, and that burns Kent even more. Kent never misses an opportunity to let Miles have it. They used to do an act together, and broke up one night after flopping with a new routine. "I'm through," yelled Jackie. "If you had

STEADY BOY!

JAY MCARDLE

to steal an act, why didn't you steal a good one?"

Lenny is very self-conscious about his former partner who made good. Buddy Lester met Lenny on the street one day. "Did you hear the new Jackie Miles story?" asked the younger of the Lesters. "Go wan," Kent snapped back, before Buddy could tell it to him, "I did it three years ago!"

Both comedians are still quarreling over who originated their "Honeysuckle Rose" routine. The ironic part of it all, the real originator, Willie Duke, can't use it himself. He died a couple of years ago . . .

Fraudway is full of hates. Sherman Billingsley has dozens of enemies because he barred them from his Cub Room. At the moment, the Stork Club host is on the Hate Parade of several hundred Broadwayites. He even barred Earl Wilson for a while because the famous saloon editor of *The Post* printed a caricature of him that he didn't like. He was sorry a couple of days later and romanced the bust man with champagne, perfume, ties, and telegrams.

Leon and Eddie's is on unfriendly terms with La Martinique. Lindy and Reuben, of the world-renowned restaurants, have been on the outs for years. John Perona, of El Morocco, and Billingsley don't exactly love each other.

The knife is more popular on Broadway for stabbing backs than it is for cutting steaks. After the last war, I wanted the knife-sharpening concession in Tokyo. Right now, I could make more with the same franchise on the Main Stem. Harry Carey and every other Broadwayite get more cuts than hari-kari did in Japan after World War No. 2.

Jon Hall and Tommy Dorsey are on each other's "unhappy-list." Some people are born with black eyes but Hall had to fight for his. Their imbroglio hit the front pages all over the world. Jon claims Dorsey isn't a comedian, but he left him in stitches.

Louis Sobol and Tommy Manville, the playboy, didn't

WHY DON'T I BUY A BAT?

J. M'A

JAY MCARDLE

speak for a long time because the *Journal-American* columnist ribbed him in print. Tommy sued Sobol and that started it. Louis swore that he would never mention the oft-married character in print again. One day Louis was annoyed at something Manville did and wrote in his column, "That moron is acting up again!" When Tommy saw it he remarked to Jack Eigen, "You see, Sobol is trying to make up with me: He's using my name again."

Danny Davis, owner of the Kitty Davis Airliner night club in Miami Beach, is always fighting with the stars of his show. He sends them notes in the middle of their act. Most entertainers dismiss him as a madman. He's really a nice guy but he can drive you batty. He once called his group together and said, "Synchronize your watches, we attack at 2 a.m. for the last show."

Leo Fuld has a unit called, "Fun For Your Money." For six weeks they broke every record at Davis' club. The seventh week, business dropped off. Danny called Leo into his office and screamed, "You got a great show, get it the hell out of my room."

Danny's feud with Billy Vine caused the rotund comedian to hurl a lot of explosives in his direction. Billy called him "the great Pigfield." "The reason an idea dies in his head," smirches Vine: "it can't stand solitary confinement."

Danny Davis tussled with Maxie Rosenbloom, the ex-light-heavyweight champion turned actor. Of course he was smart enough to confine his fighting to verbal exchanges. Slapsie Maxie went to B. S. Pully, who is no-

torious for using dirty material, to get lines to insult the
night club owner.

There are many husband-and-wife scuffles on Incan-
descent Lane. When bandleader Dick Stabile came out
of the service, he found that his beautiful and talented
wife, Gracie Barrie, was divorcing him. Being a musician, he hollered, "The least you could do is give me
two weeks' notice!"

Luba Malina is the fightin'est gal on the Main Stem.
In *Marinka* she was at the hair-pulling stage with Harry
Stockwell, Joan Roberts, Edith Fellows, and Jerry
Wayne, all at the same time. In one show she actually
threw punches at George Givot when, as she claimed,
"He speet at me."

The Maestro Dick Himber and Dunninger, the mental marvel, have put each other on the hate parade. Dick ran a concert and "exposed" all of Dunninger's tricks. In print, Himber called him a "fake," and the mental man called the bandleader many other things that are unprintable.

Pat Dane, Tommy Dorsey's lovely wife, isn't working in pictures because of her quarrel with the M.G.M. producer, Harry Rapf. Harry came to her dressing room on the lot to reprimand her for being late. "Do you know," he cautioned, "what you're costing Metro by being late?" "Do you know," slapped back the great Dane, "what you're costing Metro by being early?"

George Jean Nathan and Moss Hart are at the throat-cutting stage. Moss resented Nathan's vitriolic criticism of his *Winged Victory* show and told the famed critic so in writing. Nathan printed Moss's letter but smeared him for using Air Force stationery.

Even newspapers throw their print at each other. Winchell's favorite story is about the old *Sun* and the *N. Y. Post* when they were conservative papers. They were having an editorial feud, and one day the very proper and staid *Post* lost its temper and editorially called *The Sun* a yellow dog. To which *The Sun* replied in its starchiest manner, "*The Post* calls *The Sun* a yellow dog. The attitude of *The Sun*, however, will continue to be that of any dog towards any post."

Barry Gray is the acidy disk-jockey who rides anybody and everybody. Naturally, he makes a lot of enemies on the way. His biggest feud is with Jack Eigen.

Jack said, "Instead of reaching for a poor insult, Gray should be reaching for a good record."

Frank Fay has been at swords' ends with five members of Equity who, he claims, "appeared at a meeting where my church was insulted." The five members were upheld by the Equity Council and Fay was reprimanded. The star of *Harvey* was so incensed, he used Madison Square Garden to air his fight. Fay claimed he was fighting the "reds" in Equity, and the council countered that Fay's fellow-travelers were mixed up with un-American activities. Everybody concerned got dirty from all the mud being thrown around. Only Harvey stayed white.

Hildegarde isn't speaking to Jerry Lester because the mad comedian referred to her as "Miss Armpits of 1946." "She's not pretty," scorches the older Lester, "but she has no talent."

George Dixon, the famous Washington correspondent whose fighting shows a sense of humor, is always picking on the congressmen. He was particularly annoyed with them one day and wrote, "There is a firm in Texas that makes horses' heads and then sends them to Congress for final assembly."

Almost every act in show business that has stayed together for any length of time, has had its quarrels. Frank Mitchell and Jack Durant used to slap each other all over the stage to the delight of the customers. They would often continue their fight, with closed fists, when they returned to their dressing room.

Smith and Dale, my favorite comedy act of all time, have been together for forty-nine years. Their off-stage insults are as funny as anything they do before the foot-lights. Joe Laurie Jr. was on the same bill with them one week and eavesdropped outside their dressing room . . .

DALE: We certainly loused up the banana bit.

SMITH: We? You speak adhesively, don't you? You mean *you* loused it up.

DALE: Do me a favor: don't talk to me, y' hear. Don't talk to me.

SMITH: I wouldn't talk to you if I was in solitary con-finement and you was a mouse.

DALE: I should worry. What you say goes in one ear and stays in the other.

SMITH: Do me a favor. Go over to the window and lean out too far.

DALE: You do me a favor. Go walk under a street car.

SMITH: If I was as low as you, I'd walk under the car tracks.

DALE: A fine partner I got. Is that the way to insult me?

SMITH: If you know a better way, tell me and I'll in-sult you the way you like.

DALE: I don't have to stand for your insults! One more word from you and I'm through with you.

SMITH: Why—.

DALE: That's the word. Now I'm through with you.

SMITH: You're through with me? Well, I'm through with you, and when I say I'm through, you better look out, because I'm NOT!

That's been going on for almost fifty years. Sure they're pals, but once in a while the Broadway fever gets them and they start hostilities all over again. It never affected their act; they are still No. 1 on any laugh parade.

Billy Rose is one of the richest, most successful and talented men on the Main Stem. However, the former stenographer-songwriter-turned-producer-columnist and nightclub owner has been in more fights on Broadway than are stirred up by a Giant-Dodger double-header in Brooklyn.

His opponents say, "He hates to give up." So many stories have been written about his tightness, they have become a legend on Broadway along with the Goldwyn malapropisms and the Dorothy Parker quips. Billy never bothers to deny them. But the truth is, as Ed. Sullivan once pointed out, "Rose is tough with a buck and easy with a hundred thousand dollars."

"Billy Rose is no check dodger," kids Earl Wilson; "he merely has a slight impediment of reach."

"You can't outdo him as a producer," wails Bert Lahr. "If you furnish the ships—he'll provide the ocean."

Billy admits he mooches cigarettes from bartenders, waiters, cab drivers—anyone who may be near by. Nobody has ever seen him buy a pack. "I start out with two packs every day," he cries, "but I smoke so much I run out of them by eleven a.m."

Sitting at the round table at the Stork recently, the little Barnum took out a beautiful gold case—initials, fancy engraving, etc. "What's that for?" Jimmy Cannon asked. "I'm on a diet," said Rose: "I use it for saccharine."

"Oh!" Cannon flipped back, "I thought it was for cigarette butts."

Sam Friedman, the publicity man, brought a letter to Billy the other day. It was from a fellow who wanted the producer to send him an old suit. Friedman asked, "Have you got one?" "Yes," said Rose, "but I'm wearing it."

When Rose produced *Jumbo* at the Hippodrome in New York he spent a fortune on the production. He had just signed a $75,000 contract for a revolving stage when Will Morrissey, who was assisting, walked in and told Rose that an act called "Camellia's Birds" wanted $75 a week. "The salary is O. K.," said Billy, "but let's have it thoroughly understood that *she* feeds the birds."

Rose was sitting in Lindy's with two fellows. One was trying to sell him a huge property for two million dollars, and the other was attempting to sell him a dancer for $75. To the first guy he offered one million; to the other he said "$65." The story goes that he finally paid the two million but bought the dancer for $70.

As Ben Hecht once described him, "Billy is as wistful as a meat-axe."

Yeah, he's tough with a buck, but he did raise a million dollars for the United Jewish Appeal—and twenty thousand of those tough bucks were his.

The Rose is beloved of art salesmen. He buys paintings the way the average man buys a suit. According to legend, when the heads of the art galleries expect him, they put on a show that's bigger than any of his aquacades. Out come the fancy striped pants, ascot ties, and high hats. They dig the velvet drapes out of the cellar, put on the indirect lighting, and the organ plays "Here Comes the Sucker."

But the truth of the matter is, Billy always winds up with the right picture at the right price, and the arties are caught with their striped pants down.

"Do you have any feuds going at the moment?" my pal, Mickey Alpert, asked me the other day.

"Well," I answered, "I don't hate anybody, if that's what you mean. Oh, maybe if I look deep into my hate ball, Milton Berle will come up. But I don't really hate him. Personally, I think he's a great comedian. He gets more laughs per minute than most comedians get in their whole act. I just object to the fact that he's the object of his own affections."

"You must admit," cut in Jackie Miles, "that Milton has a lot of fan clubs." "To him," I answered, "a fan club is a group of people who tell him he's not alone in the way he feels about himself." "When a man falls in love with himself," Earl Wilson quoted from the old classic, "it's the beginning of a life-long romance."

"What burns me up," scolded Chuck Hamilton, "he never carries any money." "Never carries any?" queried Lois Andrews, "or never spends any?"

"Berle is usually in the dark about anything he can't make light of," commented Jack Durant.

"Don't get me wrong," I interposed. "I'm not jealous of the guy. I admit he's one of the greatest laugh-getters in the country, even if he did swipe a good portion of his gags. Winchell called him 'the thief of bad gags,' and Berle's even admitted, 'I laughed so hard at Bob Hope, I dropped my pencil.' Now he claims originality and objects to anybody using any gag he uses. He went so far as to send his brother to Leon and Eddie's to make me stop using a joke that he claimed. I told Milton not to worry, I wouldn't use his gags: 'I don't want to be sued by Bob Hope.' "

"Berle is responsible for selling 20,000 radio sets when he started on the air," mused Joe E. Lewis. "I know I sold mine and my brother sold his."

"He caused so much trouble in his show, *Spring in Brazil*," added Rita Angel, "they wanted to hire John J. Anthony as stage manager."

"The only good thing about Berle," suggested Chuck, "is his opinion of himself."

"I wouldn't say that," I praised; "he's a sensational comedian. He gets more laughs—."

"Money and fame will never change him," interjected Al Schenk. "He'll always be a ham."

"I think," I continued, "he's one of the foremost com—."

"He upstages you so much when you work with him," said Rose Marie, "he has you talking to the backdrop."

"He's promised to turn over a new leaf," I offered.

"Yeah," said Chuck sarcastically, "but he never seems to find the strength to lift the leaf."

"Isn't that Berle sitting there with his back towards the check?" asked Toots.

"How can you miss him?" answered Jackie Miles. "He's as anonymous as a spotlight."

Berle noticed us and walked towards the round table, throwing more lines than there are in the back yard of an East Side tenement.

"They cut me so much in *Spring in Brazil*," glibbed Milton, "I had to make up with iodine. My mother is joining the audience, maybe that will help. Trouble is, she's been laying off so much, she's forgotten how to laugh."

"How's the Number 2 company of Bob Hope?" he ribbed Lew Parker. "Okay," said Lew; "how's the Number 3 company?"

"My radio sponsors threw me a big dinner," ignored Berle, "but it didn't hit me." "There is the only guy on Columbia," heckled Jay C. Flippen, pointing to Berle, "with a Blue rating."

"Remember me when I had a long nose, a low forehead, and a low Crossley?" gagged Milton. "Everything has changed but your Crossley," flipped Hamilton.

"There's only one thing wrong with your radio personality," advised Hal Block, his gag writer: "It comes over the air."

"How's the bust man?" Berle shot at Earl Wilson, avoiding all the blurbs thrown at him. "Your show, *Spring in Brazil*," answered the saloon editor, "is a bigger bust than any girl I ever wrote about."

"Did you read my book, *Out of My Trunk*?" asked the gag bandit. "You should call it *Out of Their Trunk*,"

kidded Earl, pointing to Harry Hershfield, Joe Laurie Jr., and Senator Ford.

"Perhaps a better title," suggested Hershfield, "might be *Now It Can Be Retold.*"

Don't get me wrong, I don't dislike Berle. So what if he steals a few gags? He usually tells them better, anyhow. His three most valuable possessions are as original as they are lovely: his beautiful and talented wife, Joyce; his wonderful and faithful mother, and their recently adopted daughter, who—nicely enough—looks like Joyce.

Broadway is full of feuds and hates. Your best friend today is your worst enemy tomorrow. One broken-down little gag can start a feud that lasts a lifetime. Show people are sensitive and high-strung. It's a tough, hard business.

Sam Harris was one of the greatest and best-liked men in show business. He said a man is very rich indeed if he has one friend. He was luckier than most, he claimed; he had two friends.

Bradley, the sportsman, said, "The man who approaches the end of his life, feeling that he has as many as five friends, has been fooled five times."

How many times have you been fooled? Are you feuding, huh?

Giving Toots Shor the crum-bums' rush

CHAPTER ELEVEN

"To the Manner Born"

F R O M the time I was a little kid I've watched the stars of the entertainment world and looked upon them as gods.

The Golden Era of entertainment and sports produced some of the great of all time. They had more than a talent for the stage or their particular sport. They were "to the manner born." They had a sort of "star dust" in their eyes that lit up a room when they entered.

Babe Ruth, Bill Tilden, Bobby Jones, and Jack Dempsey reigned supreme in the sports world, John, Ethel, and Lionel Barrymore were the Royal Family of the theatre. Al Jolson, Eddie Cantor, George Jessel, Belle Baker, Bert Lahr, Will Rogers, Sophie Tucker, Ed Wynn, and Fannie Brice were the darlings of the vaudeville and musical comedy stage. Florenz Ziegfeld, George White, and Earl Carroll were the master showmen, and George M. Cohan was King.

When I saw these great walk into a room marked "Ladies" or "Gentlemen," I was disillusioned: I had never thought of them tending to their wants like ordinary mortals. To me they were minor deities. Later on, when I met them and knew them, I found them to be normal, warm, affectionate human beings who love to laugh and have fun like the rest of us.

One who is "to the manner born" can electrify a room when he enters. He is always the center of attraction without even trying. He's "big time" to his very finger tips.

The Number One man for me was Franklin Delano Roosevelt. He was sprinkled with "star dust" from the top of his head to the tip of his toes. He could excite the entire world with the warmth of his voice. He was "my friend" to every American and the idol of free people everywhere.

Yet he was normal in every way. He loved to laugh and have fun. Show people were his friends; he often had them as his guests in the White House. He had hobbies even as you and I, and he cried when his heart was hurt.

Walter Winchell once saw F.D.R. weep. It happened when ex-Congressman Lambertson and others were criticizing the war records of his sons. The President was miserable about a letter that came that morning from one of them. It concluded: "Pop, sometimes I really hope one of us gets killed so that maybe they'll stop picking on the rest of the family."

When he read it, F.D.R.'s lower lip started to quiver, and the tears came. "Will you please let me tell that Sunday night?" asked Winchell. "No, you mustn't," the President said, and changed the subject.

Anybody who ever met F.D.R. will never forget his humility and his warmth. He was loved by everybody in show business. So long as free men breathe, so long will he be remembered.

You just have the manner or you haven't. You can't buy it or manufacture it. You must be born to it.

A lot of people try to force attention by good publicity, or by throwing money around. You can't *make* people look at you. I found that out a long time ago. Don't worry about people not knowing you—but strive so that you may be worth knowing.

The people with "star dust" are always "copy." Their praises are sung all over the world.

Dorothy Parker's quips, for instance, are repeated everywhere, wherever people like to laugh. One of her famous remarks was made when she was in her room and the phone rang. "Is there a gentleman in your room?" asked the voice on the other end. "Just a moment," quipped Miss Parker, "I'll ask him!"

Dorothy was bored by a talkative actress who hadn't had a part for years. "I simply can't think of leaving the theatre," the woman gurgled. "I'm wedded to it." Miss Parker retorted, "Then why not sue it for non-support?"

In this modern age, two young fellows have taken the entertainment world by storm. They have so electrified their public that they can't walk into a public place without getting their clothes torn to shreds. They are the idols of the bobby-soxers. Their fans number millions who wear long stockings too.

Van Johnson and Frank Sinatra are like any other normal boys of 28 or 29 making a million dollars a year.

Even the laundry steals their shirts for souvenirs. I'm

not so popular—they only take pieces out of mine.

Sinatra, the voice that launched a thousand chips for his managers and agents, is in person a sweetheart of a guy. He's quite a fighter and pretty rugged in spite of the comedians' gags that he's "a little on the bony side."

His sense of humor is priceless. When he was going overseas to entertain the G.I.'s, he said, "I'm going to Europe to show the people over there we can starve too." When he was hit by an egg at the Paramount Theatre in New York he gagged, "I remember when an egg was something to eat." He gave his friend Rags Ragland a watch inscribed, "From Riches to Rags." When somebody asked him if he was a blood donor, he laughed; "I'm not even a blood owner." When I kidded him that the bobby-soxers here were going to wear their sox at half-mast when he went overseas, he answered, "Well, I heard they're going to issue G.I. bobby-sox to the WACs!"

On his radio program the rail got some howls one night when he ad-libbed, "And next week we'll have Benny Goodman and his—if you'll pardon the expression—sextet."

Frankie is the greatest idol of the opposite sex since Rudolph Valentino. None of this has gone to his head. His head has remained as small as his body.

He is very happily married but admits, "My wife is the most understanding and tolerant woman in the world. Just visualize what I have gone through in recent years and try to imagine how a wife can stand by faithfully, continue her encouragement, and raise a family! Believe me, sometimes I've sweated blood, even though there are those who say I have no blood to sweat."

His great job in teaching tolerance to the children of this country has won him the acclaim and love of decent people everywhere. He was awarded a citation by the National Conference of Christians and Jews for his outstanding work in helping to build national unity.

Sinatra has grown mentally as well as morally. His "star dust" has helped to attract record crowds. Then he uses his voice and the prestige of his name in an earnest plea for tolerance. He made a picture called *The House I Live In,* he flew to Indiana in a sincere effort to reduce racial animosities, and he sped to Harlem to urge a mixed enrollment of youngsters to apply sportsmanship in their school relationships. Kids believe him. He's their favorite and will do more for him than for any missionary.

Some performers object that Sinatra is stupid to step out of character, suggest that singing and social significance shouldn't be coupled. Ed Sullivan, who is always fighting for the little guy, thinks, "Sinatra has added something new and important to popular singing, a species of disinterested public service we should all render to the things in which we believe. The Voice strikes a grace note in a national symphony that often seems so cynical and selfish."

So when you read about Frankie's million-dollar income, don't envy him. In the first place, ninety percent of it goes to the U. S. Government for taxes. That doesn't make the Voice mad. "Say," Sinatra admits, "in what other country could a punk like me ever become a big shot?"

So don't pick on our boy—there's nothing left to pick.

Van Johnson is as plain and unaffected today, with the entertainment world and the bobby-soxers at his feet, as he was when he worked as a chorus boy in *Pal Joey* and labored on the borsht belt not too many years ago.

All this adulation is still new to the blonde star. He called Sinatra to tell him about his recent trip to New York—it was the first time he had returned to Broadway since he'd hit the "big time." "You'll never know," said Van, "how those fans can run after you."

"*I'll never know!*" Frankie screamed.

John Barrymore was really "to the manner born." Even near the end of his career, when liquor started to get the best of him, he had more "color" when he entered a room than almost any individual in the theatre. His sense of humor never failed him. He was the life of any party.

One of Hollywood's most important movie producers had his secretary call Mr. Barrymore to invite him to a party. John politely murmured into the telephone: "I have a previous engagement which I shall make as soon as possible."

When he was a youngster, acting a small part with William Collier in *The Dictator*, Jack was asked what made him look so much taller on the stage. His answer was: "Hic! Collier."

The great Barrymore tripped out of the Lambs Club

one night with a slight load on. He mumbled the address of his destination to the cab driver, who couldn't understand him. Otis Skinner, who was passing by, repeated the address to the cab driver with faultless enunciation. This annoyed John and he yelled to Skinner, "You gahdamn perfect-dictionist!"

The beloved member of the Royal Family had enough marital troubles to fill a month of Good Will Hours. In later life the Great Profile was very cynical about women and marriage. Winchell once disagreed with his disillusioned views. "Did you ever notice how happy all brides are?" Walter asked. "Brides aren't happy," John intoned, "just triumphant."

If ever a man was "to the manner born," it was Will Rogers. He was loved by presidents as well as farmers, by kings as well as paupers, by capital as well as labor. His simple homespun humor was as sweet and warm as a little girl making fudge for her mother.

Will Rogers said, "I never met a man I didn't like." I never met a man that didn't like Will Rogers. If only the world could learn that lesson!

There is a detective in New York who has "it" too. He gets "it" with his fists as well as his charm. His exploits have been heard around Broadway for years. He cleaned up the Street when racket guys were running rampant. Everybody on Broadway comes to him when they're in trouble. His name is Johnny Broderick.

Johnny is like a magnet when he is sitting in a restaurant or Hanson's drug store. They all gather around to listen to the "fighting Irishman." But when a group of tinhorns or racketeers see Broderick, the opposite happens; they scatter in every direction.

He loves show people and they feel the same way about him, but he is the kind of guy who will break a club on a phony's head and then hold him for resisting an officer and destroying public property.

A Hollywood studio offered Broadway's beloved detective $100,000 for the story of his life. His answer was right to the point: "I'd rather be a $4000-a-year real cop than a make-believe cop at $100,000 a year."

When Robert Benchley died we lost one of the best-loved men in Broadway's history. His sense of humor was out of this world. Will Rogers and Bob must be having a wonderful time up there, throwing gags at each other.

When Benchley passed away, his friends gathered at "21" and drank to him. They all sat around telling favorite anecdotes about him. They knew he would want it that way.

Leonard Lyons' eulogy of the late actor-writer-critic was a series of anecdotes, recorded in his *Lyons Den* column, that will live as long as people can laugh . . .

Robert Benchley came out of "21," tapped a uniformed man on the shoulder, and said, "Get me a taxi." "Do you know who I am?" asked the man indignantly. "I'm an Admiral." "All right," Benchley apologized, "then get me a battleship."

Another time, Bob was leaving the "21" in the midst of a rainstorm. He waited under the canopy with Donald Ogden Stewart, but no taxis were in sight. Just then a man walked by carrying an umbrella. Benchley and Stewart got on either side of him, clutched the umbrella handle, and chorused, "Yale Club, please."

When his son Nat got a job, Benchley said: "Good. Now my stuff need only be half as funny." An editor told him, "I suppose that, with typical parental pride, you hope some day to be known as young Benchley's father?" Benchley confessed, "No, I'd like some day to be known as old Benchley's father."

Bing Crosby told Leonard Lyons that he was driving with Benchley across a toll bridge where the cop on duty was impolite. Twice they drove across the bridge, and each time the cop was surly when Benchley gave him the twenty-five-cent fee. The third time, when the cop reached for Benchley's twenty-five cents, the coin could not be dislodged from Benchley's hand. In fact,

the whole arm—it was a prop—came off. Benchley drove off, leaving the startled cop holding the twenty-five cents and the arm. But the cop's whistle forced Benchley back. "Wise guy, eh?" snarled the cop. Benchley took the arm back, shook his head and said: "Y' know, officer—I never missed it."

Earl Wilson mourned the loss of Benchley by recording this anecdote:

Benchley saw elephants once at the Algonquin. Eight of them, he observed through his hangover. They were trotting outside his window, trunk to tail. Benchley instantly quit drinking, right in the middle of a pick-me-up. Later he learned they were real elephants, going to a circus nearby, so he revoked his no-drinking decision as being hasty.

During his days as a dramatic critic, Benchley covered a play on Broadway called *The Squall*. When the inevitable half-caste girl said, "Me Nubi. Me good girl. Me stay," Benchley squirmed in his seat and whispered to a companion, "Me Bobby. Me bad boy. Me go."

Bob was sitting around a night club drinking some bad liquor when a pest started bothering him. "Watcha drinkin' that stuff for?" asked the bore. "Don't you know it's slow poison?" "Well," quipped Benchley, "I'm in no hurry."

George M. Cohan had an extra portion of "star dust." An admirer once asked him how he happened to be so talented and versatile.

"Well," replied George M., "I've always been an envious cuss. As a kid in vaudeville I was often on the same bill with a hoofer that I thought was the best in the world, so I spent all my time trying to match him. It was the same with song-writing, play-writing, and acting— there was always somebody a lot better than I was, and I worked to close up the gap between us. My notion is that the guy that thinks he's the tops isn't going to do much climbing."

George Bernard Shaw rates the bows his rapier wit has earned. Anyone else who ever uttered the vitriolic squelches that he throws around so freely, would be in line for a good swift kick in the pants. However, on him it looks good.

A famous beauty once wired Shaw that she would like to have a child by him. "With your brain and my beauty," said the doll, "ours would be the most wonderful child in the world." "But," Shaw answered, "suppose it had your brain and my beauty!"

The hostess at a very dull dinner party seated herself between G.B.S. and a pretty actress and gushed, "How delighted I am to find myself between wit and beauty!" Shaw let her have it. "And without possessing either!" he added.

The famous Irish playwright was browsing through a book store one day and chanced to pick up a volume of his own plays which he had given to a friend some years back. On the flyleaf was inscribed, "With the compliments of the author." He purchased the book, took out his pen, and added, "With renewed compliments," then sent the book back to its original recipient.

Shaw's most famous remark, "Youth is a wonderful

thing—too bad it has to be wasted on children," is a classic of wit.

An acquaintance who visited the ninety-year-old genius was astonished that he didn't see a single vase of flowers in the place. "I thought you liked flowers," he remarked. Shaw answered curtly, "I am also fond of children, but I don't cut off their heads and stick them in pots around the house!"

Ever since I could understand a joke or could appreciate beautiful phrases and sweet sentiment, George Jessel has been my favorite. He is my white-haired boy on the stage or on a dais. He deserves the accolades heaped upon him as the country's Number One toastmaster. When he saw, heard, and loved Helen Morgan for the first time, he said, "You sing songs as if Whistler had painted them."

Jessel himself can paint Rembrandts with words. He delivered a beautiful speech at the Al Smith Memorial Dinner, and his closing line was: "Tonight a star in heaven tipped its hat—it was a brown derby."

George has given so many after-dinner talks around the country, he automatically starts making a speech every time he sees a grapefruit.

He was invited to speak to the senior class at Harvard University—a very great honor indeed for a boy who had never gone beyond the sixth grade in school. When his late beloved mother, who had heard show-business talk around the house for many years, was told of the occasion, "So what?" replied the venerable lady. "It's only a one-night stand!"

When Jessel appeared before the Harvard class he told them he would make a speech on any subject they'd mention. "But I only got as far as the 6B," said George, "so don't ask me any question on geometry because I won't know—same as you wouldn't know if I asked you about where's the best place to buy pastrami."

I had just finished my last show for the day at the Capitol Theatre and was in my dressing room taking my make-up off, when I heard a knock on the door. Opening the door, I was surprised to see an outstretched hand and beyond it a pair of pop-eyes.

"I enjoyed your show so much," said the visitor, "I had to come back and introduce myself. My name is Eddie Cantor."

Eddie Cantor! As if he had to tell me. Mr. Showbusiness himself! The first thing that crossed my mind was the time twenty-two years back that La Guardia called me, "you dirty little Eddie Cantor," when he wanted to call me an actor. Eddie was to the Mayor the personification of show business. He didn't know it at the time, but he was paying me the biggest compliment of my young life. It set a goal for me to reach. And, now, here was Eddie himself in my dressing room to pay me compliments!

I had three all-time favorites on the stage: Jolson, Cantor, and Jessel. I met Jessel in Mt. Freedom at "Sains" and he helped me with my imitation of him. Jolson was at the Roney Plaza in Miami Beach when Louis Sobol introduced me to him at a Bond Rally; Al was very helpful and encouraging. And now—Eddie Cantor.

Carl Schurz said: "Ideals are like stars; you will not succeed in touching them with your hands. But, like the seafaring men on the desert of waters, you choose them as your guide, and following them reach your destiny."

I chose them as my guide in show business. Eddie won't know it until he reads it here, but he made an admirer of his very happy. When he left my dressing room after throwing so many bouquets at me, the tears rolled down my face.

Tallulah Bankhead, the daughter of the late Senator Bankhead and the belle of southern society, is in reality a "regular guy." She'd rather be the first lady of the theatre than the first lady of the land. Tallu tells this story on herself: When she was touring in *The Little Foxes* in the middle west, Frank Conroy went into a little beanery next door to the theatre and overheard two local characters talking:

"What's playin' at the theaytre?"

"Stage show, live actors."

"What is it?"

"Tallulah Bankhead in *The Little Foxes*."

"Who's that?"

"You know, she does a strip-tease with little fox furs."

Tallulah and Peggy Hopkins Joyce were chatting at the Stork Club. "I met the most marvelous man," said Tallu. "He'd be wonderful for you." "Is he my type?" queried Peggy. "Sure," Tallu quickly responded, "he's alive and breathing."

A fan walked over to Tallulah and asked her: "Are you the famous Tallulah Bankhead?" "How dare you mistake me for that low, horrible woman!" Tallu replied, striding off.

Jack Benny did a magnificent job entertaining the boys in uniform all over the world. Jack, Ingrid Bergman, and Larry Adler, the harmonica wizard, were driving in a limousine in Stuttgart, Germany. It was about 10:30 at night, and they had just finished giving a show for the boys at the front line. Suddenly there was a report and at the same time Larry felt an impact against his back which knocked him to the floor of the car. Thinking he'd been shot, he shouted for Jack and Ingrid to duck down because there were probably snipers in the vicinity.

It was not, as it turned out, a sniper, but one of our own sentries who fired at them after their car passed him without acknowledging his signal to stop. No one in the car, including the army driver, had seen the sentry nor heard any signal whatsoever.

Their identity was established, and they were finally allowed to proceed. Ten minutes later, a black cat darted across their path.

"Look," said Jack bitterly, pointing at the cat, "*now* he tells us!"

Bob Hope, another great G.I. favorite, was broadcasting from a Naval Station when a pajama-clad patient walked over to the mike and began to exchange banter with the comedian. Suddenly their conversation was interrupted by two attendants who led the patient away.

After the show, someone explained to Bob that the patient had wandered away from the psychopathic ward. "What worries me," says Hope, "is that I thought we were having a perfectly normal conversation."

The man behind the nose is a warm, deeply human personality. Jimmy Durante left the East Side for greener pastures, but the East Side has never left Schnozzola.

Ever since Jimmy made his first public appearance, playing the piano for political rallies at neighbor Assemblyman Al Smith's house many years ago, Umbriago's pal has been entertaining Americans on and off stage with the same East-Side accent and manner.

He has a heart of gold. "Anyone can take me," he admits. "Dey say, 'Jimmy, you're a swell guy'—and I'm workin' for nuttin'."

His "Everybody wantsa get in duh act" and "Dere's a million good-lookin' guys, but I'm a novelty" have become bons mots for tots and teen-agers.

Jimmy never forgets a pal, even if he can't remember a name. His co-workers of long standing are still with him. Clayton is his manager, Eddie Jackson works with him in personal appearances, and Jack Roth, his drummer, is his man Friday. After twenty-five years of close association, they still think Durante is the greatest guy on earth. So do millions of kids all over the world.

Jimmy came to a broadcast shivering from the cold. His famed schnozzola was red because of the wintry winds. Some jerk heckled him with; "Hey, Umbriago, what makes your nose so red?" "It's blushin' with pride," was the squelcher, "at da way it keeps outa udder people's business!"

In 1931 a very talented young singer was making her big-time debut at Ben Marden's Riviera. As she was singing her sweetest ballad, she overheard some loud women at the ringside remark, "Isn't it a shame such a pretty and talented girl has such a large mouth!" After the show, Martha Raye went back to her dressing room and cried all night.

Now she capitalizes on it. She even pokes fun at herself. "I kissed my husband," she gags, "and he lost his head completely."

Today Martha is as hep as Times Square. She is always out for laughs. After being married to David Rose and Neal Lang, she finally met a great guy who can jive with her, Nick Condos. They go together like ham and eggs. Their beautiful daughter sits in her carriage in the wings of the theatre, and claps her hands with the music while her mother is on the stage. There is the heppest trio in show business.

Martha was at the Hollywood Canteen entertaining the boys in uniform from all over the world. After the show an English sailor asked her to dance with him. Of course, she was very happy to do so. While on the floor, he asked her if the V on her sweater was for Victory. "Yes," replied Martha, "but the bundles aren't for Britain."

Archie Robbins, the comic, and Mickey Rooney were invited to entertain at the Potsdam conference during the war. The entire show was cheered by Stalin, Churchill, Truman, and the rest of the audience.

After the performance, Archie Robbins was singled out to meet Stalin. The handsome young comedian was wild with excitement. He could picture himself getting the Russian equivalent of the Congressional Medal of Honor. What a memento to show his wife and friends! "Mr.

"The bundles aren't for Britain"

Stalin wants to know," said the interpreter, when Archie was brought face to face with the head man of Russia, "if you want to sell your watch."

Albert Einstein is always burdened with inquiries as to the meaning of relativity. After thousands of questions thrown at him and his staff all over the world, he finally decided to explain it as follows: "When you sit with your girl for an hour you think it's only a minute, but when you sit on a hot stove for a minute you think it's an hour—that's relativity."

The top mathematician and atomic-bomb authority likes to relax with his violin. He once invited the renowned pianist Arthur Schnabel to his home for a musical session. They were running through a rather involved Mozart sonata and Einstein was having trouble playing. Finally, after several explanations, Schnabel got irritated. He banged his hands down on the keyboard and groaned, "No, no, Albert. For heaven's sake, can't you count? One, two, three, four . . ."

Speaking in Paris before the war, Einstein said, "If my theory of relativity is proven successful, Germany will claim me as a German and France will declare that I am a citizen of the world. Should my theory prove untrue, France will say that I am a German and Germany will declare that I am a Jew."

Deems Taylor was a guest on *Information, Please* one evening and fumbled a question badly. When the next one was asked, he begged, "Let me have it, I want to save my face." Clifton Fadiman peered at him and then answered mildly, "I'm sure I don't know why."

"I would not have anyone believe that I am trading on the name of Edison," said Charles Edison, son of the great inventor. "I would rather be known merely as a result of one of my father's earlier experiments."

Walter Winchell tells a story about Wilson Mizner, the great wit. Mizner, according to W.W., once wrote a play that was backed by an aging dowager. During rehearsals Wilson was chatting with his backer, and

without thinking, asked her how old she was. Her icy
query gave him the shivers: "Why do you wish to know
that?" "Dear lady," he replied, "I merely wanted to know
at what age a woman is most fascinating."

Mae West has been selling the sex theme on the stage
for several decades. Her fans number in the millions. Her

lines have been quoted everywhere. Every school kid
has repeated her "Come up and see me some time."

"It's not the men in my life that counts," said Mae; "it's
the life in my men."

Quite a few years back, Mae West was in a show at
the Royale Theatre. A young reporter, Jack Eigen, went
backstage to see her about an interview for his column
in *Zit's*. It was his first assignment as a reporter, and he
tried to impress Miss West by wearing his hat on the

back of his head as he had seen all reporters do in the movies. Mae was furious at the young cub. "Remove your hat when you're in the presence of a lady," shouted the buxom star.

The next day the show was raided . . .

William Collier rarely spoke a line on the stage as it had been written. One performance he noticed Hartley Manners, his current author, sitting out front. After the show he said to a friend, "I was so embarrassed I almost remembered one of his lines."

George S. Kaufman is a great playwright and an excellent director. He possesses a wonderful sense of humor. However, he revolts, like most playwrights, when his lines are changed in a show. Florenz Ames changed the lines *Of Thee I Sing* almost beyond recognition. George sent a note backstage to Florenz which read: "I am sitting out front watching the show—wish you were with me."

Some actors make it a practice to keep changing their lines—to "fatten up their parts" by adding words or whole sentences. In a short time, unless a director or producer curbs them, they will be far away from the original script. The late George M. Cohan once posted a notice backstage, "There will be a rehearsal at 2 p.m. tomorrow to delete the improvements."

David Warfield, beloved star of the American stage, refused dozens of offers to go to Hollywood. He turned down a million-dollar certified check to do a couple of movies. "I'd rather be an actor than his photograph," he explained.

When Ole Olson and Chick Johnson's *Hellzapoppin* clicked in New York the comedians were jubilant. "We've had a lot of fun all our lives," said Ole, "but the most fun we've ever had is finding out that this terrible bogeyman, Broadway, is just Peoria blown bigger."

The two hoofers opened the bill at Keith's Theatre in Washington. For twelve minutes they did knee drops and falls, spins and splits. Their bodies were bruised and perspiration oozed from their faces as they walked off stage without a bow.

They trudged up four flights of stairs to their dressing room and lay there for twenty minutes, completely exhausted, every bone in their bodies aching. When they came to, they put on their robes and walked slowly down the stairs to see the star act.

Ethel Barrymore was on, and she delivered a soliloquy that lasted eight minutes. She didn't ruffle an eyebrow as she worked. She spoke quietly and without effort. The hoofers watched in amazement. As the curtain came down, the theatre echoed to thunderous applause. Miss Barrymore took twenty-two curtain calls.

The elder hoofer turned to his partner and pointed to Miss Barrymore. "Hey, Jim," he said, "next season, that's the kind of crap we're gonna do."

Alla Nazimova worshipped at her little shrine where she kept a picture of a character never acted by living histrion. "I keep this picture there to teach me humility," explained the star, "for even should great fame one day come to me, I never can be so famous as Mickey Mouse."

Boris Tomashevsky was a combination Al Jolson and

John Barrymore of the Jewish stage. He was completely covered with "star dust." When single he was the Errol Flynn of his day. Young hopeful actresses who came backstage to ask his help and advice about the stage, were flattered when he made love to them.

One little girl of nineteen who came to see Boris was thrilled that the famous star embraced her and paid her so much attention. As she was leaving, he gave her a pass to see his next performance, as a reward for accepting his love. "But Mr. Tomashevsky," pleaded the young thing, "I can't live on passes, I need bread. Can't you spare something for me?"

"Bread!" shouted the great Tomashevsky. "I'm an actor, I give passes. If you want bread, go make love to a baker!"

Gypsy Rose Lee, even when she worked in burlesque, was sprinkled with "star dust." Like so many of the other big names of burlesque—Jack Pearl, Fannie Brice, Bert Lahr, and Abbott and Costello—she was destined to take her place with the greats in show business.

Gypsy's sense of humor and frankness have won her thousands of friends in every walk of life. Her intimates include the who's who of society, the literati, vaudevillians, burlesque performers, and just plain Joe and Mary.

Laughs are most important with her. "My goodness, what beautiful furs you have on!" an admirer said to her. "Goodness had nothing to do with it," answered Gypsy.

"Are those real diamonds?" I asked her one night when she was bedecked with an armful of "ice." "If they aren't," answered the darling of the literati, "I've been raped."

Of course, those are only gags and signs of her sense of humor.

Gypsy was working in burlesque at the Irving Place Theatre when the Great Ziegfeld "invited" her to be a Ziegfeld Beauty at $150 a week. She refused and added, "Thanks, but I'd rather be these jerks' beauty down here at $750 a week."

All real stars are "to the manner born." Each step up the ladder makes them nicer and more humble. Danny Kaye, for instance, has never forgotten his friends and his family. He admits that his talented wife, Sylvia Fine, is responsible for his success. "Sylvia," he said, "has a fine head on my shoulders."

No, you can't buy "star dust." It's not so much what they say. It's the way Sophie Tucker and Belle Baker walk on stage, it's the way Jimmy Walker enters a room, it's the way Al Smith smiled when he tipped his brown derby, it's the way Beatrice Lillie and Gertrude Lawrence carry their heads, it's the way Babe Ruth walked over to the plate, the way Jack Dempsey stepped into the ring, the way Caruso took a bow, the way Toscanini taps his baton. It's the way F.D.R. said: "My friends."

The mere mention of their names can excite you. When they are around there's electricity in the air. They are always the center of attraction. All eyes and ears follow them as they make their rounds. They are *"to the manner born."*

CHAPTER TWELVE

Animal Crack-ers

EVER since I was able to talk, I have been telling jokes and stories. Even before I could say a word, people would look at me and laugh. And I, in turn, laugh at every comedian and scream at the anecdotes and stories in the columns. I'm a great audience for anything that has humor in it. I even like Good Humor ice cream.

I have recorded a library of jokes, stories, and anecdotes that will keep me in my old age. After all, I kept them in theirs.

Walter Winchell says a joke is new if you haven't heard it before. He claims there is a new "joke" audience born every four years.

Today a joke or story has a very short life. A comedian does it on the air, or a syndicated columnist prints it, and every man, woman, or child that can read or talk English, repeats it all over America the next day. Then it's dead until the next generation of joke audiences is born four years later.

The bottom fell out of vaudeville for this very reason. The "hicks" and "ickies" became sophisticated. There are no "hicks" today. The "ickies" are as "hep" as a jam session on Fifty-second Street.

One night I was visiting my friend Juddy Traum, and after dinner his six-year-old son Ricky asked me to tell him a story before he went to bed. Of course, I was flattered. Every comedian likes an audience that laughs out loud at his material, even if it's only a single six-year-old boy.

I put him on my knee and started to tell one of my favorite stories. Naturally, I dragged it out to give it a little color. In the middle of the story, the hep youngster interrupted: "Never mind the build-up, just come to the punch line."

"Well, er—", I stammered.

"Do you know any good animal cracks?" asked my friend's son.

Now when comedians get together, their favorite stories are about animals that talk. The columnists are pushovers for talking bird, dog, and horse stories. Ozzie Nelson was strolling in Central Park when he overheard two pigeons talking. One pigeon strutted by in snooty fashion, nose in the air and a couple of newspaper clippings under his wing. "What's the matter with him?" asked a bird. "Oh, he's got a swelled head," said another pigeon. "He got into Winchell's column three times this month!"

So when Ricky refused to go to sleep until I told him stories about animals that talk, I made a hurried call to Toots Shor's. "Who's at the round table?" I asked Joe, the head waiter. "The Ritz brothers, Earl Wilson, Ken Kling, Bert Wheeler, Bert Lahr, Jackie Miles, and Toots," was the reply. "Let me talk to all of them, one at a time," I pleaded. And each of them gave me a story to keep my protégé in good humor.

Perhaps you would like to hear some of the ones that made Ricky laugh—they're the kind of stories that make comedians hysterical. In fact, when you see a group of comics and newspapermen sitting around and having fun with jokes, they are probably telling each other some

of these—and he who laughs last was probably going to tell the story himself a little later . . .

Ken Kling's favorite animal stories are naturally about horses. The famous cartoonist and racing expert likes to tell the one about the horse who walked over to the mutuel window and neighed, "I want a two dollar ticket on myself."

"What!" screamed the man behind the window.

"Surprised that I can talk?" asked the horse.

"No," said the man, "I just don't think you can win."

Bert Lahr walked into a bird store to buy a parrot. He noticed a beautiful one with two strings, one tied to each leg.

"What are the strings for?" asked Bert.

"If you pull this one," answered the bird, "I stand on my left leg and tell jokes."

"And if I pull that one?"

"I stand on my right leg and sing, *Hubba, Hubba!*"

"Wonderful," said Bert. "What happens if I pull both strings at the same time?"

"I fall flat on my tail," answered the parrot.

Eddie Davis tells the story of the beautiful eighteen-year-old-girl who was walking in the woods and accidentally stepped on a turtle.

"Ouch!" yelled the little turtle. "Please be careful."

"Can I believe my ears?" said the startled girl. "A talking turtle! That must be the voice of the turtle."

"That's right," said the turtle.

"How come you talk?" asked the girl.

"I once was a big handsome football star, six feet tall, with curly hair and broad shoulders. A curse fell on me and I was turned into a turtle. A fairy princess told me that if some day a pretty girl picked me up and took me home and put me under her pillow and slept on me all night, I would turn into my old self again."

So the beautiful little girl took the turtle home, put it under her pillow, and slept on it all night. Lo and behold! the next morning, there lying next to her in bed was a big handsome man, six feet tall, with curly hair and broad shoulders.

And it's the strangest thing—to this day her mother doesn't believe that story.

Winchell opened his refrigerator and found a rabbit sitting inside staring at him.

"What are you doing here?" asked the newspaper man.

"Isn't this a Westinghouse?" queried the rabbit.

"Yes, it is," answered Walter.

"Well," said the rabbit, "I'm westing."

Three storks were having their nightly confab.

"I had a very busy day," said the first stork. "I flew over Pittsburgh and dropped a lovely set of twins over a coal miner's home."

"I had a busier day," said the second stork. "I flew over Boston and dropped triplets over a bartender's home."

"That's nothing," said the third stork. "I flew over New York and scared the hell out of a couple of stenographers from Brooklyn."

The Ritz brothers never fail to tell this story when showpeople are around:

Six turtles were sitting at their round table in the forest talking about this and that. Their ages ranged from a thousand to ten thousand years.

"We never have a vacation," said one of them. "We've been sitting around here for thousands of years. Let's go on a picnic."

"That's a good idea," agreed the oldest. "We'll pack sandwiches, pickles, mustard, beer, and pretzels, and we'll really have a time of it. We'll meet in the Catskill Mountains, near Grossinger's. I was there about seven thousand years ago and I know they have a beautiful field close by."

Each of the turtles went his separate way, collecting the food for the picnic. They all met at the appointed spot three hundred years later.

When they opened the food baskets they discovered that they'd forgotten to bring a bottle opener for the beer. "You're the youngest," said the biggest turtle to the littlest one; "you go and bring back a bottle opener."

"Very well," said the baby turtle, "I'll go. But don't anybody eat anything till I come back. Remember, not a morsel!"

"We promise," chorused the older five.

They waited five years for his return but the little fellow was nowhere in sight. Ten years went by, fifteen years, twenty years, and still there was no sign of the young one.

"Let's eat something," said the six thousand-year-old-one. "I'm starved."

"No," said the oldest, "we promised we'd wait."

Twenty-five years passed, forty years, sixty years, and still no turtle and no bottle opener.

"Please," said one of them, "let's eat something, just a nibble. He won't know."

The oldest one agreed, and they all started to crawl towards the food with their flippers outstretched when they heard a rustle in the bushes behind them.

"Uh-uh!" groaned the young turtle. "I knew you wouldn't keep your word. I've been watching you from behind those bushes. Just for that I'm not going for the bottle opener!"

Bert Wheeler tells the story of the old vaudevillian who walked into a booking agent's office to sell him his dog act.

"Are you kidding?" asked the annoyed booker. "Animal acts are a dime a dozen."

"I know," persisted the vaudevillian, "but this dog is different. He plays the piano."

He placed the dog on the piano and sat back as the pup proceeded to play the meanest boogie-woogie you ever heard.

"I'll give you two thousand dollars a week for the act," offered the booker.

"No," replied the vaudevillian.

"Three thousand dollars!"

"No," said the dog's owner. "Besides, you haven't seen the whole act. I also have a parrot that sings. The dog accompanies it."

He pulled a parrot from beneath his coat. The bird sang *Star Dust,* the dog assisting at the piano.

The manager was beside himself. "Five thousand dollars a week for both of them!" he shouted.

"Gosh!" confessed the young man, turning to the booker, "I can't go through with it. You see, that parrot can't really sing **a no**te. The dog is a ventriloquist!"

Ken Kling walked into a stall at the race track and noticed a man sitting at a table with ten cards in his hand. Opposite him was a horse sitting up and holding the same number of cards.

"What are you doing?" asked Ken.

"We're playing gin," answered the stranger. "What the hell does it look like?"

Just then the horse drew a card and neighed, "What's da name o' da game?"

"I've been around horses all my life," said the amazed Kling, "but that's the smartest animal I've ever seen!"

"What's so smart about him?" yelled the man. "I beat him four out of five games."

Jackie Miles panics showpeople with this story:

Three sharks met off Rockaway Beach and were talking about their day's activities.

"I caught a handsome six-foot-three movie star today," said the biggest shark. "I followed an ocean liner for three days and finally this big actor fell overboard. He had the tenderest meat I ever tasted."

"I ate a big, chubby wrestler today," said the blackest shark. "He fell off a yacht I'd been following for a week. Best meal I ever had!"

"How did you do today?" they asked the smallest shark.

"I'm starving to death," answered the little one. "I followed a canoe and Frank Sinatra fell out."

George Clarke dreamed this story. It is more logical than it dreams.

Atomic power got away from the scientists and blew the whole world to smithereens. Nothing was left—only destruction, except that on a small island off the beaten path stood one little tree, its branches torn to shreds. And sitting on a broken twig were two monkeys. "Gee!" said one to the other, "now we gotta start the whole goddam thing over again."

Ralph Edwards' favorite story concerns a family of turtles—mother turtle, father turtle, and baby turtle. As winter came on, father and mother turtle were concerned at baby turtle's habit of keeping his neck out of the shell, as several of their friends' baby turtles had already caught cold.

One day baby turtle overheard his parents talking about it. "Listen," he said to them, "why don't you stop worrying and buy me one of those people-neck sweaters?"

Howard Lindsay told Leonard Lyons about the time Monty Salmon, manager of the Rivoli Theatre, received an alarming call from one of his ushers. The usher gasped that he had just seen a man with a bear in tow, and that they were now occupying two seats in the loges. Monty rushed out of his swank office and found the man and the bear just as the usher had described them. "Sir," said the manager, "what is the idea of this? Why did you bring a bear into this theatre?"

"Why not?" the man shrugged. "He enjoyed the book so much, I thought he'd like the picture."

Henny Youngman is one of the greatest comedians, but he knows very little about horses. "I wish the horses would go as fast as the money I bet on them," says Henny. "Not that I mind losing, but when a horse comes over to me in the grandstand and says, 'Which way did they go?'—brother, that's the end."

"Ritz Brothers," the horse, has been groomed by the zany Ritz boys themselves. The stars like to talk to their namesake, and often sit up with him and tell him stories.

"What a nag!" says Harry Ritz. "He can outrun any horse in the country. The only trouble is, he's always about fifteen lengths ahead of all the other horses when they're coming down the stretch. Naturally the crowd always goes wild. They yell, cheer, scream, and applaud for 'Ritz Brothers.' Our horse, reared in show business, stops to take a bow—the big ham!—and all the other horses come in ahead of him."

Al Burnett, the famous English comedian, has told this story around the world:

A magician was doing his big trick before an assemblage on an ocean liner going from England to the U.S.A. He held a parrot in one hand and a gun in the other. "As I shoot this gun into the air," said the magic man, "the parrot will disappear from the face of the earth." Just as he shot the gun off, there was a terrible explosion in the boiler room and the ship blew to smithereens.

Two days later the parrot was seen floating on a raft, denuded of all its feathers, and saying, "Did you ever see such a silly trick!"

During the war, the favorite story of the G.I.'s was the one of the two sardines who met in a brook in Central Park.

"Let's go to California," suggested one.

"That sounds like a good idea," agreed the other. "How shall we go?"

"Let's take the train," said the first one.

"What!" screamed the other sardine, "and get packed in like soldiers?"

The master of the house was reprimanding the parrot for swearing. "If you ever say that word again," said the man, "I'll pluck every feather out of your body and stick you in the frigidaire."

"Well I'll be God-damned," said the parrot.

"Now you've done it," said the master, "and I'm going to keep my word."

He plucked every feather out of the parrot's body with a tweezer and threw him into the frigidaire. The poor, wicked little parrot was almost frozen. There he was, trying to cover his cold body with his thin little wings, when he looked up and saw a turkey, all plucked and with its head cut off and the blood dripping down, ready for the oven.

"Oh!" said the parrot, "what you **musta said!**"

Ken Kling was walking on a farm road upstate, when a horse spoke to him from behind a tree: "Hello, Ken, remember me? I won the Kentucky Derby two years ago, and you were the only one that picked me to win." A

talking horse! Ken rushed to the horse's owner, asked the sale price.

"That damned horse is no good, but if you want him, you can have him for $20," said the farmer.

"Twenty!" said Ken. "I'll give you $2,000!"

The farmer eyed Kling narrowly. "Say," he said suspiciously, "has that g.d. old haybag been giving you the baloney about winning the Kentucky Derby?"

A horse walked into a restaurant and ordered a steak. "How do you like your steak?" asked the waiter.

"I like it well done," replied the horse, "with crushed cherries on top. Then put some marinated tomatoes on it and drown it in celery tonic."

The waiter brought him the steak exactly as ordered. "Did you enjoy your dinner?" asked the waiter when he was finished.

"Very much," answered the horse.

"Good!" said the waiter, rubbing his hands.

"By the way," said the horse as he was leaving, "don't you think this is all very odd?"

"No," answered the waiter nonchalantly, "I like my steak the same way."

Allan Zee sent his homing pigeons out on a little errand. All of them came back at the expected time, except little Oscar. Everybody sat around the house and worried about the little pigeon. They waited all day, peered into the sky, and still no Oscar. When night came, rain began to fall, followed by thunder and lightning. Now they were really concerned.

In the midst of the storm they heard a tap on the window. "Open up, it's me, Oscar," yelled the lost pigeon. Little Oscar was drenched to the feathers. He really looked a mess.

"Where were you? We've been looking high and low for you, you bad bird," scolded Zee.

"Well," Oscar explained, "when I started back it was such a beautiful day I decided to walk."

Two horses were discussing a race in which they were both entered. "This is a very important race," said the dark horse. "One of us must win."

"You're not kidding," said the light horse. "First place in this race is worth quite a few bales of hay, and that ain't money!"

Patsy Flick likes to tell the story about the two little rabbits that were being chased down the road by two dogs. Suddenly one rabbit turned to the other and said: "What are we afraid of? Let's stop a minute and outnumber them!"

Charlie Zalenko bought a parrot and sent it home for his wife's birthday. The bird spoke seven languages and cost a thousand bucks. When he got in that evening he said to his wife, "Well, how did you like the bird I sent you?"

"Oh, fine," she answered, "I have it in the oven already."

When the husband came to, he said: "What! You have that bird in the oven! Why that bird could speak seven languages!"

"Then why didn't it say something?" asked the wife.

Bob Hope says that Bing Crosby got disgusted with his stable of losing horses. So he lined them up along the Santa Fe track and waited for the Super Chief. The train whizzed by at a hundred miles per hour. Whereupon Bing turned to the horses and said, "See what I mean?"

Leo Durocher was sitting on his bench worrying about his players who weren't hitting. A horse trotted up and addressed the famous manager of the Brooklyn Dodgers. "Why don't you use me on your team?" asked the horse. "I'm the answer to all your problems, I can hit and field better than anybody on your team."

"Go away," said the disgusted Lippy; "who ever heard of a horse playing baseball? I got enough troubles."

"What can you lose? Give me a chance. It can't be any worse than what you got now," pleaded the horse.

"Okay," said Leo, "go out in the field and I'll bat out a few balls to you. Let's see what happens, just for laughs."

The horse caught every ball that was hit in the field.

A line drive against the wall was a cinch for him: He reached one hoof into the air and pulled it down.

"Wonderful!" said Leo, waving him in. "How are you at bat?"

"Try me," said the horse.

Leo put his best pitcher in the box. Every ball thrown at the horse was hit over the fence.

"Great!" said Leo. "Tomorrow you join our team and go right in the line-up against the Giants."

The next day the horse was there bright and early. The first three Giants went down in quick order, thanks to the new outfielder. He caught every ball. When it came his turn at bat, the bases were loaded. The first ball pitched, the horse hit up against the wall. He stood at the plate watching the ball.

"Run!" yelled Durocher. "Don't stand there like a jerk. Run, you fool!"

"Are you kiddin'?" said the horse. "If I could run I'd be racing at Jamaica!"

"I'll buy that bird," said the man after listening to the canary sing an entire aria from *Carmen.* "How much do you want for it?"

"Three hundred dollars," said the proprietor, "but you must take this other bird too."

"All I want is this beautiful canary," said the customer. "I don't want that other beat-up bird. His nose is bashed in, his feathers are all torn, his ears are lopsided. I'll pay you the $300 just for the one."

"I'm sorry," said the proprietor; "you must take both."

"Why?" asked the man.

"This other one is the arranger."

❦

A man walked into a bird store looking for a canary that could sing. He was willing to pay any price for a bird with a lovely voice.

"I have just the bird for you," said the owner. "This one came in today and has the finest voice you ever heard."

The bird proceeded to sing six songs, each one more beautiful than the other.

"That bird has the most beautiful tone I ever heard," said the customer. "How much do you want for it?"

"Five hundred dollars," said the owner.

"Sold!"

But when the proprietor took the canary out of the cage, the man noticed that the bird limped. "Hey, wait a minute," said the man, "that bird has only one leg."

"What do you want," asked the proprietor, "a singer or a dancer?"

❦

Two little worms met in a cemetery. Said the male worm to the female worm, "Let's meet late tonight and make love in dead Ernest."

❦

Jackie Miles' favorite story is about the two brothers who went fishing in the same lake. They had the same boat, same equipment. One caught 150 fish and the other didn't even get a nibble.

"I've got all the fish because I've got all the personality," said the one with the fish, and he dragged his brother home.

The little guy couldn't sleep. He kept mumbling to himself, "Personality don't catch fish, it's luck. Fishes don't know from personality." He couldn't stand it, got up, snuck up to the middle of the lake, threw out his line, and waited. He sat there a minute, thirty minutes, an hour, a day, two days, three days, and still no fish. He got so disgusted, he broke his rod and threw it in the water. As he started to row back, a little fish stuck its head out of the water and said: "Pssst!"

"What the hell do you want now?" the guy shouted.

The little fish looked up soulfully and said, "Hey, where's your brother?"

Two cats were watching a tennis match. One turned to the other and said: "You know, my father is in that racket."

The little bird came back to its nest all beaten up. Its eyes were black, its feathers were torn, its little beak was broken—it was in a terrible mess.

"Oh my poor darling," wailed the mother bird, "what happened to you?"

"I was flying around having a wonderful time, mind-ing my own business," explained the little one, "when I noticed a group of people down below, so I swooped down to find out what was going on—and I got caught in a badminton game . . ."

Do all these stories sound strange and impossible to you? Well they shouldn't. After all, fish are smart—don't they travel in schools? How many times have you heard somebody say, "That guy has horse sense"?

Right now, in almost every night spot in the country, some wolf is talking to a girl and saying, "Come up and see my etchings."

CHAPTER THIRTEEN

They Hitch Their Braggin' to a Star

THE water was as cold as an empty night club. It wasn't June-in-January water, either. I clutched for the sides of the perambulating monster that had brought me to my roost in the middle of Biscayne Bay and silently consigned my personal press agent to a box seat in Hades.

"Is all this worth a credit line in the newspapers?" I asked myself, hoping a barracuda wouldn't catch sight of my knocking knees. "Brunn's Guide to the Tropics" warns that man-eating fish prefer man in motion.

My press agent, Leslie Simmonds, had called me that night saying frantically: "Joey, I've got the greatest publicity stunt in the world. The first amphibious jeep in this country will be in front of the Lord Tarleton Hotel at 7 P.M. sharp—newsreel men, photographers, newspapermen, columnists will be there to record the doings. I want you to be in on it," and he hung up.

When I got to the Lord Tarleton at the appointed hour, in my new white suit, they sat me in a huge aluminum bathtub on wheels. The seats were high up like the top deck of a Fifth Avenue bus. I felt like a freak, as hundreds of curious gaping spectators gathered around. The newsreel men were grinding away and before I

could say Toots Shor, we were hopping along Collins
Avenue. Before I could say Earl Wilson, I was in the
middle of Biscayne Bay, white suit and all, hanging on
to the side of the big bathtub. I didn't know till days
later what an amphibious jeep was. Anyway, it forgot to
"amphib," and I took a bath with my clothes on. For that
I pay a press agent!

Ever since the late Harry Reichenbach, a West Virginia farm boy, came to Broadway and boomeranged
ballyhoo into a newsmaking industry, press agents have
been trying to follow his pattern with stunts that often
leave their clients holding the bag.

Many of their schemes go "ashtray"; but more often
than not, they get their client's name in the paper, and
that's what they are paid to do. The Broadway "flaks" [1]

[1] *Flak.* A press agent.

are responsible for more success stories on the main stem than the Shuberts, Ziegfeld, and Horatio Alger. Sometimes it's not an easy job to make the public swallow a new star. In fact it's easier to make a fool out of some star than a star out of some fool.

There are no ethics in Broadway publicity with a Broadway praise agent; honesty is not the best policy. Many a truth is said in "guess." Some of their publicity stunts are as phony as a $35 bill.

"Man bites dog" used to be news. Now it's when a bull throws a press agent. For cash on the line he'll tell all he knows about you—for an extra few, he'll tell all he doesn't know about you. He's a blackmailer in reverse. He will *not* keep quiet for a price.

Most of them could organize their own orchestras—they're well able to play the lyre.

The daily paper is the press agent's Bible, and printer's ink is his life's blood. He worships at the shrine of the Broadway columnists. A line in a Broadway column is more important to him than a line from home.

Gags to him aren't a joking matter. He never laughs at jokes—he only writes them down. He only laughs at gags he can't use. Usually, when you're halfway through a joke he murmurs, "Yeah, I know that one."

The members of the "Froth" Estate go from club to club, getting exclusive items for the columns and looking for tips for City Editors on legitimate news stories, hoping to get a recipromention for their clients a few days later. They get more inside information than a doctor.

A press agent never enjoys reading a newspaper: he

skims it for credit lines. An average p.a. can scan a column
in three seconds flat. He can spot his client's name at
fifty paces.

They sound like a pretty ugly lot, don't they? Well,
they're not. Most of them are intelligent, hard-working
businessmen who came up the hard way. Some started
as office boys in metropolitan newspapers. Others, like
Ivan Black and Ed Weiner, went to college to study
journalism. Most of them found out soon enough about
the false lure of American journalism, of the long years
of low salaries, and of the constant struggle for promo-
tion, and having learned the ropes, naturally drifted into
press agentry.

To be a successful Broadway press agent you must
know a lot of celebrities, you must be the intimate of a
lot of big people, you must know the newspaper men,
editors, and columnists by their first names.

And you must have a sense of humor. At least, you
must develop in yourself each columnist's sense of humor
so that you can send him the type of gags he likes. You
must be correct about your news tips and you must be
a *three*-faced Janus—one face for your client, one for the
press, and one for your creditors.

A press agent is as important to a star as his material
and his wardrobe. Irving Caesar put it very well: "Now-
adays you don't build a better mousetrap—you get a better mouthpiece."

I've met almost all the Broadway flaks and find them
a wonderful lot. They are as important a part of
Broadway as its biggest stars, its famous columnists,

its fabulous characters, and its brightest lights.

The first advance man and press agent was John the Baptist. He was the advance agent for a star so great that His influence is still felt all over the world.

Unfortunately John the Baptist lost his head over a woman. The same is liable to happen to any number of Broadway press agents that I can mention.

The first press agent in America was P. T. Barnum. He started out thinking everybody is a sucker. Later he denied that he said, "There's a sucker born every minute and two to take him." Ed Sullivan said, "As smart a show-man as Barnum never could have belittled the public," and quoted Barnum as saying, "My success came from respecting the public's judgment, not sneering at it."

Most of the fabulous master press agents are dead but their stunts are used over and over again by the modern guys. Harry Reichenbach, Walter Kingsley, David Freedman, Ivy Lee, and Dexter Fellowes are some of the great who left a legacy to the Broadway press agents of this day. Charlie Washburn is the only one remaining from "the good old days."

When Harry Reichenbach was handling the picture, *Tarzan of the Apes*, he smuggled a tame lion in an old trunk into the Claridge Hotel. The bellboy who came up to Harry's room got so excited he called the police, the fire department, and the newspapers. When they went down to the desk to see who was registered in that room they found "T.R.Zan."

It broke in every newspaper in the country and made Harry $50,000 richer.

It's not so easy to pull any stunts like that these days. Editors are too "hep" to all the tricks. Anyway, Broadway press agents would rather get a mention in Winchell, Sullivan, Walker, Kilgallen, Wilson, and the rest, than a full spread in a paper or magazine. A Louis Sobol or Leonard Lyons story is more important for their clients than some cooked-up stunt.

Most press agents work hard getting exclusive items and gags for these syndicated columnists so that they can get "paid off" with their clients' names in the columns.

Walter Winchell likes to have Ed Weiner around with him. Ed is one of the better press agents and runs swell interference for the Star Spangled columnist. All-American tackle in 1928 for N.Y.U.'s championship football team, Weiner is a brilliant writer and can use his 230 lbs. to stop any would-be hecklers. He has always been known as "Horse" Weiner.

You can see Ed any morning until about 5 A.M. in Reuben's (one of his clients) looking for some hot items for Walter and the other columnists. Then he drops by at Hanson's for a last "look-see" before retiring.

The boys call Eddie a St. Bernard dog because of his size, but as Winchell said, "Once in a while a St. Bernard shows up with a keg of brandy and saves a life!" Eddie has saved the life of many an actor and night-club owner with a great publicity job. Ed is Winchell's white-haired boy, and vice-versa. Walter took the former football star with him to the San Francisco Conference. Of course, Ed worships Winchell.

Recently at the Cub Room, Winchell was sitting with

H. L. Mencken and George Jean Nathan. He left these celebrated gentlemen to join "Horse" at another table. "They used to be known as Mencken, Nathan, and God," said Winchell pointing to the table he just left, "but the combination is broken up now."

"Yes," said Eddie, "I see you left the table."

Joe Moore is Eddie's partner and one of the hardest workers on the street. He doesn't write at all but goes to every nook and corner of Broadway looking for items. He has a great sense of humor and a great nose for news. When he gives Ed Sullivan an item, Ed can use it and go to sleep without worrying whether it's correct.

Joe was Olympic Skating Champ of the 1924 Olympics and one of the great all-time skating stars. When Ed Sullivan was a sports writer on the *Graphic*, he used to follow the little champ around. Now Joe follows Eddie around. Joe is Eddie's "boy" and Joe thinks Eddie is the Number One man in the world.

Jack Tierman worked as a bus boy at the old French Casino until he decided it was easier to clean up jokes

A PRESS AGENT

A *press agent is a liar who makes under five thousand a year, eats (infrequently) in drug stores, sleeps in his underwear, has his office in a phone booth, doesn't go out with dames because dames eat*

A PUBLICIST

A *publicist is a press agent who makes over five thousand a year, eats, sleeps in his underwear, has his office in a phone booth, goes out with dames even though they eat*

and send them to columnists than to clean up dishes and send them to the kitchen.

Jack likes to make up fancy words in describing his clients. He was told that "abattoir" was a magnificent night club. The next morning he sent a release to the papers, "The La Martinique is the most beautiful 'abattoir' in the world." Dario, the owner, complimented him on the breaks in the paper until he found out, through a group of butchers who came down to inquire about prices, that "abattoir" is a public slaughtering house. La

Martinique almost turned into an abattoir when Dario got hold of Tierman that night.

Curly Harris, the publicist—any press agent that makes more than $5000 a year is a publicist or public relations man—is said by intimates to know two out of any group of five people seen in any major public place in New York. His appetite is getting as famous as he is. Earl Wilson says Curly eats meatballs the way other people eat cherries. His pal Bernie Kamber says he dines every night like a man who is going to the chair.

Two hoboes came in on a freight train in 1930. One became press agent for a Florida Hotel, and the other handled the publicity for George Price. Their own story is more interesting than any of the accounts they handled.

Carl Erbe went to Florida and Monte Proser stayed on Broadway. Their life reads like a Horatio Alger story. They really went "from rags to riches." They now own the two most famous night clubs in America. Carl owns the Zanzibar and Monte the Copacabana.

Spencer Hare, who looks like a rabbit with glasses, will plug anything from a dance hall to a broken umbrella. Spencer used to write gags for Jack Benny and Fred Allen. He now supplies gags for the Broadway columnists with credit lines for his clients.

Bunny, as his friends call him, is married about nine years now and has one child,—a daughter whom he named Hedda Hare. He admits he is not as prolific as his name.

In 1939 Bunny handled the publicity for the Fiesta Danceteria and conceived the idea of selecting a "Miss Cafeteria Society." He got several Broadway columnists and Café Society's Brenda Frazier to be the judges, and they picked a $15-a-week stenographer as "Miss Cafeteria Society of 1939."

It got a lot of publicity in the papers and made Spencer a pretty important guy around town, but the Fiesta Danceteria closed up soon after that and the little stenographer is still eating in cafeterias.

Irving Zussman, Gertrude Bayne, and George Evans all claim that they "made" Frank Sinatra. Zussman and Bayne handled the Riobamba when Frankie made his night-club debut there which started him on his rise to fame. They all did a great job on him, but the truth of the matter is that Sinatra was just a natural. Every once in a while a Rudy Vallee, a Rudolph Valentino, or a Frank Sinatra comes along that takes the country by storm. They are just "hot" copy and an easy job for a press agent.

Of course, all three can take a bow for "helping" to build Sinatra from $3000 a year in 1938 to a million or more these last few years.

George Evans has been handling Frankie Boy since January of 1943. He took the job for $60 a week, and started to go to work on the Voice. His build-up formula was old-fashioned. He started fan clubs all over the country and "sold" him to the bobby-soxers. And when those hysterical kids get behind you—that's all, brother! Now that the swooner is on top, Evans' job is to help Sinatra live down the bobby-sox sex-appeal angle. He wants the kids to stop screaming every time Sinatra sighs. He wants the grown-ups to like his man—and believe me, they do.

Dorothy Gulman is the glamor gal among the fifth estaters. She feels just as at home on the West Side as she does on the East Side. She is also as pretty on both sides and wears clothes as well as any of the stars she glamorizes.

Dorothy started her career in Chicago, where at twelve she was secretary of the Paul Ash fan club. She wrote poems about him and sent them to the Chicago papers to get them printed.

She discovered Dorothy Lamour, who had been Miss New Orleans of 1931. Gulman met the sarong girl when she was a Chicago elevator operator. She liked the New

Orleans beauty and they became pals, sharing the same apartment.

Gulman urged Lamour to get up and sing one celebrity night at the Morrison Hotel in Chicago. "Kate Smith, Dennis King, and so many others are here. Maybe one of them will like you," Gulman urged, "and then you're made."

Miss Lamour did get up and sang but no one listened. She came back to the table and wept. A few minutes later a man came over and introduced himself as Herbie Kaye, a band leader, and offered her a job as his vocalist. In the span of a few years Miss Lamour became his vocalist, his wife, and his ex-wife.

Dorothy Gulman handles Leon and Eddie's on the West Side and the Coq Rouge on the East Side and keeps both of them very happy. I'll never stop being grateful to her for getting my name in the papers when the only thing Adams meant to the columnists was a chewing gum, an express agency, a hat company, or the first man.

The press agents look up to two men in their profession as "tops." One is Irving Hoffman, who wields a lot of influence. If he says he'll make a star out of someone, the producer can go to sleep that night because the job is in the bag. Hoffman is a great caricaturist and now writes a permanent column for the *Hollywood Reporter*. Columnists and other newspapermen constantly call Irving for material and ideas. His offices and files are always available to all the press agents on the street.

Dick Maney is the other p.a. the fifth-estaters think is

tops. Maney specializes in the legitimate theatre, often handling six or seven shows at a time. He is very much in demand, and dictates his terms when he "accepts" an account. When he worked for Billy Rose he inserted a clause in his contract which said that he did not have to enter any of the Rose night clubs.

He raps any show he doesn't like, even if it's one he handles. If he doesn't like a star, Maney treats him with disdain, even if it's his own account. The editors are always anxious to get his stories because they know he can write, and write honestly.

Once, after Jed Harris had produced a string of Russian flops, Maney wrote to the *Herald Tribune,* "Mr. Harris has just combed the last Russian out of his curls."

Teddy Brooks only handles one account, Hal Winters, the young singing star. They room together and split the singer's salary. Teddy goes to other press agents for help for his star and refuses any other accounts.

Ivan Black, Curt Weinberg, Paul Coates, and Hy Gardner work with quiet dignity.

Ivan is the only Harvard graduate of the group. He found Zero Mostel and many other stars. He built Zero, Lena Horne, and Hazel Scott into national figures.

Paul is a sweet, unspoiled boy who will never get used to tough, hard Broadway. The newspaper people love him because he isn't high pressure and writes with a sincere, honest hand.

Hy is one of the best-liked men on Broadway. Of all the press agents, Hy is considered to have the greatest number of friends and the best sense of humor. His column, *Gardner's Newsreel,* is syndicated all over the country.

Joe Russel has been sitting around bus stations for years watching the young beauties stepping on New York soil for the first time, in the hope of finding another Dorothy Lamour or Betty Grable. So far, the best he's been able to do is find a lot of show girls and chorus girls for the Broadway clubs. Joe is considered by other press agents as the authority on night-club pulchritude.

Milton Rubin flopped as a song writer, but became very successful as a press agent. He made Father's Day a national thing and was largely responsible for the fame of Carol Bruce and Henny Youngman.

Harry Davies did such a great job publicizing Minsky's Burlesque Theatres that he got them closed down:

A New York newspaper ran a story one day, stating that foreign actresses were entering the United States in the guise of strip-tease artists. There was an investigation under way in Washington, directed by Congressman Dickstein. Harry sold Minsky the idea of rushing down to the Capitol. They arrived there at two o'clock in the morning, got the Congressman out of bed, and took his picture.

Business doubled at the Minsky Theatres, but then came an awful blow. License Commissioner Paul Moss suddenly ordered all burlesque theatres closed. And it was shortly after that the Commissioner stated, "If Davies hadn't publicized burlesque so much, we wouldn't have known it was around."

Steve Hannegan, former stunt man who reformed and

became a conservative public-relations counsel, is one
of the country's most successful press agents. His accounts have included Miami, Florida; Sun Valley, in
Idaho; and Henry Ford.

There was a time when Hannegan was handling the
Indianapolis speedway, where the annual 500-mile
classic takes place on May 30. It was one of Hannegan's
most successful undertakings, and when he was asked
to explain his good fortune in this enterprise, he replied,
"For five years it didn't rain on May 30. I'm a genius."

The "character" among the press agents is "The Little
Monster," Eddie Jaffe. He is scarcely five feet tall and
weighs no more than is legal. He would be an underdog
in a fist fight with a sparrow.

Eddie is the male Broadway Rose when it comes to
dressing. He seldom bothers to shave, and his hair looks
as if he combed it with an egg-beater. To him a comb is
a musical instrument.

He lives in a combination office-apartment-madhouse,
over Duffy's Tavern on 48th Street, in the apartment once
occupied by Walter Winchell. He organized "The National Order of Screwballs" to publicize Eddie Garr
but was unanimously elected president by all his pals.

The little fellow knows more about G-strings than Fritz
Kreisler, having specialized in publicity for most of the
famous strip-tease artists and snake charmers.

He called Margie Hart "The Poor Man's Garbo" and
won her national fame after Winchell used the phrase
in his column.

He brought Zorita, the snake charmer, to a psychiatrist

with the noteworthy information that she was in love with her snakes. "This girl is perfectly sane," the psychiatrist said; "but you, sir, are undoubtedly crazy."

Recently one of Jaffe's pals suggested to the editors of a picture magazine that they print a graphic story on Jaffe—"The Ugliest Man Who Publicizes the Most Beautiful Women." The editors chorused a most enthusiastic "Yes," urging Jaffe to send them pictures for the layout.

The little monster forwarded the pictures to the magazine editor. Next day his pal beheld Eddie wearing a downcast aspect. "What's the matter, didn't the editors like the picture story?" he asked Eddie.

"No," Jaffe replied. "They said I was ugly enough, but the girls I publicize weren't the prettiest in the world."

The press agents have pulled some "pips" in their time. Dave Green made Edgar Bergen draw up a will, leaving everything he had to the Actors' Fund, with a proviso that the interest would be used to take care of his dummy, Charlie McCarthy. Dave got the will printed in the *Law Journal,* then tipped a reporter to watch for the big story. It broke all over the country.

Remember the Anna Held milk baths? The famous funeral of Rudolph Valentino, when hundreds of thousands of people lined outside Campbell's Funeral Parlor, wailing their grief for their idol? The word Campbell became a household synonym for "mortuary." Remember the time New York was plastered with signs announcing the American debut of Madame Yifnuff, the great European violinist? Madame Yifnuff turned out to be one

of the losers on the Saturday night "Truth and Consequences" show.

Each of these was "cooked up" by a hard-working press
agent. So when you see some smart quip credited in one
of the Broadway columns to some bandleader who can't
even read music, you know it was the brainchild of one
of the drum beaters.

You can't tell a tooth by its porcelain jacket. That's
why press agents like Wolfe Kaufman, Chic Farmer,
Frank Law, Dorothy Ross, Jay Faggen, and S. Jay Kaufman make fabulous salaries. They cover up a multitude
of sins with good publicity.

Earl Wilson discovered one Broadway press agent who
had been reading the news flashes on the *New York
Times* electric news bulletin and then sent them out
as "exclusives" to a certain columnist.

The puff boys are the last ones to realize they are
more colorful than any of the clients they represent.
They're really backward—in an aggressive sort of a way.

The next time you see a girl nominated "Miss Droopy-
Drawers of 1953," or an actor given the honorary degree
of Squeedunk University, or some acrobat jumping from
the top of the Empire State Building into a damp rag, you
know it was thought up by some drum beater at so much
per beat.

As far as I'm concerned, they can have all their stunts.
I don't like to go swimming in Biscayne Bay with my
clothes on at eight o'clock at night. I'll be satisfied if my
press agent gets me five or six mentions a week in each
of the syndicated Broadway columns . . .

CHAPTER FOURTEEN

Dumb Belles and Beautifools

"Ya buncha creeps," shouted Toots Shor to a group of us sitting at the round table, "why dontcha have some dames at da table? You crum-bums need somethin' to dress up da joint."

"I can't stand dumb women," answered Bert Lahr.

"Aha!" said Flippen, "a woman hater."

"Yeah," added Jerry Lester, "those Broadway dolls can't add but they certainly can distract."

"I gave some of those girls the best tears of my life," said Bert Wheeler. "Women are as transparent as cellophane and as hard to remove once you get wrapped up in them."

"My girl friend gave me the sack," Jackie Gleason brooded, "but she kept the presents in it. She has a clear conscience, only because she has a poor memory. You can tell her past by her presents."

"I never fool with girls," cautioned Earl Wilson. "If I did, everybody would talk, especially my wife."

"A pretty girl is like a malady," Jack Eigen suggested. "My babe threatened to go back to her mother, so I threatened to go back to my wife."

"Women taint what they used to be," said George Clarke. "I've been watching those gals on Broadway for years; you youngsters can take some advice from me. Never go back on your word with women—without consulting your lawyer. Women are the weeper sex, and they know how to turn it on at the right time."

"What do you expect?" lectured Leo Durocher, the popular manager of the Brooklyn Dodgers. "You guys don't know how to treat dames. You cater to them too much. They get dizzy from falling off so many pedestals. Don't expect them to be smart. A girl's I.Q. is what a man should look for after he's looked at everything else."

"Mosta those dames," shouted Toots, "have more brains in their little fingers than they have in their whole head. Soma dem are such tramps, their shows should be reviewed in *The Hobo News*. Ya gotta know how to treat Broadway dames. Give a girl an inch," Shor ribbed, "and she'll buy a girdle."

"What burns me up," snarled Paul Douglas: "some of those females are ugly, besides being so dumb, and they're so independent. They can't act and they haven't a brain in their head. They stink but they're always working."

Jane Dulo, who had been sitting at the next table, got up.

"Leaving?" asked Toots.

"I sure am," said Jane. "I can't stand all those *innuendoes*."

"Are ya through, fellas?" Chuck Hamilton cut in. "Broadway women are the smartest in the world. You're talking to the kid who knows. Did you ever hear of a gal called Gypsy Rose Lee who ran a hot G-string into a cool million?"

A girl who spends any time on the Great White Way becomes sharp as a tack. She may not be well read, but give her half a chance and she'll put you in the red. She

is well reared and looks good in the front, too. Her attitude is to keep the boys guessing; she finds she is more popular when she keeps them in the dark.

Personally, I like the southern gals with their slow southern drawl. Whenever you ask them for something —before they can say no, it's done. I like bathing beauties, too, although I've never bathed any. So how come I go home every night with the morning papers under my arm?

Don't get me wrong; some of them are very dumb, but most of them are dumb like foxes. It's not an easy racket for girls on Mazda Lane.

A gal who makes good on Broadway, finds the cads stacked against her. They have the married wolves to contend with, the husband with a hobby, and the agent who wants to sign them on the dotted couch. They have to watch out for the producer who promises to star them in a show and the third assistant director from Hollywood who can "put you in pictures IF . . ." They have to be annoyed about the Latin lover with the Roman hands . . .

"She doesn't have to worry about getting ahead, she's doing very well without one," you hear some characters say. Don't believe it! Show gals are smarter and keener than most "civilians." [1]

Girls in show business are more intelligent, more honorable, and have better morals than any secretary or factory worker.

---

[1] *Civilian.* Show-business vernacular for anybody outside of the entertainment world.

From Gags to Riches

Every now and then she knocks the halo down **over** your eyes and it hurts your ears, but that can happen **in** any business.

She likes her men male and hearty. She's a lush **chick** who wants her men tall, dark, and handcuffed.

Some of the dumb stories you hear about **Broadway** gals might be interesting to record. I only mention **them** here because they are true . . .

About a decade ago, Vera Milton won fame and fortune as the "dumbest" chorus girl. Mickey Alpert **once** used a cane on her *derrière*. It irritated her enough to squeal, "Why make me the recipient of the geese?"

Mark Plant received a wire from her in Atlantic City: "Just missed the 7 P.M. train, I'll have to stay over in New York and take the train in the morning." Which was okay, except that Mark received the wire at 5 P.M. that same day, two hours before the train left.

Vera once told some friends she was in a show called *Intermission*. She bragged that she went out with a "malted millionaire."

"Silly boy," she said to one suitor, "I'm not going with you because your uncle left you a million dollars. I'd go with you no matter *who* left it to you!"

N.T.G. nicknamed Helen Gray "Caviar" after she innocently asked one night, "What kind of a drink is caviar?"

"Stuttering Sam" Dowell, the lovely showgirl, came into her dressing room at the Diamond Horseshoe with a beautiful mink coat. "Where did you get it?" the gals inquired. "I f-f-found it in the subway," she Frisco'd.[1]

Two chorus girls were great pals, although one was a live wire, the other quiet and reserved. One day Lynn, the vivacious one said, "Look, Kitty, how do you ever expect to find a feller? Every time I make a date for you, you just sit around and mope. Boys like intelligent girls. Why don't you read some books and things and get something to talk about?"

Kitty promised to try. Next city they played, Lynn arranged an appointment with two local Lotharios. As

[1] *Frisco*, or *pull a Frisco*. To stutter—after Joe Frisco (see Chapter 16).

they sat in the restaurant after the show, one of those painful silences enveloped the party. Kitty fidgeted, gulped once or twice, and then let them have it.

"Isn't it too bad," she inquired, "what happened to Marie Antoinette?"

Earl Wilson says, "The modern showgirls are the shy, home-girl type who love their mothers and can't stay out later than 6 A.M." They often play dumb, just as Marie Wilson does on the screen, but are really just as intelligent as the brilliant Wilson girl.

Louis Sobol quipped that they wrote a song about the modern showgirl: "Oh, What a Beautiful Moron!" Still, don't sell them short. Many a girl today is getting a man's salary . . . but then I guess they always have, one way or another.

Lee Mortimer calls Joan Manners, the gorgeous hunk of woman at the Copacabana, the modern "Dumb Belle." Joan has pulled some lines that are history. "Do you smoke or drink?" I asked her one day at Toots Shor's. "No," she replied, "but I eat."

She once called me at Leon and Eddie's and yelled excitedly, "It took me twenty minutes to find Leon and Eddie's number in the phone book—where are you?"

We were sitting at the round table when Joan joined us one stormy night. "I hear it's raining pretty hard," one of us said. "Yes," said the modern Vera Milton, "but you should see how hard it's raining on Fifty-seventh Street!"

We got around to discussing her career and she admitted she was only eighteen years old. "What would you like to be?" Bert Wheeler questioned her. "Nineteen" was her not-so-dumb answer.

Jackie Gleason and I were sitting in his room at the Astor Hotel, one two-o'clock-in-the-morning. "How about asking a couple of dames to join us?" suggested the rotund comic. "Okay by me," I agreed. Jackie called one of his old flames at the Copa and asked her to bring a friend. Twenty minutes later she was at the door with Rags Ragland. "I was with my friend, Rags," she announced, "so I brought him along. Okay?"

Joan Shea, the lovely La Martinique doll, has dozens of boy friends but dresses in very simple clothes. She always wears a cloth coat. "How come you haven't a fur coat, with all your stage-door Johnnies?" quizzed Ozzie Nelson one night. "Oh," she explained, "those Broadway characters—they always want to pull some Minsky business."

Chorus girls, believe it or not, discuss politics. At Nicky Blair's Carnival one asked, "Why are there two political parties? Is it that there are two sides to a question?"

"No," observed Jayne Westbrook. "It's because there are two sides to every political office—outside and inside."

Shirley Stevenson, the Latin Quarter beauty and one of the loveliest dolls ever to come out of Pittsburgh or anywhere else, knows all the answers but acts as if she didn't. One wise guy phoned her at the hotel and invited her in. "I'm always here and my door is never locked," he said. When she didn't visit him he repeated

to her, "My door is never locked." "Never?" she said.
"Never," he replied. "How dull!" said Shirley.

Billy Silleg was one of the most talented ladies on
Broadway. She married the clever comic Lou Saxon and
quit the business to have babies. When she returned
from her honeymoon I asked her how everything went.
"I never knew," she gushed, "you could have so much
fun without laughing."

One playboy spent so much on his girl in two years,
he finally married her for his money.

The gang was trying to talk beautiful Choo Choo
Johnson into going out with a certain man-about-town.
"He's one in a million, all right," said the luscious Choo
Choo, "but I'd like him better if he had a million."

"I let him kiss me once," grumbled Billy Bernice, the
charming Latin Quarter eyeful, "and he's been trying to
scrape up an acquaintance with me ever since."

Margie Little is one of the best-dressed girls on the
main stem, and her main stems are really something.
Her dresses are cut so low you have to look under the
table to see what she's wearing. Jimmy Durante is her
favorite fellow. Margie loves to talk to Schnozzola about
world events. "I'm much too worried about my own
country," she lectured to Umbriago one night, "to worry
about domestic affairs."

Joe E. Lewis told us he had a wonderful time teaching
one of the Copa girls how to swim: "I was doing fine,
too, until a life-guard came along and made us go into
the water."

Elisa Norton, the sweet young thing in Jeanette

Hackett's talented line, was late for rehearsal one evening. "Where were you?" the lovely Hackett scolded. "I'm so tired," Elisa complained. "I've been breathing all day."

Rowena Chapel and Kitty Kelly went to see *Oklahoma* one matinee. The box-office man was insistent that he had no seats left. "However," he said, "I can give you two for standing room." "Are they together?" asked Rowena.

Martha Cooper, the lovely model, wears the oddest hats in America. When she married the conservative Jerry Cooper, all his friends started to call her "The Hat." Martha met a Hollywood friend who didn't know Jerry. "Is your husband a loud dresser?" asked the pal. "Is he!" she answered. "You should hear him when he loses a collar button!"

"Junior" Standish refused to hang mistletoe at Christmas. With a twinkle in her baby blues she cooed, "No, sir! I've got too much pride to advertise for the ordinary courtesies a lady has a perfect right to expect!"

According to chorus girls' Equity, the average span of life for a chorus girl on Broadway is three years. Statistics prove that there are 3500 chorus girls who pay dues and thousands more who don't, and there are only about 500 jobs in New York. For every Joan Crawford that comes out of a chorus, thousands go back home with broken hearts and shattered dreams.

Naturally, they try to make the grade in a hurry; their beauty and youth can't wait. Some work towards a MRS. degree, others hold out for Hollywood.

In 1938 George Clarke, Morty Nathanson, and Monte Proser ran a benefit at Manhattan Center to raise money to send chorus girls home for Christmas. Each girl was given a sealed envelope with a ticket to her home town and told not to open it until they were on their way home. What they didn't know, until they opened the letter, was that it was a one-way ticket . . .

It's a tough struggle for any gal on Broadway. They

must be sharper and keener than girls in any other business. Above all, they must have a sense of humor. Contrary to all belief, their morals and honor are, for the most part, above reproach. Sure, they are more affectionate and more outspoken, but don't try to put anything over on them!

They can never resist a laugh.

Dale Belmont, the girl with the blue velvet voice, has a figure that winks at you. She became famous by wearing a sweater at all times, even to bed. Earl Wilson said about her appearance at the Belmont Plaza, "Dale Belmont is BUSTing all records."

When Dale wears a sweater once, it looks as if she'd hung it up twice. Morey Amsterdam wanted a costume for a masquerade party, so he borrowed her sweater, put it on backwards, and went as a camel. Morey claims he won first prize. Dale's picture appears on the cover of a song titled, *Oh, My Aching Back*.

Sally Rand, the famous bubble and fan dancer who recently opened her own bistro in Hollywood, often visits other clubs to attract business to her saloon. Whenever she is called upon to make a speech she says, "Come to my club and see more of me."

One of my favorite persons is Lois Andrews. Her dancing eyes and her wonderful charm and sense of humor have brought her suitors from all over the world. I was admiring her collection of furs one day. "Twenty fur coats, that's quite a collection," I remarked. "You certainly don't get them overnight." "That's exactly how you do get them!" she quipped.

Lois was sitting around Toots' with the Smithfield Ham heiress, Barbara Bannister, Melody Thompson, the beauty, and Gertrude Niesen, the star. They were discussing a woman's greatest attributes.

"I think a girl's hair is her greatest attraction," said Barbara.

"As far as I'm concerned," Gertrude commented, "a girl's eyes are most important."

Melody Thompson was definite: "It's a girl's smile— that's her greatest attraction."

"Why do you girls sit around and lie to each other?" topped the beautiful Miss Andrews.

A former Hollywood actress was suddenly taken drunk. She was complaining to Arthur Blake, the mimic, that she couldn't get any more film roles. "Oh, well," Arthur sympathized, "you can always run for Senate." The actress giggled. "I did once," she said. "The United

States Senate?" asked Blake. "No," the woman hic-coughed, "Mack Sennett."

Collette Lyons has starred in very many shows, but her friends love her off-stage even more, because she is always herself. She was a little high one night at the Havana-Madrid, celebrating her triumph in *Show Boat*. "Everybody is so blind," she stammered, "I can hardly see them."

Walter Winchell tells about the Park Avenue lady who was amazed at the extreme youth of a coat-room gal in a swank East Side club. "I can't believe you're the mother of a two-year-old child," the swankster purred, "you look so young to have a child! Are you very, very sure you're really, really married?"

"Yes, ma'am," said the girl, "I'm not one of the customers here!"

Lili St. Cyr has the wolves woofing to themselves be-cause of her lovely construction, screwball personality, and oomphy dancing. She wears green wigs on dinner dates and changes her name with the season. Her real moniker is Marie Van Schaak, but she's known as Lili Finova in San Francisco, Lili La Seur in San Diego, and Lili La Bang in Las Vegas. Her costumes are perfectly designed . . . you see her only in the best places.

The wit of the gals on Broadway is as impressive as a right-hand punch thrown by Joe Louis . . .

Margalo Gilmore was seated at a comfortably crowded dinner table next to Gregory Ratoff. "Either stop talking about your wife, Greg," chided the charming Margalo, "or take your hands off my knee."

Gertrude Lawrence was speaking at a dinner. After a long talk she said, "Pardon my long preamble. It's like a chorus girl's tights—it touches everything and covers nothing."

Maggi McNellis, the WEAF-NBC commentator (column Miss of the air), tapers up just about perfect. What's more, she has brains and intelligence to match her beauty. A gal singer was complaining to the brainy Maggi about her cold: "Everything centers in my throat because I use it so much." "You poor dear," Mag heckled, "when I have a cold, everything centers in my head."

She once remarked about a gal friend, "She doesn't select her husband's clothes, but she picks his pockets."

Chile Williams has become wealthy wearing polka dots wherever she goes, to advertise the Polka Dot King, Bill Schiller. With the money she earns she studies voice, drama, and dancing.

The lovely Billy Boze was grumbling in her dressing room. "You should be very happy," said one of the other girls; "this is your birthday." "I'm so mad I could kick myself," Billy answered. "See those flowers on my table? I met a character called Tommy Manville last night and he asked me how old I was. I told him I was eighteen years old, so tonight he sends me eighteen roses with a thousand-dollar bill wrapped around each flower. It makes me so mad—I should have told him I was 25."

Marie McDonald won fame and fortune as "The Body." She claims that in Hollywood a girl gets nowhere if she's known as "The Brain."

She made up her mind to make six million dollars and "not marry it, make it myself." She turned down bit parts because she didn't want to play straight girl to a sarong.

June Havoc and Gypsy Rose Lee are sisters. As kids they did a "sister act." Gypsy became famous as a strip dancer and later as an authoress, and June went from dancing in marathons to musical comedy and finally the Theatre Guild. Both girls have a sense of humor that is priceless. June kids her big sister: "As she shows, so shall you peep." "When I get up in the morning," says Gypsy, "it feels like the dawn of a nude day."

So you still think the Broadway gals are dumb? The total wealth of Joan Crawford, Barbara Stanwyck, Alice Faye, Betty Grable, Gypsy Rose Lee, Paulette Goddard, Gladys Glad, and Marion Davies is about thirty million dollars. All of them were chorus or show girls on the main stem. I could mention thousands of success stories that started in a chorus in a New York club.

The trouble is, the young girls today marry older men. Gloria Vanderbilt, the eighteen-year-old heiress, married the aging Leopold Stokowski. When Lois Andrews, as a child of seventeen, married the elderly toastmaster and producer, George Jessel, every paper carried the story. Tommy Manville never marries a girl past twenty; he claims any girl past nineteen is middle-aged. Charles Chaplin married the youthful Oona O'Neill. Of course, Errol Flynn is always in the market for a young doll.

Gee, I can't wait till I get old . . .

CHAPTER FIFTEEN

14-Karacters

"T ELL the boys I won't be in tonight," I told Toots Shor. "I have an appointment with a lovely debutante from Boston."

"Nobody'll miss ya, ya creepy actor," Toots answered lovingly. "It's about time ya went out wid a dame. People are beginnin' to talk."

"This girl is beautiful, Toots," I explained. "I met her while I was working at the R.K.O. Boston. She's the epitome of class, her family goes away back, a real debutante."

"Well don't bring her in here," roared Shor; "we don't want no debutramps in Toots Shor's!"

As I sat in the taxi on my way to the Grand Central Station, where I was to meet the Boston Belle, I kept trying to figure out where I would take her. I knew we couldn't go to Toots'. The gang was sure to louse me up, just for laughs, and I did want to make an impression on the society girl.

I wore my favorite blue suit and a dignified tie. My shoes were shined so well they looked like mirrors. This was one time I wanted to make good.

"Hell-o Jozif dahling," greeted my date as she stepped

off the train. "It's so good to see you agayne."

"Greetings, Barbara!" I returned. "Welcome to New York. Let's make the rounds and have some laughs."

"That sounds chahming," agreed my new gal. "I'd like to go to that girl's place everybody talks about—Toots Shor is it?"

"Toots is not a girl," I answered. "Secondly," I lied, "I don't think they're open tonight. Let's take a walk on Broadway. You've never seen our main stem and I'd like to show it to you."

"How quaint!" agreed the deb. "That sounds like fun." We hadn't walked two blocks on the Great White Way when I got a bang on the back that almost sent me sprawling in the gutter. I turned around to see a six-foot-four giant wearing a ten gallon hat, a gaudy silk handkerchief, a crimson shirt, a loud checked suit, a carnation in his lapel, and smoking a big fat cigar.

"Broadway Sam," I gulped, "I'd like you to meet—."

"Where'd ya get da babe?" guffawed the fabulous character, as he blew a mouthful of stale smoke in her face. "Ya little *momser*,[1] holding out on Broadway Sam, eh?" Sam always refers to himself as if he were someone else.

"This is our first date," I said with pleading eyes. "I'd like you to meet Miss Barbara Bassard. Barbara, this is Mr. Sam Roth. Babs is a Boston debutante and this is her first visit to New York. She can trace her ancestors away back," I said, trying to impress him. "She is a de-

[1] *Momser*. Literally, in Jewish, a bastard, but in actual use a harmless and affectionate equivalent of "little devil."

scendant of a descendant of a descendant of—oh, all the way back to the *Mayflower*."

"It just goes to show you how far she has descended," said Sam, breaking himself up. "A debutante, eh? What are ya doin' with this pluribal character? You should be wit' me. I'm a man wit' no imbitions."

"I don't think that's very clevah," answered Babs. "In fact, I think you are very uncouth."

"Broadway Sam is never discouth," said the big guy. "Don't be so exotic."

"Well!" said Babs. "Does your wife let you walk around in such bizarre clothes, blowing smoke in people's faces and acting like a prehistoric creatchah?"

"My wife?" screamed Sam. "Broadway Sam is married to his public. The constitution of marriage is for *paskudnyaks*[1] dat can't get dames. I give dem all a break. Besides, Broadway don't buy his clothes in a bazaar. All his clothes are order-made by his private tailor who never makes da pants too long for Sam. I wear a carnation a day to keep oblivion away. I'm da best-dressed character from the Catskill Mountains to Broadway and dat goes for Boston, too."

"We've got to go now," I interrupted, trying to break it up.

"No hard feelings," said Sam as he planted a kiss on my date's cheek. "I never hold no grudges. A devoured scientist friend o' mine told me to always be unanimous about t'ings like dis. Shake, sister, I'll see ya around sometime."

[1] *Paskudnyak.* Jewish word for a louse or a punk.

"Good night, Sam," I said quietly.

"So long, character," said the character.

"You certainly have some nice friends," said Babs when we had left Sam a block behind.

"He's a swell guy," I apologized. "He's a bit eccentric in his dress and manner, but he has a heart of gold. He does more charitable work than anybody on the Street. Sam is one of the most prosperous and best-liked ticket brokers in the business. He fancies himself a celebrity and very often chases a fan for blocks to give him his autograph. He loves publicity and has his entire suite at the St. Moritz covered with blowups of columns written about him by Dan Parker and others. He's a character, but a wonderful one. A genuine 14-karacter."

"When do I meet the Mayah and Alfred Vanderbilt?" she asked. "You promised to introduce me to your elite friends."

"Oh, we'll get around to the—." The words choked in my throat. As we turned the corner of Fifty-first Street and Broadway we heard a screech, "Joey, darling!" and before I could do anything about it, Broadway Rose had her arms around me in a stranglehold and was showering me with kisses. She looked like Miss Subways—during the rush hour. Her straggly hair was all over her face and her thick glasses looked like the bottoms of milk bottles. The rags on her back were from a torn page of *Vogue* of 1902.

Here I was at the corner of Fifty-first Street and Broadway, walking with my little debutante, in the arms of this character. I was the object of her afflictions. She

stood there screaming my name, yelling endearing words
and laughing hysterically. She looked like laughing gas
with legs.

"When did you get out of jail?" I asked her quietly.

"Those son-of-a—," she started.

"Please," I interrupted, "I'm with my girl. Please,
Rose, she's a lady."

"Whatta hell'a ya think I am?" she shouted. "Dem

punks can't put me in the can again. I got my rights.
Sweetheart, darling, got a few dollars for your doll?"

"Not now, Rose," I whispered. "I'm with my girl
and—."

"Why ya cheap, phony bastard!" she screamed.

I took my girl's hand and we ran, with Rose's insults
following us.

When we were out of hearing distance of "Gravel
Gertie," I tried to laugh it off. "She's the society editor
of *The Hobo News*," I laughed. "She makes the only

spit balls approved by *Good Housekeeping*." By this time Babs was walking with her nose so high in the air, if a rain came it would drown her. "She's so homely," I said, trying to get a smile from my little deb, "she sleeps with her face in the pillow to be kind to burglars."

My alleged comedy was making no impression on her. "She's been around Broadway for years," I said seriously. "She loves Abe Lyman, Ted Eddy, and Bob Hope. She waits for hours in the rain, outside of Lindy's, just to put her arms around them. All the guys are very nice to her. She's really harmless."

"When do we start to meet your *human* friends?" she inquired sardonically. "Don't you know anybody but characters? You told me you know the best people in New Yaark."

"Well, doll," I said blandly, "I do, but it seems we are meeting all the—." I stopped short. Coming towards us were two of the most sensational characters of all, B. S. Pully and H. S. Gump. They were trotting along Seventh Avenue at a leisurely pace. Gump was in his underwear and wore a number on his chest. The little dwarf-like chap looked so funny in his striped shorts, I started to howl, forgetting for a moment the little deb on my arm. The six-foot Pully was alongside of him, yelling at passers-by to get out of the way. They ran square into us.

"Hiya, comic?" greeted Pully. "Watcha know, Joe?" saluted Gump. "Who's da tomata?"

"Darling," I said to Babs, "I'd like you to meet B. S. Pully and H. S. Gump."

"How do you do?" she said icily.

"How do you do?" answered Gump haughtily, mimicking my Boston deb.

"Why the underwear—is it the new style?" I asked the boys.

"I had a hot tip on a horse," explained Pully. "I was broke, so I took Gump into the men's room in the subway, took off his clothes, and hocked them. I was sure the nag would win. Then I could get his clothes out of hock, bring them back to him, and we would have a bundle of cabbage besides. They're still looking for the horse and we're still broke. I had to get the little character out of the men's room and get him home somehow —he's been in there for six hours—so I put a number on his chest and he's making like he's a long-distance runner."

"Hey, it's cold," yelled the little fellow. "Let's go."

"Be careful how you talk to your master," answered Pully as he gave him a slap across the face, followed by a bang on the head. "I'm going to Hollywood to make another picture for Zanuck," he said to me as they started to leave. "Write to me."

"Where will you be? What's your address?" I asked.

"Just address it: B. S. Pully, c/o 1940 Convertible Buick, Hollywood, California."

"What's the B.S. stand for?" I shot after him.

"It's not Bernard Shaw," he yelled.

As Babs and I walked along in silence, I was beginning to realize how funny this all was. I giggled to myself as I recalled some of the things B. S. Pully has done in the past.

When the character went out to Hollywood to make his first picture for 20th Century Fox, he was introduced to the great Darryl Zanuck for the first time. "You're a smart man," B.S. complimented, "bringing me on your lot. You and me will make a lot of money together."

Zanuck took to him and kept him around for laughs. He is the favorite of Fanny Brice, Abbott and Costello, Don Ameche, George Raft, Phil Silvers, Bob Hope, and many others. He is liable to do anything at a party. He tells the dirtiest stories and even is known to whistle dirty songs. The Broadway and Hollywood mob take it from him. They say, on him it's becoming.

He once called Zanuck on the phone and yelled, "I'm sorry I can't be at the conference today, I'm in bed with a dame."

"We have no conference today," answered the startled executive.

"Well," said Pully as he hung up, "I just want you to know that if you had a conference, I wouldn't be there."

When he worked at La Martinique recently, Dario stood at the light switch and Jimmy Vernon at the microphone switch ready to pull them if he said anything dirty. "It's a new Pully that's working tonight," said B.S.; "no more dirt." He hadn't finished his sentence when a heckler started on him. "How dya like that crummy bastard?" answered the clean Pully, as the lights went out and the microphone went dead.

Pully was worried about a part he had in the picture, *Eve of St. Mark*. He went to his friend Phil Silvers for advice. "Go to the director, John Stahl," Phil suggested, "and ask him what your attitude should be." He came back to Phil the next day. "Did you see Stahl?" asked the former burlesque comedian.

"Yeah, he said my attitude should be one of chagrin," answered B. S.

"Do you know what chagrin means?" queried Silvers.

"I don't even know what attitude means," answered Pully.

He consistently refused to play the part of a stool pigeon in *Within These Walls* because he was afraid his racket friends wouldn't like it.

He has been dispossessed from dozens of buildings. He brags about the fact that tenants have signed petitions to make him move. "All I do is bang Gump's head against the wall, throw a few pieces of furniture out of the window, and run a party every night until five in the morning," he explains. "Is that any reason for people to sign a petition?"

A real estate agent in Hollywood took Pully out for lunch every day for three weeks, because he thought the character wanted to buy a home. B.S. was having a free lunch every day and riding around in a beautiful car, looking at lovely homes. He finally decided on a gorgeous $85,000 house.

"Here's a $16 deposit on it," offered Pully. "I'll move in tomorrow."

"Sixteen-dollar deposit on an $85,000 home?" screamed the agent. "You must be joking!"

"Joking, hell! That's all I got," answered the wacky one. "Take it before I change my mind. I'll give you $10 a week. At least you'll know where I live, and you won't have to look for me to collect your money."

His best pals are the biggest racket guys in the country. He would rather be a member of the "mob" than the biggest star in Hollywood. Every night before he goes to bed, his last prayers are, "Please, God, make me a tough guy."

Babs and I had walked ten blocks and she was still as silent as a henpecked husband who came home late for dinner. I could feel what she was thinking. She was out with the wrong guy. She walked with an air of superficial refinement, annoyed with it all. She had the ability to yawn without opening her mouth.

Now I didn't care what she thought about me. I was going to have some fun. These characters are as important a part of Broadway as any of its brightest stars. I love every one of them, and I wouldn't exchange a little finger on any of them for all the blue-bloods in Boston.

I set out to look for the rest of the fabulous characters on Broadway. "Let's go to Lindy's," I suggested.

"Veddy well," she said frigidly.

"Who is that distinguished-looking grey-haired gentleman with the white tie and blue shirt?" asked Babs when we were seated in Leo Lindy's "store."

"That distinguished-looking gentleman," I answered, "is the wholesale husband, Tommy Manville. He's the biggest character of them all. That's B.S. Pully with money."

"I've read about him in the newspapers at home, and

I've seen his pictures in magazines," said the deb, "but I didn't recognize him."

"Yes, it's hard to recognize him standing up," I said. "He looks more natural horizontal."

"Why does he marry so often?" she asked.

"Oh," I oh'd, "I think he's queer for rice. He has a one-track mind from walking down the middle aisle so often."

"Is he wealthy?" she quizzed.

"Wealthy?" I yelled. "He's so rich he has mink ulcers."

"Well, anyhow," she said, "he must be a romantic figure to marry so many girls. He certainly must be an authority on women."

"He's as romantic as an appendectomy," I answered. "All he knows about women is what he reads in his check book. He just marries in haste and repeats at leisure. He believes in cafeteria marriages: get what you want and pay for it later."

"It all sounds so revolting," said the young snob.

"Would you like to meet the distinguished grey-haired gentleman?" I ribbed. "He's probably looking for another wife. He goes for blondes; I'm sure he'll like your type."

"No, thank you," she said haughtily. "Don't be jocular. I don't appreciate your levity."

"It's too late now, doll," I said; "he spied us. Here he comes now."

"Hello, Joey," greeted the asbestos heir. "I'd like to meet the beautiful blonde doll."

"At your age, are you still looking for girls?" I kidded.

"A man never gets so old that he isn't in there pinching," he laughed.

"What happened to your last wife, Georgina Campbell, the *Hobo News* reporter?" I asked. "You only got married the other week. How many does that make?"

"I'm now behind my eighth ball and chain," gagged Tommy. "Furthermore, she is too old for me. She's a middle-aged girl of twenty-seven."

"How long were you married?" I asked.

"This time or altogether?" he giggled.

"I mean this last one," I said.

"Oh, Georgina? She was very nice. I liked her so much, I held her over for another week."

"Isn't it true," I asked the playboy, "that they are changing the wedding ceremony line from 'until death do us part' to 'until trains do depart—for Reno'?"

"Aren't you going to introduce me to the lady?" asked Tommy.

"Barbara," I hesitated, "I'd like you to meet Tommy Manville. Tommy, this is Barbara Bassard."

"Would you like to be the ninth Mrs. Manville?" he threw at Babs as he kissed her hand, totally ignoring me.

"No, thank you," she said acidly, "and please go."

"Let's go through that old ritual, doll," insisted the aging lover boy. "I haven't had my name in the papers for eighteen hours."

"Can't you get rid of this horrible creatchah?" asked Babs in her most contemptuous manner.

"The easiest way to get rid of me," laughed Tommy,

"is to marry me. If you change your mind, let me know. So long, beautiful."

"All these crude people," she said with pique. "Don't you know any normal persons?"

"Yes, doll," I kidded, "I know you."

"You certainly are disappointing," she said acidly. "I thought you told me you know the nicest people."

"Well," I answered, laughing to myself, "these are the nicest people. See that fine-looking man sitting over there? That's a pal of mine, his name is Nick the Greek. He's the most fabulous gambler in the world. He'll bet you $100,000 on the flip of a coin."

"Well I don't wish to meet him. Don't you know any aristocratic people—I mean the Park Avenue type?"

"Nick the Greek," I continued, ignoring her last statement, "has more class and more intestinal fortitude than any Park Avenuite. He is considered the greatest gambler of them all."

"Why," she asked coldly, "is he considered the greatest gambler of them all?"

"Well," I answered, "he says it's because it took him longer to go broke than anybody else."

Barbara could never understand what makes these characters of Broadway tick. She lives in a different world. She could never understand men like Broadway Sam, Tommy Manville, or Nick the Greek. Yet I love each one for a different reason.

Nick the Greek loved the excitement that went with gambling. He was never concerned with his surroundings. He was only interested in gambling. He played in the most aristocratic homes and gambling rooms in the country. He also took part in "floating" crap games in hotel rooms, garages, and subway platforms.

One night Nick walked into a dice game in a garment loft. Without a cent, he stood watching a game for a while. Then one of his friends, winning quite a bit, handed him a twenty-dollar bill, saying, "You've often slipped me something. See what you can do with this." Nick took it, watched the dice awhile, and then bet. He won the bet. In an hour, Nick had run the twenty dollars up to thirty thousand. Nick played all night long and, toward morning, with the dice going against him, he was completely wiped out. Without any comment, Nick started to walk out of the garment loft. A man stopped him near the door and asked, "How did you make out, Nick?"

"I lost twenty dollars," was the reply.

On another occasion, a panhandler approached Nick on Broadway to make a touch. "I'm a little tired of this place," he said. "Things have been tough, and I want to go back to California. I've an idea they might be better there."

"How much do you need?" asked Nick.

"Fifty cents," replied the panhandler.

Nick was amazed. "How are you going to get there with fifty cents?" he asked.

"I'm going to hitch-hike there," said the panhandler, "and all I need is money for coffee."

"Have you ever been to California?" asked Nick.

"No," replied the panhandler.

"Here's a dollar for you," said Nick. "You mightn't like it there."

Nick always says, "Money isn't everything. I just like it the best."

He was playing in a high-stake crap game and was being bothered by some stooge who wanted to make a touch. The hanger-on kept annoying him until the exasperated Nick finally paused in rolling the dice and shouted, "Please, please, do you have to bother me during business hours?"

All the characters were out in full force. It looked like a bargain day at Lindy's. As each character greeted us at our table, Babs' nose went higher in the air and I gave each one a bigger greeting. I was really getting my kicks.

Kingfish Levinsky came over to peddle his ties and kibitz awhile. Commodore Dutch joined us long enough to sell me a couple of tickets to his annual ball at Webster Hall. Everybody buys tickets every year but nobody attends. However, he hires the hall and the band and they play for an empty house, even though the affair is sold out.

Willie Howard's new secretary, who looks like a hangover, drops by for a chat and Petey Wells comes over to meet my little deb. "That's the kind of a girl for me," says Pete, " a girl with plenty of loot. My ambition is to marry a rich girl who is too proud to let her husband work."

"What are you doing in Lindy's?" I asked him.

"Well," he replied, "after I eat here, I'll have to cut

14-*Karacters*   **249**

my budget and stay out of Kellogg's Cafeteria for four
days."

Jack Zero is there too. His face looks as if it had worn
out three bodies. The veins in his completely bald head
come out as he tells you his latest experiences.

"How dya like that?" he hisses. "I go on at the Havana-
Madrid celebrity show. I'm the hit of the whole evening.
A producer is sitting there and laughs himself sick. After
the show the big gee from Hollywood says, 'Who does
Zero look like?' Then he gives the other guy the job."

The erstwhile songwriter (his *Please Don't Squeeze
duh Banana* is a big hit), straight man, and comic, broke
me up with his latest anecdote about his first radio shot.
My Boston Belle just stared.

"After rehearsing all day," said Jack, "we went on at
night. When my spot came up I started to read my lines,
but the director waved me back. I finished and he came
over and told me that I was too nervous and the mike
was too sensitive. I shouldn't stand too close. On the repeat, the director again waved me back. I stepped back
about four feet. Suddenly a door closed between me
and the mike. That was my one and only radio shot and
it took a closed door to get me off."

The Prince himself, Michael Romanoff, is in New
York for a short visit and drops into Lindy's to reminisce.
The bogus Prince is a successful restaurateur in Hollywood now, but he is still one of the biggest characters on
the street. However, he'll never forget his troubled,
harassed days—his penniless years.

Romanoff, the Prince, was once the lowliest pauper.

He was the "guest" of Broadwayites for years. They were amused by his royal manner and his regal sense of humor.

Michael once ate at the Tavern for eight months in a row, three meals a day. He not only signed the tabs but he even put the tip on the check and the manager paid it.

One day, Romanoff was offered a part in a show and he finally decided to go to work. The show was a hit and the Prince was working steady. He never showed up at the Tavern while he was in the show.

"How come we haven't seen you at the Tavern?" asked one of the waiters, when he met him on the street.

"Now that I'm working," answered the last of the Romanoffs, "who can afford their prices?"

"Would you like to meet Prince Michael Romanoff?" I asked Babs.

"Veddy much," she answered, lowering her nose about six inches. "It's about time you introduced me to some nobility. I mean, people with culture and breeding."

"Prince," I called to the Brooklyn royalty, "would you be kind enough to come over for a moment?"

"Are you really Prince Michael Romanoff?" asked the deb, all atwitter. For the first time her eyes shone and her face was wreathed in smiles.

"If I'm not," answered Michael, as he walked away, "I'm having a helluva time with his girl."

Her face dropped all its glee and her nose soared into the stratosphere.

I invited Ken MacSarin, who keeps a who's who of chorus girls and show gals. He has an appetite that has an appetite. I wanted him to polish her off good. "Have something to eat," I suggested to the character.

"Okay," he said reluctantly, "order me four or five omelettes to start." By the time he'd finished his twentieth omelette and his twelfth cup of coffee, the plates were piled so high you couldn't see the supercilious look on the snob from Boston.

"I'd like to add this babe's name to my list," said Ken, between gulps. "I keep a list of all the gals in town, what they drink, the kind of flowers they like, phone numbers, type of jewelry, etc. What's your name and phone number?"

Praise the Lord and pass the Alka Seltzer! I thought she would burst a blood vessel. "I think I've had quite enough," she said to me. "Please take me to Grand Central Station, I'm going home."

"Gladly," I answered. I was never so anxious to get rid of anybody. Some men dislike women without reason. Others like them that way. I didn't like her any way.

As we got up to leave, Ken gagged to Babs, "Why don't you come up to my room and see the handwriting on the wall—I'm too poor to afford etchings."

That was the final blow. She stormed out of Lindy's and I followed leisurely. I was only sorry that she had to miss Sol Violinsky and Swifty Morgan, two of my all-time favorite Broadwayites. They would really have made her evening complete.

The fabulous Swifty Morgan has been all over the world, and is the intimate of all the bigs in every walk of life. The aristocratic peddler will only sell you ties or jewelry if he likes you. When he is invited to a table in Lindy's or any other restaurant, he always orders caviar and demands only the best imported variety. Then he has it put in a special package and takes it home for his dog. "Blackie," he explains, "don't eat nothin' but caviar."

The eminent tie salesman gives advice on how to beat the horses: "Play nothin' but winnin' long shots."

The bizarre Broadway character once offered to sell J. Edgar Hoover, the G man, a watch. He wanted $300 and Hoover protested it was too much.

"Too much!" snorted Mr. Morgan. "Why let me tell you somethin'—the reward alone for this watch is $500!"

Sol Violinsky has been around Broadway for a long, long time. His wit has been repeated around the world. The beloved ex-vaudevillian claims, "I have had my violin in hock so long that my pawnbroker knows how to play it better than I do."

Solly admits that he has laid off under four presidents. When he was ill recently he phoned for a doctor, who at once diagnosed the case and gave him the verdict, "overwork."

Violinsky fell and broke his leg a few years ago. "Luckily I have insurance," he said between sobs. "Wonderful! What kind?" asked Earl Wilson. "Fire and theft," said Solly.

Solly likes to recall his terrific triumph in England about 1910. During the coronation of King George V, he had an apartment overlooking the procession. As the royal carriage passed, he threw open the window and played his violin. Next day he ran advertisements about the great Solly Violinsky—"who played before the King and Queen."

He told Ken Kling he was going to sign a non-aggression pact with his landlady: "If she doesn't ask me for money, I won't ask her for a receipt."

The lovable wit copyrighted the "Sol Violinsky Plan" with Earl Wilson. It's for guys who are always being asked to contribute to some fund. When Solly is asked to give something for somebody he never cared about he says, "Sure" and then he scribbles on a small piece of paper, "I.O.U. $50. Sol Violinsky."

Well, my stuffy deb and I were just about to get into a taxi in front of Lindy's when Swifty Morgan approached us. "I have some great ties for you, actor," he sneered. "Come on over to Nat Lewis' haberdashery store and I'll show them to you."

I couldn't resist this last touch of Broadway for my Boston Belle. I took Babs under the arm and we followed Swifty into the Lewis shop.

"Let me see those ties," he said to one of the clerks, when we were in the store. "Do you like them?" he asked me. "Yes, I do," I answered.

"How much do you charge for them?" he asked the clerk. "Five dollars," was the answer.

Then he opened the box he was carrying under his arm and brought out his stock of ties. "Here's the same ties and I'll let you have them for three dollars because you're my friend and I like you," said Swifty.

"Okay," I said, "I'll take a dozen."

"Let me have a box," he said to the clerk. "You don't mind carrying my ties in a Nat Lewis box, do you?" he asked me.

As we were riding in the cab to Grand Central Station, I couldn't help laughing at the deb's discomfort. She couldn't wait to get on the train and leave me and my character friends behind. The more I laughed, the more furious she became. We had words, but I didn't get a chance to use them. She told me off in no uncertain terms.

"You and your creatchahs are certainly not welcome in Bahston," she burned. "I've never been so veddy, veddy anxious to leave anybody or anything behind in my life, as I am to leave you and your characters. I rahthah think you should be ashamed of yourself."

"Parting is such sweet sorrow . . ." Shakespeare had something there. If we had parted sooner, it would have been sweeter. What a relief to put the deb back on the train, and send the bahstard back to Bahston. Now I could go back to Toots' and laugh again.

CHAPTER SIXTEEN

Joe Frisco, Broadwayite

"ARE ya through, fellas?" whispered Chuck Hamilton sarcastically. "Hear me good and I'll tell ya the most fabulous character that ever hit Fraudway, and then ya can close the book."

"Well, ya creep, you're on! Who's a bigger character than me?" barked Toots.

"Hear me out," ignored Chuck. "When I mention his name, ya can bet all the cabbage [1] on this street, there never was any greater one. I didn't make it that way—he just is."

"Okay, chowderhead, who is it?" queried Shor.

"I go away back with characters on this street," drawled Chuck, "and the Number One man is still Joe Frisco."

"You're right, Chuck," agreed Paul Denis, who is Earl Wilson's Bust Assistant on the *N. Y. Evening Post.* "I've been covering Broadway for seventeen years and I have yet to find a more colorful character. I'll never forget the time he was harassed by a process server. He broke into a run down Seventh Avenue, with the process server running breathlessly after him. Suddenly Joe

[1] *Cabbage.* Broadway vernacular for money.

255

swung left into his favorite Fifty-second Street and shouted to the man following him, 'Th-th-this is where we turn'."

"My favorite Frisco story," added Rags Ragland, who is always a welcome visitor to the round table, "hap-

pened a short time ago. Abe Attell, the sixty-eight-year-old former featherweight champion of the world, was hit by a car and was in pretty bad condition . . . 'Poor Abe,' said Frisco, 'h-h-he'll never be able to fight again'."

George Clarke, one of the best-liked newspaper men in the country, former editor of the *Daily Mirror* in New York and now doing a great column for the *Boston Record*, joined in the praise of our hero: "I love that guy because his sense of humor is terrific. One night at the Mayfair in Boston, we were sitting around having our nightly schmooze [1] when a heavily bearded sailor, just back from overseas, entered. 'Ain't that n-n-nice,' said Joe, 'L-L-Lincoln's son's joined the navy'."

The yarns about Joe Frisco have become part of the legend of Broadway and Hollywood. He is invariably broke and cares little about it, as long as his credit is good with the bookmakers. He'd rather make a mental bet on a nag, than star in a picture. He eats mostly at diners. "Those swank joints are too rich for my blood," he says. His friends include vaudevillians, gamblers, night-club owners, murderers, and ladies of the evening. He never heard of Katharine Cornell, Galli-Curci,

[1] *Schmooze.* Chewing the rag, as when a group of people get together and "cut up" everybody and everything.

or James Byrnes. Society is the name of a club, for all he knows about it. But he knows every bartender from coast to coast by his first name, and every bookmaker by his number.

Joe was working at Grace Hayes' Lodge in Hollywood and, as usual, was in the diner across the street, making mind bets on the ponies. It was celebrity night and Grace introduced Lawrence Tibbett. The world-famous baritone started to sing his famous *Glory Road,* and his magnificent voice was booming around the room as Joe entered. "Th-th-there's a guy with a v-v-voice!" he said as he approached Miss Hayes. "W-w-w-why don't you sign him up, p-p-put him in the show?" "Are you kiddin', you dope?" reprimanded the lovely owner of the Lodge. "That man's name is Lawrence Tibbett." "Th-th-the hell with it!" screamed Joe. "Change his n-name, put him in the sh-sh-show!"

His loyal followers include the great in show business from coast to coast. Bing Crosby who screams with laughter at everything Frisco says, is a good touch for the little guy with the cigar and scratch-sheets. Crosby had been lending Joe one $20 bill after another to go to the races, and Joe didn't pay them back. Finally, at Santa Anita, Joe got on a long shot and won a bundle. He began treating everybody at the bar, and soon a mob was around him. Bing came up, and from the outer fringe of the crowd he called to the celebrity, "Hey, Frisco, what about me?" Joe grandiosely peeled off a twenty and said, "H-h-here, boy, sing two ch-choruses of *Melancholy Baby.*"

He once cautioned Peter Lind Hayes, who was about to open at New York's Roxy Theatre (it has one of the largest stages in the world), "Don't get c-c-caught in the middle of the stage without b-b-bread and water!"

One early morning, about six ayem, "our boy" entered the lobby of the Sherman Hotel in Chicago. The scrub women had shined up all the cuspidors and piled them in a corner in front of a large picture of Abe Lyman that was posted there to advertise the coming appearance of the popular maestro. "H-h-h-he's a g-g-great guy, that Lyman," praised Joe, "b-b-but he never won all those cups."

The little vaudevillian is well aware of the fact that he

stutters, and it strikes his sense of humor. Jack O'Brian recalled the time Joe called a Western Union boy who stuttered worse than Frisco. "G-g-go back to the office," Joe warned him, "and tell them to s-s-send me a straight man."

Leonard Lyons, one of my favorite fourth-estaters, always drops by the round table long enough to tell us one of his great anecdotes. Bing Crosby saw Joe Frisco at the race track and asked him how he was doing. Frisco opened his scratch-sheet. "I have this one in the first race," he said, circling the name of the horse, "and I got it parlayed with this in the third, then with this one in the daily double." Frisco continued circling names in pencil, and drawing connecting lines with his parlaying bets. After he had circled and linked the names of all the horses he was betting, Joe studied the lined and circled scratch-sheet, then drew a heavy line across one spot and said, ". . . and the G-Germans went this way."

Even Chuck Hamilton listened without interrupting one night, when Oscar Hammerstein 2nd sat at our round table and told this tale about "our Joe":

During the first world war a monster benefit was staged at the Metropolitan Opera House, and there was almost no entertainer of any prominence in show business who was not there. All three Barrymores were on the bill, and Al Jolson and all of those who had reached the pinnacle in their respective lines.

Big as they were, however, there was one who seemed to top all in importance, and this was Enrico Caruso. He was one of those geniuses recognized in his own lifetime as a rare phenomenon. The other artists on the bill had a respect for him that amounted to awe. As Caruso stood in the wings awaiting his entrance, no one actually had the courage to walk up to the great tenor and address him—no one, that is, except Joe Frisco. Joe came out of his dressing room onto the stage, saw Caruso, and without a moment's hesitation, walked up to him, tapped him on the shoulder, and said, "Hey, C-C-C-Caruso, l-l-lay off *Strutters' Ball*. I'm doing it in the s-second half."

No matter how broke Frisco was, he always held out for "his price" and headline billing. Which often meant that jobs weren't too plentiful. In addition, the horses kept him short, no matter how much he earned or how often he worked.

Joe was in his room at the Belvedere Hotel in New York when the phone rang. It was his manager. "I can get you three thousand a week at the Palace and top billing," said the ten percenter with glee. "Are you k-k-kiddin'?" said Joe. "You know my p-p-price is thirty-five hundred dollars and not a n-n-nickel less." "Well, I'll see what I can do," said the manager. "Anyway, come on over to my office and we'll talk it over." "What!" yelled Frisco, "and g-get locked out of my room?"

Joe had many lean days. In fact, even the prosperous days were lean ones for Joseph—the ponies saw to that. However, he never lost his sense of humor. He had a particularly long string of bad luck on the coast one year, was really up against it, and Hollywood, the land of

"Ah! Bewilderness," is a helluva place to be broke. Joe would stand in front of the Brown Derby waiting for his friends to invite him for a bite to eat. Everybody who knew him offered to buy him a "cup of coffee." After weeks of "Join me for a cup of coffee?" or "How about some coffee, Joe?" from many pals, Joe finally blurted out to one of them, "Doesn't anybody eat m-m-meat in there?"

Romo Vincent met Frisco at Hollywood and Vine, where all the actors hang out. "You've been out here a long time," said the fat boy; "how have you been doing in pictures?" "Are you k-k-kiddin'?" answered Joe. "I've been here f-f-four years and I've n-n-never even been before a Brownie camera."

At the height of his career he was called down to the Income Tax Bureau for neglecting to pay $12,000 in taxes. "I h-h-haven't g-g-got it right now," Joe apologized. "The horses t-t-took it, but I'm g-g-good for it. K-k-keep in touch with me." Luckily the inspector was a fan of the little vaudevillian's. "Listen, Mr. Frisco," he pleaded, "pay us a little every week and we'll straighten it out." Joe promised to be a good boy. As he stepped away from the desk, he noticed that Pat Rooney Jr. was called next. It seems that Rooney owed about $900. Frisco walked back to the desk, put his arm around the youngest of the Rooneys, and said to the income-tax man, "This is a great little k-k-kid, I know his whole f-family. Put his b-b-bill on my tab."

Another vaudevillian suddenly came into a lot of money and was on his way to pay his room rent in full.

"G-g-go ahead, wise guy," Frisco cautioned him, "pay your r-r-rent and spoil it for everybody."

Joe likes to tell this story on himself: He was in debt to a midget. It seems a four-horse parlay didn't work out for him. Frisco left town and didn't see the little guy for months. One day while eating at a restaurant on the coast, Joe turned his head to give the waiter his order, when the midget spied him and approached the table to collect his money. His head just reached the top of the table. Frisco turned to the waiter and inquired, "Who ordered J-J-John the Baptist?"

On one of his infrequent visits to New York, Sidney Skolsky, the half-pint Hollywood reporter, joined the "crum-bums' round table" long enough to tell us the latest anecdote about our "pal":

Frisco was working at Charley Foy's night club in the Valley and was living with Foy in a room over the night club. One night, after the show, Foy said he had a date and wouldn't be back. He was going to sleep at a friend's house. This was okay with Frisco, who then went upstairs to bed.

Now when Frisco goes to bed, it's practically a vaudeville act in itself. He gets undressed down to his underwear. Then he starts dressing. He puts on several suits of underwear. Then a clean shirt and tie, just in case. Then over this he puts a bathrobe. He is now fairly well bundled and ready for bed. But before going to bed, he locks the door. Then he puts the bureau against the door, and he puts a chair against the bureau. He wants to make certain no one will enter.

At about four in the morning there was a knock on the door. "Who is it?" shouted Frisco, surprised and frightened. "It's me, Charley," was the reply.

"Ch-Ch-Charley who?" asked Frisco.

"Charley Foy, you fool!" answered Charley Foy.

"No, it isn't," Frisco answered. "Charley Foy is staying over with f-f-friends and won't be home tonight."

"Listen, it's me, please let me in."

"If you're Ch-Ch-Charley Foy, give me the first h-h-half of that routine we do d-downstairs."

And Charley Foy, standing in the hallway at four in the morning, had to do the first half of their night-club routine before Joe Frisco would open the door . . .

CHAPTER SEVENTEEN

They Pan Everything But Gold

LEE SULLIVAN, the singer, was telling Walter Winchell the yarn about the two shipwrecked critics. They drifted for weeks on a raft, and the more frightened of the two started seeking forgiveness for his sins.

"I've been a louse all my life," he said. "I've been cruel to actors. Too often I went out of my way to hurt them. If I'm spared, I promise . . ." "Just a moment," shouted the other, "don't go too far. I think I see smoke from a ship!"

Most of the ladies and gentlemen who review the shows on the radio, in the night clubs and theatres, and on the screen are kindly and tolerant away from their fascinating chores. In their personal lives the critics are meek, lovable, tender, and thoughtful human beings who don't beat their wives or put poison in their children's soup.

But as soon as the "first knifer" sits down to review a show, the pen turns into a sword. The charming intellectual becomes a stinging insectual.

Some critics think more of putting over a sharp line than delivering a just and constructive criticism. Don't get me wrong—the critics are honest, but they would rather throw hisses than kisses.

Few shows survive an explosion of adverse reviews at the hands of the dramorticians. On the other hand, orchids and love pats from the critics are usually translated into long lines of customers at the box office.

Very often they do hiss wrong. *Hellzapoppin'*, *Tobacco Road*, and *Abie's Irish Rose* were roasted by al-

In their personal lives the critics are meek, lovable, tender, and thoughtful human beings

most all the aisle assassins. They were three of the biggest hits Broadway ever had.

Please don't misunderstand, there are many more bad shows than there are hits. It's the job of the "boys in boo," as Louis Sobol calls them, to give their readers their honest recommendations. Some plays don't even deserve a Broadway showing. Morey Amsterdam saw a show that was so bad, "the actors walked out on the critics." Hal Block, ducking out of the theatre to miss something boring, quipped, "This looks like a four-drink act."

Actors are the severest critics. Groucho Marx remarked to Winchell after a flopperoo some years ago: "I saw the show at a disadvantage: the curtain was up."

Nobody has ever escaped the critics' sledgehammer. Even Katharine Cornell and Helen Hayes have had to fight through a lot of scallions thrown at them.

Percy Hammond said, "Drama criticism is venom from contented rattlesnakes." He proved it when he wrote of one show, "I find I have knocked everything except the knees of the chorus girls, and the Creator has anticipated me there."

Channing Pollock admitted, "A critic is a legless man who teaches running."

Arthur Guiterman wrote,

"The stones that critics hurl with harsh content,
A man may use to build his monument."

The members of "The Death Watch" are an actor's sneering acquaintance. Their vitriolic criticisms cause more feuds with actors and producers than a bad decision by an umpire at a baseball game. One prominent star bought a radio just to turn off Barry Gray, the radio critic.

Irving Hoffman, the critic who writes the scalding and witty reviews for the *Hollywood Reporter*, is a sweetheart of a guy personally, who would give you the glasses off his nearsighted eyes. But when he sits down at a typewriter he is feared by actors, actresses, and pro-

ducers. He talks about the "best smellers" he sees in
theatres. His blast at Max Gordon's play, *Ethan Frome,*
moved Gordon to squawk to Hoffman's boss about per-
mitting a review by a man who didn't see very well.
Hoffman's reply settled the argument: "I may not see
very well, but there's nothing wrong with my nose."

Irving telegraphs the opinions of the film critics in
New York to his West Coast paper every week. A box
prefaces them; it reads:

> *The authors of the criticisms capsuled below are given the
> widest possible latitude. Their opinions do not necessarily
> reflect those of the paper in which they appear. In fact, their
> opinions do not necessarily reflect anything but the state of
> their digestion, the location of their seats, the holes in their
> bobby-sox, the tenacity of their hangovers, the efficacy of their
> sleeping pills, the promptness of their laundry, the angle of
> their political leanings, and the number of their prejudices.*

Earl Wilson is one of the few columnists and critics
that don't bite the ham that feeds him. He is never
known to give an actor or a show a bad notice. If he
doesn't like a show, he avoids saying anything.

The Belmont Plaza's Glass Hat put on one show that
was pretty bad. Earl went to the opening with Frank
Law, who produced it. The next day the *Post's* Saloon
Editor wrote a review that was a classic: "The dinner
was fine, the waiters wore starched dickeys, the head-
waiter wore a white coat, and the band was dressed in
blue. The telephone booth was air-conditioned and the
carpeting was shocking pink, which matched the chairs.
The pro in the men's rooms wore an immaculate white
coat. There were many celebrities at the opening. To-

morrow night I will review the show at the Versailles."

"You're a doll," I said to Earl one night while sitting at the round table. "You always give the actor a break. Especially on those horrible opening nights. There's nothing like an opening to make the performer wish he were temporarily dead."

"Does a bad notice by 'the pallbearers' make you slightly ill?" asked Earl.

"Well," I said, "it's not exactly a vitamin pill. I always put a black pencil mark around a bad notice in my scrapbook."

"Ya must have worn out a lotta pencils, ya creepy ham," taunted the benign Toots Shor.

Paul Martin, the former columnist and night-club critic of the *World-Telegram,* loved to razz me in and out of his paper. Whenever he sat down at his tripe-writer he would stick his tongue out at me in print. Martin wrote a column called *Tips on Tables*. Six days a week he would write about food, and on the seventh he became a George Jean Nothin'.

"The only way you could review me," I told Paul one day, "is if I wore a poached egg on my head."

"An expert on food is just da kinda guy ta cover your act," slammed Toots. "Yer a big ham."

"Don't worry about a little thing like that," consoled Joe E. Lewis. "Look at the Milton Berle flopperoo, *Spring in Brazil:* $300,000 thrown in the sewer. It's not a bad show, either. The only trouble is, the theatre is constructed wrong—the seats face the stage."

"Instead of opening the show in New York," jibed Jackie Miles, "they should call it *Spring in New York* and open it in Brazil."

"The show can't be too bad," Bob Goldstein interjected. "It did receive mixed notices: Some thought it wasn't much good and some thought it was horrible."

"Elliot Norton's review in Boston really was a killer," Earl Wilson commented. "He said, 'Two girls chase Berle around the stage all through the show—and they can have him!'"

"I don't know," I don't-know'd, "I saw the show in Philadelphia and I found it very refreshing. I think Berle was very funny in it."

"I found it very refreshing, too," put in Jerry Lester. "I felt like a new man when I awoke."

"After they played *The Star-Spangled Banner,*" embalmed Jay C. Flippen, "there was a helluva let-down."

"Why ya buncha crumbums," Shor bellowed, "ya object ta critics lousing you up, but ya do a pretty good job tearing yer fella hams apart yerselves!"

Of course, critics don't need any help from actors to massacre a show or a performer. Down through the years they have found ways and means to make players and producers jump at the crack of their quips.

John Chapman said about the Mae West show, *Catherine Was Great*, "Miss West now has one more bust than she needs." Dorothy Parker murdered Katharine Hepburn in *The Lake* with: "Hepburn ran the gamut of emotions from A to B." Irving Hoffman fouled Ilka Chase when the authoress appeared in her own play, *In Bed We Cry*. The witty critic of the *Hollywood Reporter* said, "She makes me Ilka." That made Ilka a little Ilka, too.

In reviewing the Carole Landis show, the brilliant Hoffman wrote, "Its humor is bedpan; its music tinpan."

Charles Gentry of the *Detroit Times* didn't like June Havoc in the musical version of *Sadie Thompson*. As he wrote it the next morning, "It never rains but it bores."

Kelcey Allen of *Women's Wear* is recognized as the dean of the current crop of Broadway aisle sitters. The seventy-year-old veteran admits that he has been blasting shows "ever since N.B.C. meant National Biscuit Company." It was Kelcey who said of one play, "If the guy who wrote this had a lot of enemies, he's even with them now."

The rotund, jolly-mannered Allen has thrown some poisonous darts in his time. In 1936 he reviewed a picture for his paper by saying, "In the past year two terrible things happened to the movies—Laurel and Hardy."

When the donkey that appeared in the musical comedy, *Rainbow,* in 1928, forgot its stage manners, the event created a furore in theatrical circles. The following morning Allen's report of the show did not appear. The producer, desirous of the critic's decision, phoned for it. "What is there left for me to say," answered Kelcey, "after the donkey said it so eloquently?"

Asked some years ago if he was going to review *Kismet,* he sense-of-humored, "No, we're sending our rug buyer."

George Jean Nathan of the cameo-brooch features has been coughing and sneezing at first nights for thirty years or more. Nathan is the fellow who invented riding in cabs, even when the distance is two blocks. "Don't you ever walk and get some fresh air?" Winchell queried one night. "Walking is dangerous," he answered; "when you walk you get cinders in your eye." His caustic comment has thrown more than cinders in the eyes of producers and showpeople.

The pungent Mr. Nathan, covering John Barrymore in *My Dear Children,* belted the eccentric member of the royal family: "I always said that I would like Barrymore's acting until the cows came home. Well, sir, last night the cows came home."

The actorturer doesn't dislike all actors—only the ones he sees in shows. They say that Mr. Nathan once gave a blood transfusion to an actor and the poor guy froze to death. The only rave notices the brilliant G.J. gives are in the obituary columns. The immaculate critic of the *Journal-American* and *Esquire* has given the best jeers of his life to the theatre.

Once in a great while he does embrace an actor or a show. He is a hallelujah shouter for anything turned out by William Saroyan. But then, fewer people understand Saroyan or his plays than could figure out the Einstein relativity theory.

George "Mean" Nathan, as he is called by many actors and producers, really loves the theatre, but usually writes as if he got up on the wrong side of the aisle.

Once in a while a play comes along that is so bad it's a field day for "the grave diggers."

The Girl from Nantucket stuck her head out at the Adelphi Theatre and the "boys in boo" promptly chopped it off.

Barry Gray gave it a short funeral: "I saw *The Girl From Nantucket*—duck it."

It caused Earl Wilson, who loves everybody, to resort to prose:

"Oh, there was a young girl from Nantucket,
   But there probably won't be next week this time."

Robert Coleman's stinger in *The Mirror* was the clincher: "An entire page of the Adelphi Theatre program is devoted to credits for *The Girl From Nantucket*. The list of writers alone runs to four lines. Which provokes the paraphrase that seldom has so little been owed so many."

The morning after John van Druten brought his *The*

Mermaids Singing into the Empire Theatre, Robert
Coleman started his review with: "The mermaids' singing is out of tune."

John Chapman was even more biting: "In *The Voice
of the Turtle* Mr. van Druten ran a bedroom skit into
three acts and made it the most diverting comedy of a
couple of seasons. In his new affair, his indelicacies seem
a little too delicate. The girl wants to and the man wants
to but nobody does, and somehow, base fellow that I
am, I think everybody would have more fun, including
the characters in the play, if they did along about the
end of the second act."

Walter Winchell doesn't cover shows any more as a
critic; he confines himself to keeping score for his former
plague-mates. "*The Girl From Nantucket* was snubbed
as though she had a bad reputation," he noted after taking a count. "*The Secret Room*," wrote the orchid man,
"was pushed around like a revolving door. It was
knocked by everyone except opportunity." The film,
Dangerous Intruder, was brushed off by Mrs. Winchell's
little boy Walter with, "It is a murder meller that merely
kills time." After Carole Landis opened in *The Lady
Says Yes*, he summed up for the aisle assassins: "Lady
says yes—critics say no!"

When Winchell was covering shows for *The Mirror* he
offended the powerful Shuberts by some flippant comments and was barred from all their houses. But the
Bund-Belter always liked a good fight. He was about to
be readmitted to first nights when he tossed another
barb: "A certain critic barred from the Shubert open-

ings," he wrote, "says he'll wait three nights and go to their closings."

Even beloved men like Heywood Broun and Robert Benchley, who had hearts as big as themselves, couldn't resist a little pants-kicking when they covered first nights.

When Benchley was writing drama reviews for *The New Yorker*, he said about *Tortilla Flat*, "It will probably go down as one of the worst cases of miscasting since I played a red-headed manicurist in the Hasty Pudding show of 1912."

Heywood Broun was always for the underdog. But when he covered a show for his paper, he always carried an axe. His review of one actor made the thespian jump: "Sidney Blackmer has been accused of being a very good actor. By his performance in last night's drama he was tried and acquitted." Asked by Tallulah Bankhead about a play in which she was starring, the baggy-pants founder of the Newspaper Guild murmured, "Don't look now, Tallu, but your show is slipping."

Every once in a while, producers get so burned up at criticisms of their plays, they decide to eliminate the play jurors entirely. In fact, playwright-director George S. Kaufman once tried the experiment of keeping the critics away on opening night. However, acid-tossers keep coming and cutting.

Robert Garland wrote about *Nellie Bly*, "I see by the papers that Joy Hodges is the only actress that gets up at seven every morning—she shoulda stood in bed."

G. J. Nathan ended a review thuswise: "We will concede that Lionel Hall, as the lead, could do better if he were given the right vehicle—a truck."

Gilbert Gabriel, covering the debut of *The Women,* the controversial play by Clare Booth Luce, observed dyspeptically, "One can get the same effect by sticking a finger down one's throat."

Jim O'Connor said about a recent show, "*January Thaw,* as seen on a cold February night, is not so hot."

When Archer Winsten reviewed the picture, *Hollywood and Vine,* he wrote, "Prince Michael Romanoff, playing himself, the restaurateur, is so bad as an actor that you begin to suspect he must be a real prince."

Lee Mortimer saw a picture that was so bad, "it should be retaken and then put on the shelf." About another stinker, Lee said, "It was so horrible, two people called up to have their names taken off the free list."

Barry Gray, radio's robot ribber, was born with a silver knife in his mouth. He hates everybody and everything. "Old songs never die," he said about Carl Ravazza, "until he sings them." About another singer he burned, "He couldn't carry a tune if it had a handle. That's not a voice, it's a vocal hotfoot." He let one singer have it, but good: "Phil has proved that you can't talk without a voice but you certainly can sing without one."

A certain glamor girl who insisted on a stage career, the vitriolic WOR broadcaster described as "Personality plus—and everything else minus." About a bad play he wailed, "A good finish to his show, would be—a match." He even pans his sponsor, the famous theatrical weekly.

"*Variety* is useless," he tells his radio audience; "it has no race results."

It's Barry who admits that he "pans everything but gold." The acidy young radio spieler doesn't adore many people. He said, "Milton Berle is so stingy, you'd think he was saving for a rainy century."

He receives enough pan mail to prove he is being heard. Last year he decided to go into competition with the comedians he had been heckling. He opened at the Greenwich Village Inn but confessed he laid the biggest egg of the year. Barry was the first to give a bad notice to his own performance at the Village bistro. "I can only do better," he admitted on the air; "there is no other direction left to go."

His friends and critics made it unanimous. Henny Youngman phoned from Chicago and suggested that streets to the Village be marked "*Smellbound.*" Lee Mortimer advised the owners to "fumigate the room." Earl Wilson consoled him with, "Who isn't bad the first time?"

After five unhappy days, the flip-quipper quit his job at the Inn and swore, "From now on, I'll be very lenient with comedians. I didn't realize how tough it was to make people laugh in night clubs."

So what happened? The very next night he said about a famous clown, "I don't think there is more to his comedy than meets the smell."

When *The Duchess Misbehaves* opened in New York, Lewis Nichols, who does the drama obituaries for *The Times*, wrote an opening line that bears repeating: "Another musical has come to town, dragging its book like a tin can tied to the tail of a cat."

Robert Sylvester atom-bombed a new show before it came to Broadway. "Word from Montreal yesterday," said the *Daily News* critic, "indicated that there may not be enough aspirin on the shelves of St. Lazare's Pharmacy to cure the headaches of everybody involved in the production."

Burton Rascoe, when *World-Telegram* dramurderer, hissed *Variety,* his confrères, the critics' circle, and the actors. Burton was invariably blasted back in good measure, even by the actors. *Variety* roared that praise from Rascoe was "a kiss of death." The dramanhandler unchivalrously commented about Annabella in the hit, *Jacobowsky and the Colonel,* calling her an "incredibly talentless" actress who made him "spiritually ill." When the beautiful Annabella read his notice, she promptly mailed him a bottle of castor oil.

Gypsy Rose Lee reviewed Clare Luce's performance in *Candida.* "Candida Dry," she called it.

The cuss-tomers who are paid to axe the acts, were annoyed with Spencer Tracy for closing *The Rugged Path.* The movie star's answer was right to the point: "The show is closing for a very old-fashioned reason—empty seats."

Robert Garland, the *Journal-American* crepe-hanger, sent a Happy New Year greeting to Rose Ingraham in *Polonaise*—"for stealing the show from Ham'n'Eggerth." Meaning, of course, Jan Kiepura and his lovely wife Marta Eggerth.

Al Bloomingdale, the department store biggie, is one of the best-known angels on Broadway. When he opened *Allah Be Praised,* a critic sent the show on its way to Cain's Warehouse with: "Bloomingdale should close the show and keep the store open nights."

Michael Todd questioned a critic who had doubted the worth of one of his productions, then quickly added, "But I'd never bar you. If I did, it would be just my luck for your boss to take Pegler off Democrats and put him on Drama."

The critikill first-nighters have let up a little since the *Variety* box score came into existence. The theatrical trade paper gives the professional larrupers a rating for their guesses on shows. Now they only massacre every other show.

It was Lee Mortimer who said about the Warner Brothers star, "Bette Davis has given the best tears of her life to the screen." Then he added in his best poetic fashion:

"Little handkerchief, don't you cry,
   You'll be in a Bette Davis picture, by and by."

Bill Cahn, the youthful producer, was being heckled by his pals at Toots Shor's after his *Devils Galore* was buried by the critics. "How come the show was so bad?" asked Ted Husing. "Well," Bill welled, "next time I'm going to read the script." "What do you want for your epitaph?" taunted Jack O'Brian. "Born 1909—Died 2009," was the producer's answer.

Some show producers have claimed that the critics are the theatre's worst enemies. Especially after their newest flops get sour notices. "If we're the theatre's worst enemies," countered one critic, "why do you producers persist in sending your worst enemies the best tickets to opening nights?"

A lot of actors and producers have discovered the formula for gaining the love of the first night dramanglers: Just do a good show and the love pats will follow.

The trouble is, the people on stage are scared out of their wits, and very often their lines, by the critics. Sir Herbert Beerbohm Tree, England's most widely panned histrionic, admitted: "My gravest fault is a too great deference to dramatic criticism."

Of course, the dramaimers know that they make new enemies with every crack of their whip. They are aware, too, that as soon as their typewriters stop clicking, so do the heels of the actors and the producers.

When the old *N. Y. American* folded and left critic Gilbert W. Gabriel jobless for the moment, the dramenace philosophized, "Now I can be hated for myself alone."

In other words, ham, don't pick an argument with the criticlique out front if you get a bad review. Conversely, don't let a good notice go to your head. The critics who carry you on their shoulders today, may be your pallbearers tomorrow.

CHAPTER EIGHTEEN

"Confusion Says . . ."

My father, without being aware of it, writes and talks the most natural "double talk." Whenever I receive a letter from him I have to read it forwards and backwards and both ways from the middle. Then I play it over slowly on my guitar—and I still don't understand it.

In person he is even worse. "I saw what's-his-name at what d'ya call it," he said to me one day, "and he asked me to remind you about what'sit." If I told my pater that I didn't understand him, he would get furious: "Big actor—he don't know what his own father is talking about!"

Oddly enough, my pop never became a Hollywood director or producer . . .

Sam Goldwyn is alleged to have uttered so many malaprops and had so many confusing lines credited to him, that when anybody pulls a verbal boner, they call it a Goldwynism. Like my dad, Sam has always been unaware that he mutilates the English language or that he has a dialect.

When the Great Goldwyn left for a European tour, his staff took pictures of the entire trip. The modern

Ziegfeld was astounded when he saw and heard himself on the screen for the first time. "Dot's pacular," he said to his wife. "In netural life I spik wonderful Anglish, but on de screen, I tuk wid a dialect."

The round table at Toots Shor's was particularly crowded one midnight when Toots approached the table, voice first: "They tell me dat crum-bum producer talks worse dan me." "Who," inquired Orson Welles, "could louse up the language worse than you?" "Listen, Hoople-Head," answered the lovable fat man, "why don't ya go back ta Mars where ya belong? I'm talkin' about Sam Goldwyn; he just come in da joint."

"Sam certainly has pulled some lulus," interjected Jack Pearl. "He once invited me to his home in California. 'Why do you need three swimming pools?' I asked him. 'You don't understand,' said Goldwyn. 'One is for people who like hot water and the other is for people who like cold water.' 'What's about the third?' I inquired. 'Oh, that! That's for people who don't like to swim.'"

"He's a fabulous guy," added Bert Lahr. "Some of the stories about him have become legends. He once said to an associate in a heated argument, 'For your information, let me ask you a question.'"

"The funniest of all the Goldwynisms," Bert Wheeler suggested, "happened not so long ago. One of Sam's yes-men complained to him about a certain star that the boss was anxious to get under contract. 'But she's a Lesbian,' cautioned the uh-huh man. 'I don't care what her religion is,' Sam yelled; 'sign her!'"

"I think Gregory Ratoff out-Goldwyns Goldwyn," commented Earl Wilson. "His dialect has a dialect. I interviewed him many times and his language, as Ratoff puts it, is 'abdominable.' I asked him if he approved of monogamy. 'No,' said the Russian, 'I like oak better.' I asked him in one interview if he rhumba'd. 'No,' he answered, 'only when I eat'."

"There's a guy called Mike Curtiz—he directs a few pictures once in a while," broke in Chuck Hamilton—"who ain't tin when it comes to moiderin' the English language. And I should know about English, I been talkin' it for years. Hear me good. Curtiz had lost his wallet on the train, and was complainin' to his friend, Ernst Lubitsch. 'So you lost $80 in cash and $3000 in checks,' Ernst commented. 'What are you worrying about, you can always stop the checks.' 'Yeh,' growled Mike, 'you can stop the checks, but you can't stop the cash'."

Mike Curtiz once asked a friend to "go into the Western Union office and fill out a telegraph blanket."

About an actor he said, "He is a modest man who has plenty to be modest about."

Mike loves to play golf, but the more he plays, the worse it turns out. While golfing one day he stepped up to the tee, took one swing at the ball, and made a hole-in-one. He turned to the caddie and inquired earnestly, "What did I do right?"

Phil Spitalny, renowned leader of the all-girl orchestra, is another fracturer of the English language. He once made a mistake on the air and referred to "my old-girl orchestra." He accidentally walked into the undressing room of his violin section one night. "I'm sorry," he apologized later, "to have walked in on you when you were starch naked."

When the famous leader of the "Hour of Charm" orchestra was suffering from indigestion, he told a friend, "I have information of the stomach."

Another guy that massacres the language is the concert violinist, Dave Rubinoff. The temperamental musician talks worse now than he did when he first came to this country from Russia some twenty-five years ago. A few pals invited Dave to go fishing. The fish weren't

biting. Suddenly Rubinoff yelled, "Boy, have I got a haddock, have I got a haddock!" "That's impossible," said his host. "How can you catch a haddock in these shallow waters?" "You dun't understend," said the artist furiously. "My had is spleeting, I got a tarrible haddock."

There's a little theatrical booking agent around Broadway called Johnny Singer, who has a lingo all his own. After he gets through kicking the English language around, even Webster couldn't straighten it out. When F.D.R. was elected for the third time, the little ten-percenter was elated. "Roosevelt won by a landslide," he shouted; "he got 364 electrical volts."

"Where are you bounding?" he asked Lew Parker, when he met him on the street one afternoon. "I can give you a lift in my new Plymouth. It has wonderful shock observers."

Johnny finished writing a letter in longhand and said to his secretary, "The ink is all wet, will you lend me your bladder?"

He lives in a regular "chubby hole" but pays his sister's "intuition to school." "She's taking an epidemic course at Columbia University," he explains.

Broadway Sam, the lovable character, doesn't exactly destroy the spoken word, he just mangles it a little. He is proud of his "very-close veins" and loves to ride horses, but complains that "I always gets my feet caught in da syrup."

B.B.B., the talented master of ceremonies from California, was all excited one night when the charming charactress of the cinema, Vera Gordon, entered his club. He insisted on introducing her to his audience. "Ladies and gentlemen," he said, "may I present a wonderful lady who betrays mother parts on the screen."

"I always gets my feet caught in da syrup"

One of my favorite song stars, Sid Gary, is the greatest double-talk artist in the country. He has amused thousands of stars with his sense of the ridiculous. He is quite serious at home, however, where his father is the natural double-talker. Sid was going to Madison Square Garden to see the Allie Stolz-Beau Jack match one Friday night. "Where are you going?" asked his dad when he saw the singer put his coat on. "To the fights," answered Sid, as he started to go out the door. "Don't mix in," cautioned the head of the house.

Joe Jacobs' famous saying, "I shoulda stood in bed," has become a classic.

Glenn Schmid, the young proprietor of Glenn's Rendezvous in Newport, Kentucky, was raving about a great act: "I think the four Ink Spots are the greatest trio in the business. Furthermore," continued the youthful night club owner, "all their songs have beautiful words and excellent lyrics."

When I worked at Leon and Eddie's, Leon was my inseparable pal. When a critic knocked my brains out, he consoled me with, "Don't worry, the public domain likes you."

The world-famous Fifty-second Street club has a big sign in the lobby announcing the minimum, usually $3.50. Once a year, however, the night of the Army-Notre Dame game, they raise the minimum to $5.00, and post the sign accordingly. Leon was working hard one night, trying to get football fans from all over the country comfortably seated. He was holding the rope in the lobby, when one of his pest friends came in and slapped him a wallop on the back. Leon turned on his assailant. "You're about as funny," he screamed, pointing to the sign, "as my minimum."

As a youngster, Leon had an ambition to live at the famous Roney Plaza Hotel in Miami Beach. He used

every connection to get a reservation there. He bought
special luggage and hired a car and chauffeur, just to
make the right entrance. He even had his bank call the
management to recommend him. After two days of

luxurious living, he checked out. "You go through all the
trouble to get into the Roney," a friend scolded, "and
then you check out after two days. What's the idea?"
"Who could afford it?" Leon answered . . .

The round table was just getting ready to break up for
the night. It was about 3 A.M. and, as usual, Chuck
Hamilton was "on." "The kid can tell you," he was saying, pointing to himself, "the funniest Goldwynism was

pulled by Goldwyn himself when he said, 'Include me out.' "

"That's an old one," said Jack O'Brian. "My favorite of all of Sam's remarks is known by everyone who ever heard of the great Goldwyn: 'A verbal contract isn't worth the paper it's written on.' "

"Cut it, ya creeps," said Toots. "Here comes Goldwyn now, let's not embarrass da bum." All of us waited to hear the latest Goldwynism born.

"I hate to take you away from your repast," said the renowned producer, as he approached the table, "but I do wish to thank Mr. Shor for his raucous hospitality. I enjoyed it with infinite delight," he continued in perfect English. "The cuisine was prepared by a culinary expert, and I should know—I'm a gourmet. A million thanks, gentlemen. Till we meet again! *Au revoir* . . ."

CHAPTER NINETEEN

Broadway Foxholes

I F L I N D Y ' S , Reuben's, Toots Shor's, The Lambs Club, The Friars Club, 21, El Morocco, The Cub Room, Kellogg's Cafeteria, The Theatrical Pharmacy, Moscowitz and Lupowitz, Café Royal, Walgreen's Forty-fourth Street Drug Store, Sardi's, and Hanson's Pharmacy all burned down in one day, every actor, actress, chorus girl, columnist, press agent, and producer in New York would be homeless.

The big and the little in show business, each has his own particular hangout. They sit around until the "whee" hours of the morning discussing their ambitions, their enemies, and their torches, some of which could light up the Great White Way.

When a group of actors get together, the night has a thousand I's. At the end of the night, they are so tired talking about themselves, they can hardly keep their mouths open.

Somebody is always holding court in one of the Broadway foxholes. In the Cub Room of the Stork Club, it's Winchell. In Lindy's, Leonard Lyons is king. At Sardi's, Renée Carrol is the queen. Earl Wilson is top man at Toots Shor's, Jack Adler of the famous Adler family is the royal prince at Walgreen's, and Menashe Skulnick is the Number One man at Café Royal. Sam Newgold is Mr. Big at two places, the Theatrical Pharmacy during the day and Kellogg's Cafeteria at night. At Hanson's, the man to know is Johnny Broderick.

The Lambs Club on Forty-fourth Street and the Friars Club on Forty-seventh are the retreats for the intelligentsia of the theatre. All the great veterans of the entertainment world, from John Barrymore on down, have made the Lambs their home in New York. Both clubs are strictly stag. Not a woman has passed their doors since they opened.

The Friars Club has been the meeting place for show-people since George M. Cohan and Sam Harris were members many years ago. Any night you can find Michael Todd in a hot gin game with Lew Walters of Latin Quarter fame, or Milton Berle holding ten cards against Benny Davis, the songwriting genius.

Lou Holtz, Benny Fields, Sid Gary, Harry Rose, Sid Marion, or Bert Frohman can be seen playing cards or kibitzing a game, any time you visit the famous club. Some of the biggest deals have been signed over a card table at the Friars.

If you're angling for a part in a show or you would like to appear at the Latin Quarter, for instance, you can get to Mike Todd or Lew Walters very easily—if you're a member of the Friars. Just make sure you get to them when they're winning.

I should know. I was anxious for a part in a Todd show and asked Benny Fields, the minstrel man, a buddy of mine, to invite me to the Friars. I was discussing the part with Mr. Todd while he was playing a hectic gin game with Walters. Everything was going fine until Lew hollered, "What's da name o' da game?" I answered "Gin." Mike forgot to break his kings and I wound up without the part.

Maybe I'm not John J. Anthony or Confucius, but take a little advice from me. If you must talk business to a producer while he's playing cards, make sure he's winning. If he gets blitzed in gin, he's bound to do the same to you and your part.

The Lambs Club did a magnificent job in entertaining the boys in uniform all through the war. Smith and Dale, Joe Laurie Jr., Horace MacMahon, and all the Lambs ran shows for the boys with the greatest stars in the entertainment world participating.

An actor's home is where he hangs his hat. All around the country there are foxholes where the people of the entertainment world gather to have laughs and talk about "how I killed 'em last night."

Showpeople are the warmest, most sensitive, most affectionate human beings in the world. In show business, for the most part, you are judged by your talent, ability and character, and not by your race, creed, or color. We are one big family. Sure there are feuds, fights, and heartaches. But don't let some outsider come in and try to louse one of us up!

That's why, no matter what city we play, the people of the entertainment world are drawn together like a magnet, to one or more spots in every burg.

People of the theatre are always on the lookout for laughs. Wherever showpeople gather there must be "kicks." [1] Every angle of the amusement business is discussed, and everybody is on the "pan."

When an actor tells the gang: "I'm not happy in that joint," you know he didn't do good. "I fractured that audience" or "nobody could follow my act," is the universal language of vaudevillians, heard above the din of the dishes, from Toots Shor's in New York to the Brown Derby in Hollywood.

When Tony Canzoneri, Mark Plant, and I get through with four or five shows a day at the theatre, trying to make people laugh, we look for laughs ourselves. When we're in Miami Beach, after our last show we make a beeline for Mammy's Restaurant at Twenty-first Street and Collins Avenue because we know we're bound to find the gang there. Lou Holtz, B. S. Pully, and whoever else is in town is sure to be kicking the gags around after their shows are over. Bob Feinstein, who owns Mammy's, lets the gang run loose and they really take over.

We walked in, one two-ayem, and found the Ritz brothers behind the counter selling pies, Max Baer and Maxie Rosenbloom cutting up the turkeys, Billy Vine taking cash at the register, and Sophie Tucker hostessing, while Jan Murray and Henny Youngman waited on tables. When Tony, Mark, and I entered, they put us in the cold cuts department . . .

If we are in Cleveland, at the R.K.O. Palace Theatre

[1] *Kicks.* Show-business vernacular for having fun.

or the Mounds Club, we can't take our make-up off fast
enough to join Joe E. Lewis, Guy Lombardo and the
brothers Lombardo, Bert Wheeler, and the rest of our
buddies at Willie Langer's Hickory House.

In Philadelphia the round table moves to Lew Tendler's or Benny the Bum's. In Baltimore the boys are
divided between Nate's and Leon's and Mandell's. In
Cincinnati, it's the Netherlands Plaza, where Max Schul-
man makes showpeople comfortable. In San Francisco
it's the International Settlement. If you get to Hollywood and you want to be with the gang, you go
to Mike Lyman's, the Brown Derby, or Dave's Blue
Room. In Montreal, the clan gathers at Dinty Moore's.

You can't go to Hartford without joining the actor's
table at Mike and Mickey's Empire Villanova. The boys
love showpeople and turn their successful restaurant
over to them. In Washington it's the Spotlight Club and
in Chicago it's Henrici's. The gathering of the gagsters
is a big thing at Ruby Foo's when you're in Boston.
There, George Clarke sits with all the clan and Ruby
Foo herself, and we swap jokes and yarns until dawn
comes up.

In New York there were three famous landmarks
where our folks "cut up the jackpot." Dave's Blue Room
was the rendezvous for the night-club people, the racket
boys, showpeople, and the hangers-on in show business.
The Palace Cafeteria on Forty-sixth Street was the
hangout for the struggling entertainers and writers. The
front of the Palace Theatre was the gathering place for
all the vaudevillians, big and small.

But Dave's Blue Room is now a Chinese Restaurant, and Dave has moved to Hollywood. The Palace Cafeteria is now a clothing store, and the cops keep the gang moving from the front of the Palace Theatre.

Oh, the boys have found other places to have their laughs and say, "Would I lie to you, I was the hit of the show!" or "There's a conspiracy in the Shubert office against me" or "That louse is doing my whole act."

Leo Lindy is as famous as any of the stars who frequent his "store," as he calls it. Only in New York can you see a man-eating shark at the museum and a man eating herring at Lindy's. Lindy has been host to the big of the entertainment world for more years than he can remember. He gives them advice and sends them hot soup and chicken between shows. He sends his cheese cake and marinated herring to the Broadway mob all over the world.

Though the famous restaurateur has no publicity man, he garners more publicity than any other restaurant or night club in the country. All the columnists drop in to talk to the stars, and to find out "what's new?" Lindy divides the "dope" with all the fourth-estaters.

Earl Wilson, the sturgeon general of Lindy's, dropped in at two one morning to inquire about the latest happenings. He fought his way through a large crowd and finally reached Leo Lindy. "Who is in your store tonight?" asked the saloon editor. "Nobody especially famous tonight," answered Leo—"just plain people with money."

The "ickies" [1] follow the mob. Wherever showpeople gather, the "squares" are sure to follow. That's why restaurant owners look for the "actortainers'" patronage. You can't "buy" a guy in show business. He either likes you and your "joint" or he doesn't. Everybody loves Lindy, and they know they are welcome.

The civilians come to Lindy's to have their cheese cake and to see Damon Runyon sitting in the corner with his lovely wife and her strange hats. They love to watch Danny Kaye having laughs with Jack Benny over a plate of borsht. Or watch Bing Crosby eating sour cream, and Bob Hope hanging on to a cream cheese and lox sandwich on bagel.

I was sitting at one of the front tables with Lindy, Danny Kaye, and Bing Crosby one night, when a typical "ickie," who looked as if he comes out once a year, approached "the groaner." "Remember me?" It was the same question that has haunted entertainers ever since the beginning of time. "You look familiar" was "der Bingle's" answer, the same dodge all actors use.

"Remember when you worked for my organization, The Knights of Pythias, about eighteen years ago," the stranger continued, "and after the show we all had something to eat together? Remember you told us that some day you would be a big star on the radio, the stage, and the screen?"

"Yes, I do recall," said Crosby, trying to be polite.

---

[1] *Ickies* or *squares*, as they are often called in show-business vernacular, are people who are not "hep" or "in the know" on Broadway. Just plain, nice people who pay to see what's going on.

"So tell me, Bing," pressed the square, "what happened?"

Lindy's is the home for all the song writers, song pluggers and music publishers in town. Some of America's famous songs were written on the back of a Lindy menu, napkin, or tablecloth. Lew Brown wrote *Sonny Boy* in sixteen minutes while imbibing a piece of cheese cake. Walter Donaldson scribbled *My Blue Heaven* on the tablecloth over a second cup of coffee. Benny Davis composed *Goodbye, Broadway—Hello, France* and *Margie* while finishing a Lindy pancake. Irving Berlin, when he was torching for Ellen, consoled himself at the famous hangout by tearing a herring. In between herrings he wrote *Always*, *All Alone*, and *Remember*.

If you walk into the famous restaurant and you see a mob scene around one table, don't get nervous. What looks like a free-for-all or a riot, is probably a group of song pluggers or music publishers who have spotted Guy Lombardo or some other famous bandleader and are trying to get him to play their songs on the air.

The first day we were at the Capitol Theatre, Guy, Carmen, Victor, and Liebert Lombardo and I decided to have lunch at Lindy's, only a few steps from the theatre. We found song writers in our soup, song pluggers in the chopped liver, and music publishers in the turkey sandwich. After that, Lindy sent our food backstage.

The "rib" is always on at the famous eating place. Fred Fradkin, the radio violinist, smuggled some sliced tongue into Lindy's, then ordered a sliced-tongue sandwich. He added the smuggled tongue to that brought to him and built an enormous sandwich. When Lindy came over, Fradkin howled with delight over the huge sandwich, and Lindy, seeing the monument of meat, rushed to the kitchen and started throwing dishes.

Lindy will name a sandwich after you if he likes you. If he doesn't, he'll name you after a crumb cake.

Before you "arrive" at Lindy's, there are two places where the "five-cent-coffee buyers" congregate, the Theatrical Pharmacy and Kellogg's Cafeteria. Here the future stars meet to cut up the Mr. Big in showbiz.

During the day, at the Theatrical Pharmacy on Forty-sixth Street, you can find the borsht-circuit stars, and the unhappy comedians, selling five Milton Berle jokes for two Bob Hope gags. The last time I was there, twenty of my jokes were selling for one of Eddie Cantor's.

After dark, the gang moves to Kellogg's on Forty-ninth

Street just east of Broadway. First they go home to dinner and then they rush to Kellogg's for their coffee, which lasts until five or six in the morning.

Joe E. Ross, the comic, is king at the Forty-ninth Street hangout. Petey Wells, who bills himself as the world's worst comedian, is president of the alumni of disillusioned masters of ceremonies.

Everybody is a comedian in Kellogg's. The counterman throws jokes at you as you pick up your cup of coffee, the manager hits you with gags all night, and Johnny Shepard, the bouncer, who fought such greats of the ring as Benny Leonard and Leach Cross when he was a fighter, is always "making with the comedy."

The writers of hot, stolen gags and parodies, go from table to table peddling their wares. They will sell you a Henny Youngman gag for one Eddie Davis parody.

All the comedians from the smaller night clubs and theatres, sit around and "burn" at the stars who make $2000 a week or more.

"I can't understand it," Petey Wells complained to me one night; "Milton Berle makes $10,000 a week, Bob Hope fifteen thousand, Jackie Miles three thousand, Joe E. Lewis five thousand. I swear I do the same jokes and I don't make fifty dollars a week."

The chief booking agent of these disgruntled comedians is Sam Newgold. He has two offices, during the day at the Theatrical Pharmacy where he books the acts, and at night in Kellogg's where he waits for his commission. Sam claims he is the biggest booking agent of the best comedians in the low-priced field.

Visiting our old hangout one night, Morey Amsterdam and I noticed that Newgold looked disturbed. "What's wrong with Sam?" we asked Joe E. Ross. "Every night he dreams he booked me at the N. Y. Paramount at $5000 a week," explained Joe, "plus three radio shots at $2000 apiece and a picture for $100,000."

"What's he worried about?" I asked.

"Oh," said the comic, "he keeps waking up before he gets his commission."

Sam once booked Duke Granada, a clever little comedian, in a night club in Jersey. After three weeks of three shows a night, the club owners told Duke they didn't have the money to pay his salary. "Take anything in the joint," they told him. Granada took everything in sight, including dishes, ash trays, silverware, and napkins.

When he got back to Kellogg's that night, he dumped three saltshakers, four napkins, three tablespoons, and four knives in Newgold's lap and said, "Here's your commission."

Duke took the rest of the equipment and opened a spaghetti joint on Eighth Avenue called "Duke and Charlie's." He'll always be indebted to Sam for turning him from a flop M.C. into a successful restaurateur.

It wasn't so very long ago that I sat at the very same round table in Kellogg's with Henny Youngman, Jackie Miles, Milton Berle, Jack Durant, Jan Murray, Lew Parker, the Lester Brothers, Jackie Gleason, and many others who are stars today. Pretty soon these youngsters will move over to Lindy's, Reuben's, and Toots Shor's and make room for a new generation of "disillusioned comedians."

The swank hangout of the literati in show business is the exclusive "21" on Fifty-second Street, right next door to the democratic Leon and Eddie's. To be a member of the "21" set is supposed to be an honor. The membership requirements are very stiff—and so are a lot of the patrons. They are so exclusive, even the lamb chops have nylon panties.

Goodman Ace, the radio star, was excluded from the famous bistro by somebody who didn't recognize his kisser. After this had happened several times, his wife remarked: "Poor Goodie, he's free, white, and can't get in 21."

Don't misunderstand, Jack and Charlie who run the saloon—oops! I mean salon—give nothing away.

Milton Berle told Winchell that he dined at the swank Fifty-second Street delicatessen one night, and was amazed when the waiter whispered to him after dinner, "I lost your check and I can't remember everything you had. Can you recall?" "Of course," Milton obliged. "I had a shrimp cocktail, Vichyssoise, roast beef, cherry tart, demi-tasse, and two glasses of water." "Thanks," said the waiter, "but you didn't have to mention the water. We don't charge for it any more."

Winchell has been spanking Jack and Charlie for many years. He once swore that he would never set foot in the 21 again. He enjoys ribbing the swank club at every opportunity he gets, and his "story of the week" about it is worth repeating:

A man-about-town died and was stopped at the Pearly Gates. "Just a minute!" said St. Pete. "Before you get in here, you must prove you've acquired some patience. Now take this spoon and go and remove that mountain over there. Then come back and we'll think it over." A hundred years later the fellow returned to the Pearly Gates and said, "I did what you told me. Here's your spoon. Let me in." "Oh, no," said St. Pete, "you haven't proved you've acquired patience yet. Now take this cup and dump the Pacific Ocean into the Atlantic— we've got too many oceans, anyhow." Three hundred years later the chap returned. "I did what you said," he sighed. "Lemme in, fer the lovapete!" "My!" said St. Peter, "you're impatient. But we'll try you once more. You simply must acquire patience. Now look down there on Fifty-second Street. See that electric sign, a big 21? Well, go in there—and wait until Jack and Charlie buy you a drink!"

On the lower East Side are two restaurants that are famous as the meeting place of the people of the Yiddish Theatre. One is Moscowitz and Lupowitz at Second Avenue and Second Street; the other is the Café Royal at Twelfth Street and Second Avenue.

Moscowitz and Lupowitz is owned by a swell guy called Louie Anzelowitz. The head waiter's name is Abramowitz. Oddly enough, the telephone number is GRamowitz 9-8245. Any night you will find some of the gang uptown joining their brothers from the Jewish Broadway in a round-table session.

Peter Donald, the comedian with the floor-walker

face, likes to go there to swap jokes with the gang and eat what he calls "Jewish crepes Suzettes"—blintzes served in blazing celery tonic.

Paul Muni, Jimmy Cagney, George Raft, Bob Hope, and Eddie Cantor are frequent visitors when they hit New York. George Burns, of Burns and Allen, loves to go there to reminisce about the days when he was George Biernbaum and used to order the blue seltzer bottle. He still orders the seltzer because, as he puts it, "I love to *grepps* [1]—it brings back such memories . . ."

It's fun sitting down there with Aaron Lebedeff, the Jacobson brothers, Diana Goldberg, Irving Grossman, Molly Picon, Moishe Oyshe, and the other greats of the Yiddish Theatre, and listen to them spill their yarns. Café Royal is the headquarters for the intelligentsia of the Jewish entertainment world. All the writers, newspapermen, stars, and producers do their kibitzing there and eat *palachinken*.

The "head man" at the Royal is Herman, the bus boy, who has been at his job for forty years. He has consistently refused to be elevated to waiter. He admits he isn't smart enough, but he is smart enough to own the building where the restaurant stands and several other buildings to boot.

Herman cashes checks for the East Siders, and has financed dozens of shows on the Yiddish Broadway. However, although known as the biggest "angel" in the Jewish Theatre, he doesn't invest money in the shows, he only lends them money at a percentage of interest.

[1] *Grepps.* To belch.

At one time, Menashe Skulnick owed the bus boy $50,000.

Almost all contracts and plans for new shows are born and carried out in some corner of the Royal. It is the casting office, the producing office, and the actors' headquarters, all rolled into one. When the show is all set and ready to go, Herman is called over. The aging bus boy drops his dishes in somebody's lap, starts his negotiations, and a new show is on its way.

Just a stone's throw away from Second Avenue is Greenwich Village, where the ambisextrous characters of show business meet to exchange swishes. One spot, now defunct, was noted for its boys-will-be-girls shows. There they switched the old gag to: "Who was that girl I saw you with last night?" "That was no girl—that was my brother. He just walks that way."

Jackie Miles, Lenny Kent, and Milton Berle were some of the better comedians who visited the "she-hes" at their round-table sessions to get first-hand information on their swish characterizations. It was Miles who first said: "Greenwich Village is where boy meets girl and you can't tell the difference."

I joined Earl Wilson and Jackie one night to see how the other half of the show world lives. We were just about to enter the famous meeting place of the "doll-boys" when we noticed a pedestrian approach a fellow in front of the club. "Can you direct me to the Christopher Street ferry?" asked the stranger. The one addressed replied, "Thpeaking!"

El Morocco and the Stork Club are two of the most

famous rendezvous in the world. John Perona and Sherman Billingsley have been vying for the patronage of the stars and society ever since they started in business. They are still running a neck-and-neck race.

The round table at El Morocco is supervised by John Perona himself. Macoco and Pancho are his chief lieutenants. It's a great kick sitting at the table near the

door. Sometimes you watch the frauds go by, but most often the patrons of the swank Fifty-fourth Street room are the famous of society and the entertainment world. Perona insists on "the best people" and gets them. He claims it's easy to see through people who make a spectacle of themselves.

Perona's round table of wolves is famous the world over. The playboys are often joined by Jimmy Roosevelt, Douglas Fairbanks Jr., Arturo de Cordova, and other famous personalities. I was sitting with the boys one Friday night when the luscious Marlene Dietrich came into the club. Natch, the boys all turned to look. Marlene noticed it and remarked to the famous host as she passed the table, "When people look me over, it always reminds me of the gallery at a tennis match—except that the heads go up and down."

In the Cub Room of the Stork Club, Winchell holds court every night. A few tables away Louis Sobol is in session, and in another part of the room Dorothy Kilgallen holds sway. The exuberant Leonard Lyons goes from table to table getting his famous anecdotes, while Damon Runyon relaxes with Billingsley and W.W.

The Cub Room is exclusively for the inner circle. Once in a great while a "non-belonger" gets in. Then Mr. Big gives the codeword—"Thirteen"—to one of his lieutenants, and the intruder is out of the Cub Room and out of the club.

The Cub Room round-table soirées have gathered all the greats of the theatre and screen, as well as the literary world. The members of the Fourth Estate have found some of their greatest stories at these sessions.

A dozen clubs could be filled with the celebs, actors, producers, and society snobs who have been barred from the house of Billingsley.

The people of the dramatic theatre have their special gathering places. For the gang that haven't "arrived," the meeting place is Walgreen's Drugstore at Forty-fourth Street and Broadway, the Kellogg's of the drama

world. The hopefuls and the understudies sit around
and pray for the star to fall down a sewer or fracture a
leg so they can get their break.

Just a few doors west on Forty-fourth Street is the
world-renowned Sardi's, where all the greats and near-
greats of the theatre congregate. Here the "head man"
is Renée Carroll, who has been checking hats for eighteen years at the same stand. Renée is the intimate and
confidante of the producers and the stars as well as of
the would-be stars. She has fed hundreds of entertainers
down on their luck. Or, as they like to put it, when they
were "at liberty" or "free-lancing."

Renée backs shows, lends money to actors, actresses,
writers, and producers, collects data for newspapermen,
and even found time to write a best seller, *In Your Hat*.
She does all this while checking hats. When a producer
is casting a show, Renée suggests people for the part,
and puts actors and actresses "in the know" when a part
is available.

If the producer comes into Sardi's and she knows he
is looking for talent, Renée calls any number of actress-
friends and warns, "Dress to kill and hurry over. Brock
Pemberton is here, and I know he'll grab you for the
part if he sees you. Don't be nervous, just stroll in nonchalantly and take a table by yourself. I'll see to it that
you sit facing him, so he can't help but notice you." Then
she'll pick up the girl's check and slip the waiter a few
for his trouble.

June Havoc is one of the many stars who got her break
that way. The lovely Havoc would sit around all day

nursing a glass of milk when Renée told her that Vinton
Freedley or Oscar Serlin was expected.

All the producers hold court at Sardi's regularly. The
stars usually sit under their own caricatures that were
created by Gard. Pop Sardi goes from table to table,
talking to all the members of his dramatic family. He
sees to it that Miss Cornell has her steak as she likes it,
and that Miss George has her soup hot. He helps this
one with money and cashes a check for another.

They're a queer bunch, these people of the dramatic
world. Their struggles, their disappointments, their
heartaches and set-backs are covered up by their ability
to "play a part." More drama is unfolded at the round
table in Sardi's than in any of the plays in which they
participate.

When the night clubs close and the city is asleep, the
theatrical clan begins to gather at Reuben's famous
Fifty-eighth Street restaurant. The night-club owners
and the entertainers, the celebrities and the would-be
celebs, the actors who can't sleep and the Hollywood
stars who are having their fling, arrive between four and
six A.M. to chew the fat and relax after a hectic night in
the smoke-filled saloons. The press agents are all there,
too, going from table to table, getting news for their
favorite syndicated Broadway columnists, who are fast
asleep in their penthouse apartments.

Billingsley exchanges greetings with Leon, of Leon
and Eddie's; Orson Welles embraces Luise Rainer.
Sinatra and Van Johnson compare notes, and Joe E.
Lewis, Jackie Miles, Jerry Lester, the Ritz brothers,

Martha Raye, Nick Condos, Bert Wheeler, Jackie Gleason, Phil Silvers, and the Slate brothers sit around and
throw "ribs" at each other. Natch, I join the "sense of
humor" boys.

"If you're such a big hit at the Capitol," Jerry Lester
rides me, "how come you can't get a job?"

"Well, if you're making so much money," I return,
"how come you have to warm up sandwiches in your
dressing room at the Roxy?"

"What are you characters arguing about?" Phil Silvers
throws in. "I came here for a vacation. May we have
the pleasure of your absence?"

"Get a load of the big Hollywood comedian!" Joe E.
Lewis protects us. "He rose from obscurity to oblivion,
whatever that means."

"Watch your diction, Joe, don't talk dirty; Martha
Raye is at the table," reminds Jackie Miles.

"Thank you very large," says Martha. "You're a nice
boy. I wish I'd known you when you were alive."

Peter Donald and his lovely wife are there, eating
their favorite dish, an onion sandwich. "Are you kiddin'?" ribs Harry Ritz. "An onion sandwich? Don't you
know Reuben's motto? 'The taste of an onion can be
greatly improved by adding a pound of steak to it'."

There's romance at the famous rendezvous of celebs,
too. In the corner booths the blues singer and the comic
aren't laughing as they hold hands. The hat-check girl
and the crooner are looking at each other with bated
breath. The night-club owner forgets his worries in a fond
embrace with the chorus girl, and the star is cooing to

the cigarette gal. Arnold Reuben himself met a lovely girl in his restaurant and recently married her.

There's drama in every corner. Two typical-looking collegiates were sitting in a booth one night throwing jibes at every waiter and passer-by. Their language was loud and filthy. They challenged everyone to a fight. Their anti-Semitic remarks were accentuated with dirty curse words.

Johnny Broderick watched the entire proceedings from the corner of his eye. Broadway's favorite "hero" was off duty, but he was beginning to lose patience with the jerks. An elderly man, sitting in the booth next to the loud-mouth characters, leaned over and asked them, "Please watch your language; I'm here with my daughter." At this, one of the punks, a six-foot three-inch giant, hit the little grey-haired man and sent him sprawling to the floor.

The famous detective couldn't take any more of it. He walked over to the trouble-makers, showed his badge, and pulled them out of the booth.

"I know who you are," one of the loudmouths threatened, "Johnny Broderick, but I wouldn't fool with us if I were you. I'm the intercollegiate light-heavyweight champion of the U.S.A. and my pal is heavyweight champ."

A left to the chin of one and a right to the nose of the other, and both lice were on the floor. "Meet the new light-heavy and heavyweight champ," said Johnny as he picked them off the floor.

Arnold Reuben doesn't pay much attention to the

business of running his restaurant any more. He leaves that to his son, and busies himself with his many charities. He goes from table to table, getting money for the Father Duffy Canteen or the Hospital for Crippled Children, selling bonds, collecting for the Infantile Paralysis Fund. His buttons, pins, and medals from grateful organizations that he has helped, cover his entire vest.

When he needs a show for one of his charities, to promote money for crippled or poor, all A. R. has to do is to make the rounds of the tables in his restaurant, and he has a show with the biggest names on Broadway. Do the people of show business have hearts? Ask Arnold Reuben, or the charities that he helps sponsor.

The Algonquin Hotel has long been the favorite retreat of the literati. The late Robert Benchley, Heywood Broun, and Alexander Woollcott were the round-table boys there for many years. Thornton Wilder, Ernest Hemingway, Dorothy Parker, Dorothy Thompson, Quentin Reynolds, and the critics' circle are some of the great of "letters" who frequent the renowned rendezvous today.

The late Frank Case, the Algonquin owner and host, helped many a promising writer on his way. He paid their board bill and let them charge their food and phone calls. He even introduced them to his literary pals and patrons. Few of them ever forgot, though Case did get fooled once in a while. He was very nice to a prosperous writer, who departed and left a bill of many hundreds, half of it in long distance calls. "I've charged it off to profit and louse," Case said.

Hanson's Drug Store, at Fifty-first Street and Seventh Avenue, has been tabbed "the El Morocco of the drug stores" and "the poor man's Stork Club." It's the only place where the chorus girls and show gals can sign "tabs." All the Roxy and Radio City Music Hall chorines use it as their hangout. More beautiful girls pass through Hanson's than ever passed through the portals of a Ziegfeld, Earl Carroll, or George White theatre.

Willie Yuran, one of the owners, lends the girls money without interest and takes their phone calls and messages. He gives them credit until they find a job. Some of the biggest stars have remembered and still send him money, even after they have "arrived" in Hollywood.

Hanson's is the melting pot of the big and the little in the entertainment world. Their greatest business is done with showgirls and showpeople. Their biggest calls are for make-up and pills. Some want pills to stay awake to study scripts. Others want pills to go to sleep so they can be fresh in the morning for their broadcast or show.

The showbiz drug store is open all night. After all the hangouts are closed, the clan starts to gather at Hanson's. Hat-check and cigarette girls rub shoulders with showgirls and restaurant owners. Winchell, Billingsley, and the press agents drop in for a last schmooze before going to bed. An actor who is in trouble, drops over to see Johnny Broderick for a little help. The comedian stops off to throw the final joke before retiring.

The dawn is coming up . . . and so from bedlam to bed.

CHAPTER TWENTY

Things I Wish I'd Said

IT WAS my last day at the Capitol Theatre. I walked over to the round table wreathed in smiles. I had just broken the attendance record at the theatre. Oh yes, Guy Lombardo and June Havoc were on the show with me, and Van Johnson was on the screen in *Thrill of a Romance*.

"What are you doing, wearing my old nose?" asked Milton Berle, who was wearing a new one.

"That's good," I admitted. "Wish I'd said it."

"You probably will," replied Berle.

At that moment, Toots Shor steamed up to the table. "How d'ya like that hoople-head doctor of mine?" he shouted. "He tells me drinking is harmful. 'Listen,' I told him, 'I don't knock your racket! Don't knock mine!'"

"Swell!" I applauded. "I wish I'd said that."

"Ya gotta have a brain to say somethin' like that," answered Toots, "and you're an actor."

"Maybe I shoulda stood in bed," I said sheepishly, and "Doc" Marcus sneered, "I suppose you wish you'd said *that* before Yussel-the-Muscle Jacobs."

Sitting in the intelligentsia corner were a group of Toots Shor fans, some of the world's outstanding person-

alities. Among them were Quentin Reynolds, Jimmy
Walker, Arthur Garfield Hayes, Harry Wismer, Horace
Stoneham, and Mel Ott. Each of these has ripped off
lines I wish I had said. In fact, at almost any table, any
night, bons mots are being tossed about that I'd be
proud to claim as my own.

So many times when I was onstage, or at a speaker's
table, I've wished for the silver tongue of Jimmy Walker
—the lovable and brilliant Jimmy, who said, "The applause of yesterday has but a short echo." (It proved
all too true for the ex-mayor of New York City.) After
worshipping at Catholic, Protestant, and Jewish chapels
with Eddie Cantor, Jimmy turned to him and said, "Con-
gratulations, Eddie, you've just played God across the
board!"

Fred Allen has always beaten me to the punch when
it comes to ad libs. I always remember them after he
says them. Fred was once asked how it happened that
so many comedians who couldn't shine his shoes when
it came to comedy, had higher ratings than his on the
air. "Woolworth's will always sell more than Tiffany's,"
answered Fred. Another time he just saved a kid from
being hit by an automobile. "Take it easy, son," said the
wit. "Don't you want to grow up and have tro bles?"

Don't sell women short when it comes to wit. They
are always ya-ta-ta, ya-ta-ta, ya-ta-ta. The female of the
species is very often wittier than the male. When the
authoress of *Forever Amber*, Kathleen Winsor, was
asked if her book was autobiographical, she replied, "If
it had been, I'd never have had time to write it."

Sylvia Fine, the brilliant writer who is Mrs. Danny Kaye in private life, sent a wire to Benay Venuta on the birth of her daughter Deborah, which read: "I'm glad you lost that great big blister that turned out to be Patty's sister."

Joan Davis admitted, "I've got what Betty Grable's got

—what's more, I've got it longer. When I was a girl," Joan continued, "I couldn't keep my mind on my lessons—gosh, I was boy-crazy! That's all I thought about —boys, boys, boys. But I grew out of that—now all I think about is men."

Paulette Goddard's advice is worth repeating: "If a girl doesn't watch her figure, the boys won't!"

One of my favorite gals is Gertrude Niesen. I love her description of a music lover (masculine) "who on hearing a soprano in a bathroom—puts his ear to the keyhole."

Rosemarie and Stephen Vincent Benét dedicated *A Book of Americans* to their children thus: "To Stephanie, Thomas, and Rachel, our other works in collaboration."

Of course—talking about women wits—I'll always wish I'd said Dorothy Parker's line to a girl friend who had a baby. She wired, "I knew you had it in you."

Belle Baker once philosophized, "You know you're getting old when men look at you East and West instead of North and South."

How often I've sat at tables in Toots' and listened to the greats of Broadway throw their wit around, thinking to myself, "Gee, I wish I'd said that!"

Some of the boys were whooping it up in Toots' when the talk turned to a local gambler who always won at cards but invariably lost at the track.

"The answer is very simple," explained Damon Runyon, "he can't get a horse up his sleeve."

"Doc" Marcus, the mad magician, is the favorite wit of the wits in show business. He has invented such words as "schissors," "sheese," "rangletangle," "phohodo-hydascope," and "stinky-hi-diddle." Only he knows what they mean.

"There's just one thing worse than playing with loaded dice," says "Doc": "loaded women." Doc's description of a diplomat is "a man who can convince his wife that she looks fat in a fur coat."

Louis Sobol was sitting at a table in the Barberry Room when he saw Sally Rand, foremost exponent of the art commonly called strip-tease, rise from her table and accidentally drop a glove. Where-upon playwright Marc Connelly, sitting at an adjoin-ing table, rose, applauded loudly, and yelled, "More! More!"

Ken Kling, who has gone from "nags to riches," warned us many times, "At the race track there are more phonies than ponies."

My friend Harvey Stone was on a rampage one night. He had just gotten out of the army and couldn't get an apartment. "The OPA," Harvey raged, "has put a ceil-ing over everything but me. I got footprints all over my chest from sleeping in doorways. They are so crowded in New York, *Helen Trent* and *Our Gal Sunday* moved in with *One Man's Family*. *Portia Faces Life* out on the sidewalk, and even John can't find a room for his *Other Wife*. And they tell me *Life Can Be Beautiful!*"

Cully Richards said, "If I'm going to keep my health, I must lose some weight—about 118 lbs. of blonde."

Ruby Zwerling was watching a "ham" go through encore after encore at a benefit. "He's from Milton Berle out of Benny Davis," commented Ruby.

Not all the great lines are comedy. Joe Louis, the champ, was onstage at Madison Square Garden when he said, simply, "We can't lose the war. God is on our side."

The other Lewis, Joe E., has said many things I wish I'd said first. "I follow the horses," wails Joe. "The trouble is, the horses I follow—follow the horses."

"I'm working under a handicap," cries the comic, "I have no talent."

When Joe married the lovely Martha Stewart of Hollywood, he wired Earl Wilson: "Marriage is a wonderful thing. No family should be without it."

"Poor guy," says Joe of his millionaire friend, Jorge Sanchez, "he's got all his money tied up in cash."

Zero Mostel, the comicoliberal, was denouncing a group of liberals with lorgnettes: "You guys will do everything for the working man—except get off his back."

Marty Bohn: "Since I got married to Nancy and my daughter Lee was born, the only chance I get to open my mouth at home is to yawn."

Al Kelly, the double-talk expert, was in a romantic mood and was complaining to his buddy Willie Howard, "Getting the baby to sleep is hardest when she's about eighteen."

Monsignor Fulton J. Sheen once said of a girl, "She was in her early flirties." Another time the Monsignor commented, "A halo need drop but a few inches to become a noose."

Yes, if I were given one wish by a fairy godmother, I wouldn't ask to be as handsome as Gable or as talented as Barrymore. Nor would I ask for the voice of Crosby or the following of Sinatra. If I had one wish I would ask for the combined wit of all my favorite wits, so that I could say *first* the things I wish I said after they said it.

Oscar Levant, who always looks as if he had just missed somebody by two minutes, is one of the brains I would wish for. "Alimony," said Oscar, "is something like the time payment plan—pay as you burn." Oscar described a Broadway gal-about-town: "She's such a phony she even tells the truth if she has to lie about it."

Elsa Maxwell, Benny Rubin, Harry Morton, Jimmie Jemail, Henny Youngman, Phil Baker, Col. T. J. J. Christian, and Dan Healy are others who have pulled lines that I would love to have said first.

Elsa Maxwell said, "One way to get along with women is to let them think they have their own way—and then let them have it."

"Don't wear out your welcome," commented John J. Anthony. "It's one of the toughest things to replace."

Bob Christenberry, managing director of the Astor Hotel, said, "The only indispensable man the world has ever known was Adam."

"Sure I'm the father of those famous five daughters," said Eddie Cantor. "I'm Dionne in slow motion!"

The beloved Powers Gouraud said, "There's just one pretty child in the world, and every mother has it."

As Mitzi Green put it, "An egotist is a man who talks about himself when you want him to talk about you."

Phil Baker: "An optimist is a guy who can always see the bright side of other people's troubles."

Sheila Rogers: "A kibitzer is a guy who picks up a girl on another guy's whistle."

Fred Allen: "A bore is a yawn with skin on it."

Ex-Champ Max Baer to Louis Sobol, "I'm the only guy who never bet on a fight—unless I knew what round I was going to lose in."

"I don't want to be smart like other producers," admitted the successful Mike Todd; "I just want to be lucky."

"I just saw the greatest comedian in the world," said Jerry Lester modestly; "I worked in front of a mirror tonight."

"It's easy to be rich and not haughty," said Alan Corelli. "What's difficult is to be poor and not grumble!"

Col. T. J. J. Christian, the grandson of Stonewall Jackson and my favorite soldier, has always lived by the words of James M. Barrie: "Those who bring sunshine to the lives of others—cannot keep it from themselves."

Jack Benny: "When Fred Allen thinks, it's a violation of the child labor law."

Mrs. Eleanor Roosevelt, who was known at the White House as Public Energy No. 1, is one of the great women of all time. "No one can make you feel inferior without your consent," said the former First Lady.

Will Rogers' observation: "A friend will remember a hundred good deeds and forget one mistake; an enemy will never forget the one mistake you make."

"I'm not interested in horse races," said Bernard Baruch. "I find the human race a whole lot more interesting to watch."

Buddy Lester said he saw critic Kelcey Allen at a premiere incognito—"He was awake."

When John Barrymore was in the Santa Barbara Hospital they had him on a strict diet. For breakfast he got an ounce of orange juice, for lunch they gave him a cup of tea, and his dinner consisted of half a slice of toast. Finally the meagre diet got on his nerves and he rang for the nurse. "Bring me a postage stamp," he yelled; "I want to do some reading."

Sid Gary, the baritone who is famous for his double talk, was talking about a used-to-be: "He's been up against the wall so much—the handwriting is on *him*."

MATERNITY

Billy Gleason: "She has the shape of an hour glass— after the sand has seeped all into one place."

Winston Churchill was interviewed by a young woman journalist who coyly remarked, "Mr. Churchill, the two things I don't like about you are your politics and your moustache." "My dear girl," he chuckled, "pray do not disturb yourself—you are not likely to come into contact with either."

Harry Morton is a manager-agent who gets more

laughs from comedians than the comics get from their audiences. Harry was about to become the father of a brand-new baby. He paced up and down the waiting room at the hospital as millions of expectant fathers have done before him. He bit every nail on his fingers and almost wore the carpet out. Finally he rushed into the room where his wife was waiting for the final word and asked earnestly, "Darling, are you sure you want to go through with this?"

Lillian E. Smith said, "No one is emotionally mature who has any type of racial prejudice."

"Philadelphia is a wonderful city," said Milton Berle. "Where else do traffic cops wipe your windshields before giving you a ticket?"

Orson Welles: "When you're down and out, something always turns up—usually the noses of your friends."

Fibber McGee: "She looked at me as if she'd just stepped off Plymouth Rock and I'd just crawled out from under it."

Frank Coniff, who went from covering the entertainment beat in New York to the war in Europe, came back with many tales. "The Nazi war criminals," Frank reported, "are going to be hung Von by Von."

Judd Whiting, the Baltimore *Chronicler*, was complaining to his lovely wife about women's clothes. "A man's clothes," said Judd, "reveal his tailor; a woman's clothes reveal her."

Bob Steele, the sportscaster of WTIC in Hartford, has a great sense of humor. He was telling me about a lovey-

dovey couple from his home town that finally **reached** the preacher. "Before they were married," said Bob, "he told her how much he yearned for her lips; but after they were wed he informed her that he wanted none of her lip!"

Coleman Jacoby: "When she first came to Broadway, her eyes were big blue question marks—but before long they were big green dollar marks."

Sid Reiss knows "an intoxicated couple that are keeping unsteady company together"; and Jack Leonard said, "I fell for one of those beautiful acrobats **at the** circus, but she wouldn't give me a tumble."

Jerry Lewis is a funny little guy with **a very original**

style. He admits that he's quite a jitterbug: "That's because the first job I ever had was as a Western Union messenger, and now it's easy to send me."

Phil Foster says, "A word to the wife is never sufficient."

Harry Wismer has been fighting for good fellowship in sports ever since he started broadcasting years ago. He is very proud of the job our boys and girls have done in that field. "In sports," says Harry, "there is no such thing as race, creed, or color. Whether your skin is white, yellow, or black, you'll come out on top when you remember the red, white, and blue."

The famous columnists are men and women of both wit and wisdom. Columning used to be known as "the peek of professions"; but since, as Winchell says, there are no more keyholes in smart doors, they now delve into politics, economics, civic planning, advice to the lovelorn, tips on the market, Americana, and the Art of Begetting and Building Better Babies.

On top of it all, these scribes, who used to burn the scandal at both ends, are as famous for their witticisms (in and out of their typewriters) as any of the great comedians. In fact, many big-time comics have built good parts of their acts on pilferings from Winchell, Walker, Wilson, Kilgallen, Sullivan, and Lyons.

Many times my ears hear and my eyes read cleverisms by Lee Mortimer, Nick Kenny, Robert Dana, Virginia Forbes, Gene Knight, Paul Denis, and the Wit-at-Large, Hy Gardner, that make my brain envious.

Chroniclers of the entertainment world, who alter-

nately fill their pens with carbolic acid, Chanel No. 5,
or a simple solution of humor, have also set a standard
of wit for professional funny men.

Nor does this apply only to Gotham. In Chicago I have
Irving Kupcinet and his *Kup's Kolumn* for my laugh
breakfast, and Nate Gross for my laugh dinner. In Detroit it's Charlie Gentry; and in Philadelphia, Jerry Gag-
han and Jeff Keen. In Boston it's George Clarke, who
left a high editorial post in New York and now pours
forth endless bons mots from his Boston bean. The hangout of the Cabots also boasts such great fourth-estaters
as Joe Dinneen, George Holland, and Mal Massuca. In
Miami the actor's bible is written by Jack Kofoed,
George Bourke, Dorothy Raymer, Paul Bruun, and, for-
merly, by my favorite wits, Les and Peggy Simmonds.

One half of the world laughs with Hollywood's
Prophets of Journalism—Jimmy Fidler, Sidney Skolsky,
Louella Parsons, and Hedda Hopper—while the other
half (the population of Brooklyn) clocks its chuckles by
the staccato stutterings of Eddie Zeltner and Lew Sheaf-
fer. Of course, the All-American Great is Damon Runyon.

If I could rub my head like Aladdin's Lamp, I—instead
of Winchell—would have coined "making whoopee," "Is
my face red!" and "bundles from heaven"—as well as
many other examples of what H. L. Mencken calls
"Winchellingo." And I'd better be careful not to use
them, or I'll become one of his famous "Copy Cads."
Earl Wilson says Winchell imitates nobody but has been
imitated by everybody. Not so long ago, Winchell called
the Southern Senator, Bilbo, a "Bilbigot."

Mark Hellinger said, "Winchell's greatest thrill is writing a line." The atomic Nazi-fighter was recognized by the Newspaper Guild when it gave him a headliner award, "For making the fifth column fear the fourth estate." One of Winchell's funniest lines was about Wallace Beery, from Hollywood, and Polly Adler, "girl about town," when he wrote: "I saw Wallace Beery and Polly Adler walking down Fifth Avenue arm in arm, each waving to their respective fans."

Winchell's tribute to Franklin Delano Roosevelt on the first anniversary of his death is a monument that will live forever: "And wherever a child sleeps in peace —F.D.R. lives."

"Those of us who still fight under the Roosevelt banner," wrote W.W., "know that F.D.R. can no longer lead us: we are guided by his words and deeds . . . If men follow his ideals, civilization can never lose its way."

Irving Hoffman expressed the sentiments of millions of Americans when he said of Winchell: "W.W.'s got guts, heart, brains, and the respect of all respectable people."

Ed Sullivan, who did a magnificent job in bringing entertainment to the boys in the hospitals, was awarded a scroll of honor by the Secretary of War and his staff. More than that, he received the love and undying thanks of the boys and their families all over the world.

"Ten thousand memories are concentrated in that scroll," said the Number One civilian G.I., "as well as a constant reminder of a pledge that so long as one wounded American soldier remains in a military hospital, we will continue to bring him entertainment."

Earl Wilson brought an original style to columning, and it took Broadway and the country by storm. He brings you news "hot off the girdle," and talks about Jane Russell as "the treasure chest." "Jane wore a low-cut bathing suit," reported Earl, "that revealed her two best features."

Earl picked the "ten bust women" for his readers. Actress Constance Moore chose Lana Turner as Number One and columnist Edith Gwynn immediately tagged Lana "the community chest."

Wilson said, "Success has turned more heads than halitosis."

Although Earl thinks nothing of writing about Gypsy Rose Lee's unadorned torso, Mae West's bust, and Joan Crawford's *derrière*, he will blush if you tell him an off-color story.

Little Sidney Skolsky, the columnist hypochondriac who switched from Broadway to Hollywood, was the topic of conversation in Toots' one night. "How is Sidney doing?" someone asked. "Wonderful!" said a friend; "he has a good job, a fine family, owns his own home and stethoscope!"

Eddie Cantor, Phil Rapp, and Skolsky are three post-graduate hypochondriacs, and when they get together it's practically a clinic. One evening, in Eddie's Beverly Hills tepee, all three began complaining about their aches and pains. Finally Eddie suggested they all visit the doctor. "Okay," agreed Skolsky, "and low-pressure man pays."

Paul Denis was cautioning a run-around pal. "Remember," said the *Post* scribe, "variety is the vice of life!"

Former columnist Dorothy Dey was about to marry Dean Murphy. The bride-to-be told friends, "The only thing new will be the cake!"

Nick Kenny, the *N. Y. Daily Mirror* columnist and benefit king, is famous for his poems. However, his wit is as sharp as his famous nose. Nick describes a jitterbug as "a convulsion with white shoes." He explained a rumba as "simply a matter of making both ends meet."

Lee Mortimer is one of our favorite guys. His column in the *N. Y. Daily Mirror* is a must for showpeople and a guide to night clubs for New Yorkers and visiting firemen. China's unofficial ambassador of good will, he will drink nothing but sidecars and even walks on a bias.

"Henny Youngman is so skinny," said Lee, "he looks like a microphone wearing shorts."

"The difference between a Broadway wolf and a Broadway gal," he comments, "is that she knows what she wants and he wants what she no's."

H. L. Mencken says, "There are two times in every man's life when he is thoroughly happy. Just after he has met his first love and just after he has parted from his last one."

"On one issue at least, men and women agree," said Mencken: "they both distrust women."

Mencken also said, "It is hard to believe that a man is telling the truth when you know that you would lie if you were in his place."

The glamor girl of Manhattan's columnar fraternity

is Dorothy Kilgallen. Her column in the *Journal-American* is syndicated all over the country. She uses beautiful phrases like "a young couple with softening of the hearteries." Another time she described a lovely thing as "a woman wrapped in ermine and male glances."

Jimmy Fiddler describes Hollywood as "a place where people spend more time two-facing friends than facing cameras."

Jimmy Cannon is the *N. Y. Evening Post's* ambassador-at-large of the sport world and Broadway. He was covering a fight for his paper at Madison Square Garden one night. After a dull fifteen rounds Jimmy quipped in his column, "It was plenty crowded at the Garden, everybody was pushing and shoving. The safest place was the ring—nobody got hurt there."

Another time he wrote of a bad decision, "They would give him the decision even if they had to give it to his widow."

O.O. McIntyre's famous description still holds true: "New York—where everyone mutinies but no one deserts."

Dale Harrison's comment when a strip-tease dancer was arrested: "For no gauze at all!"

George Jean Nathan's classic description of Hollywood: "Hollywood impresses me as ten million dollars' worth of intricate and highly ingenious machinery functioning elaborately to put skin on baloney!"

Irving Hoffman: "It's finally been revealed how they made room for Frank Sinatra on his flight overseas. They removed two airmail letters."

The late Robert Benchley's remark upon seeing two matinee idols: "I bet the hair of their combined chests wouldn't make a wig for a grape!"

John Chapman: "Joan Crawford can do a fan dance just by lifting her eyebrows!"

Henry Morgan's radio weather report: "Cloudy, disturbing fog over Senator Bilbo's head."

Danton Walker is the kind of guy who takes up both sides of an argument. He and Winchell had been quarreling for a long time. Danton told Louis Sobol one day, "Every time I open my mouth, Winchell puts a feud in it."

Louis Sobol was talking about a typical Broadway columnist. "He thinks he's writing his column for posterity," said Louis, "but by the following day it's usually wrapped with the rest of the paper around the garbage."

Describing the jokester, Sobol said, "He always has a gag on his tongue but you often wish his mouth were covered with one." As for the chorus girl, according to Sobol, "she learns in her career how to be foxy around the wildest wolves." He nominated for the best play of the year "a certain chorus girl's for Howard Hughes, the millionaire."

When Tony, Mark, and I opened at La Martinique in New York, all the gang turned out to give us a big send-off. Danton Walker, Lee Mortimer, Earl Wilson, Bob Dana, L. L. Stevenson, Louis Sobol, Ed Sullivan, Nat Kahn of *Variety*, and Bill Smith of *Billboard* represented the fourth estate. There were so many agents there, it

looked like the waiting room of the William Morris office.
All the comics showed up, including Milton Berle, Lew
Parker, Eddie Bracken, Red Buttons, Harvey Stone,
Henny Youngman, B. S. Pully, Julie Oshins, the Slate
brothers, the Ritz brothers, the Radio Aces, Rags Ragland, and Jan Murray. For a while it looked like a comedians' convention.

My buddy Toots Shor was there big as life and twice
as fat. Sinatra was there to cheer us on. So were Barry
Gray, Sophie Tucker, Tommy Manville, Carole Landis,
and Lana Turner. Jerry Cooper, Jack O'Brian, Nicky
Blair, Dr. Ralph Slater, Russell Patterson, Pete Donald,
Xavier Cugat, Renée de Marco, Maureen Cannon, Jane
Dulo, Joan Roberts, Jane Kean, and Gene Baylos were
there to wish us well. Of course there were a lot of other
pals—not celebrities, just the schmoes who pay the check,
but equally important to us.

And (talking about things I wish I'd said) I was too
excited to thank them all for being in our corner when
we needed them most. I don't know if I was nervous, but
when the girl brought me a telegram, I tipped the telegram and opened the girl's dress. I wish I'd been able
to say "Thanks" to all of them. Anyway, this is to say
it with a full heart!

CHAPTER TWENTY-ONE

A Wit's End

I LOOKED at my watch. It was ten-thirty. I had just ten minutes to get back to the Capitol Theatre and join Tony Canzoneri and Mark Plant for the last performance of our engagement. It had been everything I always thought Success should be. For six weeks we'd heard the plaudits of full houses; we'd signed hundreds of autographs for the stage-door Janes; we'd received picture, radio, and theatre offers. Our pal and manager, Leo Cohen, had inflated our egos daily with what for him is high flattery: "Not bad, fellows." We'd even been dreaming of taking Frankie's and Van's places as the bobby-soxers' idols.

I was feeling great—really great. I got up from my seat at the round table to leave.

"So long, fellows!" I said. "It's time for my last show."

"There's a guy with a lot of talent," said Milton Berle, pointing at me, "but it's in Mark Plant's name."

"Hey, Cleopatra," one of the Slate brothers threw at me, "you'd be lost without Mark An'-Tony."

"I'm going over to see your last show," muttered Lew Parker. "I know the eggs will be there, so I'll just bring the ham."

"Just bring yourself," I answered meekly.

Every table threw a line as I passed. "I hear you're getting left back to Loew's Pitkin," kidded J.C. Flippen.

"What time are you due back in Macy's window?" questioned the Mad Auctioneer, Lionel Kaye.

"There goes the Number One alumnus of *It Pays To Be Ignorant*," said Danny Thomas.

"I understand you got the Capitol Theatre audience jumpin'—out the window," ribbed Henny Youngman.

"I hear you're packing them out," added Harvey Stone.

The killer was thrown at me just as I was going out the door. "There goes UNO's biggest problem," was Toots' parting shot.

Even though they had let the air out of my head, I was still content as I left the hangout that night. I knew it was only the boys' way of wishing me luck. Raucous humor invariably cloaks the sentimentalities of show-people. Actually, there are no more tolerant, generous, warm-hearted, and affectionate souls on earth than those of the entertainment world.

An actor's home is where he hangs his hat, and that hat is always welcome among show folks, regardless of race, creed, or color. I'm proud to belong to the profession which judges its members by talent and character, and not by the color of their skin or the church in which they worship. A true example of fellowship is the sight of Bill Robinson, Eddie Cantor, Ed Sullivan, and Fred Allen, their arms entwined on the same stage at some benefit. It is not uncommon to see a galaxy of

Jewish, Protestant, and Negro stars helping to lift the mortgage from a Catholic church. In the past year or two there has been one notable exception—but we don't talk about that.

Sure, there are a lot of arguments and feuds about gag-stealing, and accusations of "big head" and "for-

Any entertainer is an easy target

getting," but showpeople are generally right there when the chips are down and some colleague needs a friend. 'Most any entertainer is an easy target for anyone down on his luck. At one time or another, many of the theatrical greats have "eaten on the house" at Toots Shor's, Lindy's, Reuben's, The Tavern, and other Broadway foxholes.

It's a tough racket, this show business of ours, and it

takes a long time to get to the top. Few make it in less than fifteen to twenty years of struggle, hardship, and a trunkful of aggravation, but through it all run hope and laughter. Many a cloudy day has seen the sun because of their gallant gaiety.

A guy with a sense of humor—whether he dishes it out or only takes it—*must* be a great guy. And laughter is the foundation of show business.